T0332737

FPGA Algorithms and Applications for the Internet of Things

Preeti Sharma
Bansal College of Engineering, Mandideep, India

Rajit Nair
Jagran Lakecity University, Bhopal, India

A volume in the Advances in
Systems Analysis, Software
Engineering, and High Performance
Computing (ASASEHPC) Book Series

Published in the United States of America by
    IGI Global
    Engineering Science Reference (an imprint of IGI Global)
    701 E. Chocolate Avenue
    Hershey PA, USA 17033
    Tel: 717-533-8845
    Fax: 717-533-8661
    E-mail: cust@igi-global.com
    Web site: http://www.igi-global.com

Library of Congress Cataloging-in-Publication Data

Names: Sharma, Preeti (Professor of history) editor.
Title: FPGA algorithms and applications for the Internet of Things / Preeti
    Sharma and Rajit Nair, editors.
Description: Hershey, PA : Engineering Science Reference, an imprint of IGI
    Global, [2020] | Includes bibliographical references and index. |
    Summary: "This book examines the application of field-programmable gate
    array algorithms in internet of things, artificial intelligence, and
    high-performance computing"-- Provided by publisher.
Identifiers: LCCN 2019010458 | ISBN 9781522598060 (hardcover) | ISBN
    9781522598084 (ebook) | ISBN 9781522598077 (softcover)
Subjects: LCSH: Field programmable gate arrays--Industrial applications. |
    High performance computing--Equipment and supplies.
Classification: LCC TK7895.G36 F63 2020 | DDC 621.39/5--dc23
LC record available at https://lccn.loc.gov/2019010458

This book is published in the IGI Global book series Advances in Systems Analysis, Software
Engineering, and High Performance Computing (ASASEHPC) (ISSN: 2327-3453; eISSN: 2327-
3461)

British Cataloguing in Publication Data
A Cataloguing in Publication record for this book is available from the British Library.

All work contributed to this book is new, previously-unpublished material.
The views expressed in this book are those of the authors, but not necessarily of the publisher.

For electronic access to this publication, please contact: eresources@igi-global.com.

Advances in Systems Analysis, Software Engineering, and High Performance Computing (ASASEHPC) Book Series

ISSN:2327-3453
EISSN:2327-3461

Editor-in-Chief: Vijayan Sugumaran, Oakland University, USA

MISSION

The theory and practice of computing applications and distributed systems has emerged as one of the key areas of research driving innovations in business, engineering, and science. The fields of software engineering, systems analysis, and high performance computing offer a wide range of applications and solutions in solving computational problems for any modern organization.

The **Advances in Systems Analysis, Software Engineering, and High Performance Computing (ASASEHPC) Book Series** brings together research in the areas of distributed computing, systems and software engineering, high performance computing, and service science. This collection of publications is useful for academics, researchers, and practitioners seeking the latest practices and knowledge in this field.

COVERAGE

- Distributed Cloud Computing
- Engineering Environments
- Software Engineering
- Metadata and Semantic Web
- Network Management
- Enterprise Information Systems
- Storage Systems
- Computer Networking
- Performance Modelling
- Virtual Data Systems

IGI Global is currently accepting manuscripts for publication within this series. To submit a proposal for a volume in this series, please contact our Acquisition Editors at Acquisitions@igi-global.com or visit: http://www.igi-global.com/publish/.

Titles in this Series

For a list of additional titles in this series, please visit:
http://www.igi-global.com/book-series/advances-systems-analysis-software-engineering/73689

Urban Spatial Data Handling and Computing
Mainak Bandyopadhyay (DIT University-Dehradun, India) and Varun Singh (MNNIT-Allahabad, India)
Engineering Science Reference • © 2020 • 300pp • H/C (ISBN: 9781799801221) • US $245.00

Formal and Adaptive Methods for Automation of Parallel Programs Construction Emerging Research and Opportunities
Anatoliy Doroshenko (National Academy of Sciences of Ukraine, Ukraine) and Olena Yatsenko (National Academy of Sciences of Ukraine, Ukraine)
Engineering Science Reference • © 2020 • 195pp • H/C (ISBN: 9781522593843) • US $195.00

Cloud-Based Big Data Analytics in Vehicular Ad-Hoc Networks
Ram Shringar Rao (Ambedkar Institute of Advanced Communication Technologies and Research, India) Nanhay Singh (Ambedkar Institute of Advanced Communication Technologies and Research, India) Omprakash Kaiwartya (School of Science and Technology, Nottingham Trent University, UK) and Sanjoy Das (Indira Gandhi National Tribal University, India)
Engineering Science Reference • © 2020 • 300pp • H/C (ISBN: 9781799827641) • US $245.00

Advancements in Instrumentation and Control in Applied System Applications
Srijan Bhattacharya (RCC Institute of Information Technology, India)
Engineering Science Reference • © 2020 • 298pp • H/C (ISBN: 9781799825845) • US $225.00

Cloud Computing Applications and Techniques for E-Commerce
Saikat Gochhait (Symbiosis Institute of Digital and Telecom Management, Symbiosis International University, India) David Tawei Shou (University of Taipei, Taiwan) and Sabiha Fazalbhoy (Symbiosis Centre for Management Studies, Symbiosis International University, India)
Engineering Science Reference • © 2020 • 185pp • H/C (ISBN: 9781799812944) • US $215.00

701 East Chocolate Avenue, Hershey, PA 17033, USA
Tel: 717-533-8845 x100 • Fax: 717-533-8661
E-Mail: cust@igi-global.com • www.igi-global.com

Editorial Advisory Board

Table of Contents

Detailed Table of Contents

Internet of things (IoT) is a recent technology, and it will become the next generation of internet that connects several physical objects to interact amongst themselves without the assistance of human beings. It plays a significant role in our day-to-day lives and is used in several applications. IoT is a boon to this modern world, but it lacks in security. It cannot protect the user data from assailants, hackers, and vulnerabilities. Field programmable gate arrays (FPGA) helps to achieve all these objectives by incorporating secured end-to-end layer into its architecture. In this chapter, ultralow power and reduced area AES architecture with energy efficient DSE-S box techniques and clock gating for IoT applications are introduced. The proposed AES architecture is implemented over different FPGA families such as Cyclone I, Cyclone II, Virtex 5, and Kintex 7, respectively. From the experimental results, it is observed that the Kintex 7 FPGA kit consumes less power than other FPGA families.

In this chapter, the authors discuss the utilization of FPGA technology in providing the Internet of Things (IoT) with security and privacy services through means of cryptographic realizations. The first part of the chapter focuses on the practical aspects of using FPGAs for providing the IoT with security and privacy. The authors explore the feasibility of using these devices in constrained environments and the features attractive for their use in security applications. The second part is a revision of case studies reported in the literature where FPGAs have been employed for security applications in the context of IoT and related technologies. The main goal of this chapter is to present a general perspective of the role played by FPGA technologies in protecting the IoT.

Chapter 3

Mingjie Lin, University of Central Florida, USA
Juan Escobedo, University of Central Florida, USA

High-level synthesis (HLS) with FPGA can achieve significant performance improvements through effective memory partitioning and meticulous data reuse. In this chapter, the authors will first explore techniques that have been adopted directly from systems that possess a fixed memory subsystem such as CPUs and GPUs (Section 2). Section 3 will focus on techniques that have been developed specifically for reconfigurable architectures which generate custom memory subsystems to take advantage of the peculiarities of a family of affine code called stencil code. The authors will focus on techniques that exploit memory banking to allow for parallel, conflict-free memory accesses in Section 3.1 and techniques that generate an optimal memory micro-architecture for data reuse in Section 3.2. Finally, Section 4 will explore the technique handling code still belonging to the affine family but the relative distance between the addresses.

Chapter 4

Rajit Nair, Jagran Lakecity University, India
Preeti Nair, Bansal College of Engineering, India
Vidya Kant Dwivedi, Bansal College of Engineering, India

Today, in cyber-physical systems, there is a transformation in which processing has been done on distributed mode rather than performing on centralized manner. Usually this type of approach is known as Edge computing, which demands hardware time to time when requirements in computing performance get increased. Considering this situation, we must remain energy efficient and adaptable. So, to meet the above requirements, SRAM-based FPGAs and their inherent run-time reconfigurability are integrated with smart power management strategies. Sometimes this approach fails in the case of user accessibility and easy development. This chapter presents an integrated framework to develop FPGA-based high-performance embedded systems for Edge computing in cyber-physical systems. The processing architecture will be based on hardware that helps us to manage reconfigurable systems from high level systems without any human intervention.

Chapter 5

Neuroscience is a multidisciplinary science that is focused with the study of the structure and function of the nervous system. It contains the evolution, development, cellular and molecular biology, physiology, anatomy, and pharmacology of the nervous system, as well as computational, interactive, and cognitive neuroscience. A field-programmable gate array (FPGA) is an integrated circuit (IC) that can be programmed in the field after production. FPGAs are likely in principle to have vastly wider potential application than programmable read-only memory (PROM) chips. Internet of things (IoT) is an integrated part of future internet including existing and evolving internet and network developments and could be conceptually defined as a worldwide dynamic network infrastructure with self-configuring capabilities based on standard and interoperable protocols communication where physical and virtual "things" have identities, physical attributes, and virtual personalities.

Chapter 6

Modern vehicles are very complex by incorporating various computational signals and critical information transactions. Electronic control units (ECUs) are embedded with various software functions, network information, sensor/actuator communication, and dedicated hardware. Altogether, the special hardware needs to be adaptable to the current needs of next-generation vehicles. This chapter will give a broad idea about modern automotive systems by considering various factors. Finding the best reconfigurable field programmable gate array (FPGA)-based hardware, intelligent assistance systems for drivers and various communication protocols are elaborated in this chapter. Moreover, it also provides the essential knowledge of IoT-based smart automotive systems along with its pros and cons. This chapter also gives the awareness and comparative study of artificial intelligence (AI) systems in the present smart automotive systems. The overall observation of this chapter will satisfy the audience by knowing the reconfigurable FPGA, IoT, and artificial intelligence-based automotive systems.

Chapter 7

Saber Krim, University of Monastir, Tunisia
Mohamed Faouzi Mimouni, National Engineering School of Monastir,
Tunisia

The conventional direct torque control (DTC) of induction motors has become the most used control strategy. This control method is known by its simplicity, fast torque response, and its lack of dependence on machine parameters. Despite the cited advantages, the conventional DTC suffers from several limitations, like the torque ripples. This chapter aims to improve the conventional DTC performances by keeping its advantages. These ripples depend on the hysteresis bandwidth of the torque and the sampling frequency. The conventional DTC limitations can be prevented by increasing the sampling frequency. Nevertheless, the operation with higher sampling frequency is not possible with the software solutions, like the digital signal processor (DSP), due to the serial processing of the implemented algorithm. To overcome the DSP limitations, the field programmable gate array (FPGA) can be chosen as an alternative solution to implement the DTC algorithm with shorter execution time. In this chapter, the FPGA is chosen thanks to its parallel processing.

Chapter 8

Chandrasekaran R., Vels Institute of Science, Technology and Advanced
Studies, India
Hemalatha R. J., Vels Institute of Science, Technology and Advanced
Studies, India
Josephin Arockia Dhivya A., Vels Institute of Science Technology and
Advanced Studies, India
Thamizhvani T. R., Vels Institute of Science Technology and Advanced
Studies, India

Wireless sensor networking plays an important role in sensor signal communication and data transfer. The WSN is one of the trending fields in medical data mining. WSN provides the connecting link between the real physical world and virtual environment. In this study, the various WSN network algorithm, topologies, architectures, and their applications to medical technology are discussed. This study will be useful for the readers to know about various communicative technologies and standards followed in biomedical technology.

    Annu Priya, Birla Institute of Technology, Mesra, India
    Sudip Kumar Sahana, Birla Institute of Technology, Mesra, India

Processor scheduling is one of the thrust areas in the field of computer science. The future technologies use a huge amount of processors for execution of their tasks like huge games, programming software, and in the field of quantum computing. In hard real-time, many complex problems are solved by GPU programming. The primary concern of scheduling is to reduce the time complexity and manpower. There are several traditional techniques for processor scheduling. The performance of traditional techniques is reduced when it comes under huge processing of tasks. Most scheduling problems are NP-hard in nature. Many of the complex problems are recently solved by the GPU programming. GPU scheduling is another complex issue as it runs thousands of threads in parallel and needs to be scheduled efficiently. For such large-scale scheduling problem, the performance of state-of-the-art algorithms is very poor. It is observed that evolutionary and genetic-based algorithms exhibit better performance for large-scale combinatorial problems.

Foreword

Internet of Things (IoT) is a promising technology that continues to spread around the world, contributing to many challenges faced by cryptographic designers who are trying to meet IoT-constrained system safety standards. IoT stands in various applications of modern world such as smart home automation, elder people caring system, transportation, medical, health care application, Manufacturing industries, agriculture, energy management and environment monitoring system. IoT in nowadays is driven by field-programmable gate array (FPGA)-like devices, because these devices can interface with the outside world very easily and provide lowest power, lowest latency and best determinism. This book basically reflects all the application and implementation aspects of FPGA to make IOT as a real frontier in modern age. From the challenges in FPGA to Neuro Science in FPGA, every important aspect has been described in this book which leads to an effective IoT Implementation.

An FPGA can be called a programmable special-purpose processor because it can receive, process, and drive signals on its output pins at its input pins. The method described above is very deterministic. Such major benefits of FPGA with IoT have been incorporated in the book.

Some other practical applications of IoT using FPGA and their relevant conclusions have been included in different chapters of the book. The book also focuses on various security issues raised in IoT which can be resolved with the help of FPGA by incorporating secured end to end layer into its architecture. To perform this application, ultralow power and reduced area AES architecture with energy efficient DSE-S box techniques and clock gating for IoT applications are introduced in this book. Along with this, utilization of FPGA technology in providing the Internet of Things (IoT) with security and privacy services through means of cryptographic realizations have been examined in the book.

The book has enlightened various techniques that have been developed specifically for reconfigurable architectures which generate custom memory subsystems to take advantage of the peculiarities of a family of affine code called stencil code. It also focuses on techniques that exploit memory banking to allow for parallel and conflict-free memory accesses.

The book will provide an overview on an integrated framework to develop FPGA-based high-performance embedded systems for Edge Computing in Cyber-Physical Systems. SRAM-based FPGAs and their inherent run-time reconfigurability are integrated with smart power management strategies which have been described in the book. Reconfigurable FPGA, IoT and Artificial Intelligence based automotive systems have been also explained in this book. Modern vehicles are very complex by incorporating various computational signals and critical information transactions. Electronic Control Units (ECUs), which is embedded with various software functions, network information, sensor / actuator communication and dedicated hardware. Altogether, the special hardware needs to be adaptable to the current needs of next-generation vehicles. This book will give a broad idea about modern automotive systems by considering various factors. Finding the best reconfigurable Field Programmable Gate Array (FPGA) based hardware, intelligent assistance system for drivers and various communication protocols are elaborated in this chapter. Moreover, it also provides the essential knowledge of IoT based smart automotive systems along with its pros and cons.

High-Performance Computing Using FPGAs for Improving the DTC Performances of Induction Motors, High Performance of on-Chip Communication for FPGA based SoC for application of IoT have been also explored in this book.

In my opinion, this book has taken a very good first step towards the development of a methodology that helps to identify the most critical issues, and to create answers by collecting best practices from experts and early adaptors in the field of FPGA for IoT applications. The Ignite FPGA based IoT methodology is a very valuable tool for IoT product managers, IoT project managers, and IoT solution architects.

With best regards,

Vaibhav Jain
Department of CSE, School of Engineering and Technology, Jagran Lakecity University, Bhopal, India

Preface

In the last few decades we have witnessed several unpredictable works on IoT (Internet of Things). It works for the different applications like smart homes, wearable, smart cities, Industries, Health care, smart farming and smart supply chain etc. This textbook covers all the aspects of IoT applications used with FPGA. An FPGA can be considered a special purpose programmable processor, it can handle signals, process them and control signals on its output pins. If higher processing rates are needed, FPGA can be combined with the ARM processor to exploit higher levels of software functions, such as web servers or protection packages. The programmable feature of an FPGA is the key consideration. A manufacturer development kit is used for the configuration of FPGA during a standard development cycle. A printed circuit board with different sensor, communication and display components is developed using FPGA.

This book will provide an idea to the researchers as well as the students that how FPGA is beneficial from the other source. Also it will meet the need of those readers who would like to gain knowledge and understanding the use of FPGA in IoT application. This book is divided into nine chapters each chapter of this book has been specially prepared and corrected to cover different FPGA based IOT technology with its future application. It contains the application of FPGA in different areas.

This textbook is based on series of lectures on how FPGA's be used in IoT applications required for the researchers and the students. This has shown the working of FPGA with internet. It covers many topics which provide a brief idea about the research in the field of IoT. Through this book research and students will get a topic on which they can work and write research papers based on it. This provides various methodology and future work in which further research can be done.

The first chapter discuss about the challenges in FPGA technology paradigm for the implementation of IoT applications. Internet of things (IoT) is a recent technology and it will become a future of next generation of internet that connects several physical objects to interact amongst themselves without the assistance of human beings. It plays a significant role in our day to day life and used in several applications. IoT is a boon to this modern world but it lacks in security. It cannot prevent the user data from assailants, hackers and vulnerabilities. Field Programmable Gate Arrays (FPGA) helps to achieve all these objectives by incorporating secured end to end layer into its architecture. In this work, ultralow power and reduced area AES architecture with energy efficient DSE-S box techniques and clock gating for IoT applications are introduced. The proposed AES architecture is implemented over different FPGA families such as Cyclone I, Cyclone II, Virtex 5 and Kintex 7 respectively. From the experimental results, it is observed that the Kintex 7 FPGA kit consumes less power than other FPGA families.

In the second chapter authors discuss about the utilization of FPGA technology in providing the Internet of Things (IoT) with security and privacy services through means of cryptographic realizations. The first part of the chapter focuses on the practical aspects of using FPGAs for providing the IoT with security and privacy. The authors explore the feasibility of using these devices in constrained environments and the features that result attractive for their use in security applications. The second part is a revision of case studies reported in the literature where FPGAs have been employed for security applications in the context of IoT and related technologies. The main goal of this chapter is to present a general perspective of the role played by FPGA technologies in protecting the IoT.

The third chapter will first explore techniques that have been adopted directly from systems that posses a fixed memory subsystem such as CPU's and GPU's . Section 3 will focus on techniques that have been developed specifically for reconfigurable architectures which generate custom memory subsystems to take advantage of the peculiarities of a family of affine code called stencil code. The authors will focus on techniques that exploit memory banking to allow for parallel, conflict-free memory accesses in section 3.1 and techniques that generate an optimal memory micro-architecture for data reuse in section 3.2. Finally, Section 4 will explore the technique handling code still belonging to the affine family but the relative distance between the addresses.

The fourth chapter will provide an overview on an integrated framework to develop FPGA-based high-performance embedded systems for Edge Computing in Cyber-Physical Systems. Today, in Cyber – Physical systems, there is a transformation in which processing has been done on distributed mode rather than performing on centralized manner. Usually this type of approach is known as Edge computing, which demands hardware time to time when requirements in computing performance get increased. Considering this situations we must keep energy efficient and adaptability with the physical world. So to meet the above requirements, SRAM-based FPGAs and their inherent run-time reconfigurability are integrated with smart power management strategies. Sometime this approach fails in case of user accessibility and easy development. This chapter presents an integrated framework to develop FPGA-based high-performance embedded systems for Edge Computing in Cyber-

Physical Systems. The processing architecture will be based on hardware that helps us to manage reconfigurable systems from high level system without any human intervention.

The fifth chapter introduced Neuroscience In FPGA & Application in IOT. Neuroscience is a multidisciplinary science that is focused with the study of the structure and function of the nervous system. It contains the evolution, development, cellular and molecular biology, physiology, anatomy, and pharmacology of the nervous system, as well as computational, interactive and cognitive neuroscience. FPGA: Field Programmable Gate Array. A field-programmable gate array (FPGA) is an integrated circuit (IC) that can be programmed in the field after production. FPGAs are likely in principle to but have vastly wider potential application than, programmable read-only memory (PROM) chips. Internet of Things (IoT) is an integrated part of future internet including existing and evolving internet and network developments and could be conceptually defined as a worldwide dynamic network infrastructure with self-configuring capabilities based on standard and interoperable protocols communication where physical and virtual "things" have identities, physical attributes, and virtual personalities.

The sixth chapter provides the knowledge about the reconfigurable FPGA, IoT and Artificial Intelligence based automotive systems. Modern vehicles are very complex by incorporating various computational signals and critical information transactions. Electronic Control Units (ECUs), which is embedded with various software functions, network information, sensor / actuator communication and dedicated hardware. Altogether, the special hardware needs to be adaptable to the current needs of next-generation vehicles. This chapter will give a broad idea about modern automotive systems by considering various factors. Finding the best reconfigurable Field Programmable Gate Array (FPGA) based hardware, intelligent assistance system for drivers and various communication protocols are elaborated in this chapter. Moreover, it also provides the essential knowledge of IoT based smart automotive systems along with its pros and cons.

The seventh chapter based on High-Performance Computing Using FPGAs for Improving the DTC Performances of Induction Motors. The conventional Direct Torque Control (DTC) of induction motors becomes the most used control strategy. This control method is featured by its simplicity, fast torque response and it's less depending on the machine parameters. Despite the cited advantages, the conventional DTC suffers from several limitations, like the torque ripples. This chapter aims to improve the conventional DTC performances by keeping its advantages. These ripples depend on the hysteresis bandwidth of the torque and the sampling frequency. To accomplish, the conventional DTC limitations can be prevented by increasing the sampling frequency. Nevertheless, the operation with higher sampling frequency is not possible with the software solutions, like the Digital Signal Processor (DSP), due to the serial processing of the implemented algorithm. To overcome the DSP limitations, the Field Programmable Gate Array (FPGA) can be chosen as an alternative solution to implement the DTC algorithm with shorter execution time. In this work, the FPGA is chosen, thanks to its parallel processing.

In Chapter 8, processor scheduling is one of the thrust areas in the field of computer science. The future technologies use a huge amount of processor for execution of their tasks like huge games, programming software, and in the field of quantum computing. In hard real-time, many complex problems are solved by GPU programming. The primary concern of scheduling is to reduce the time complexity and manpower also. There are several traditional techniques exits for processor scheduling. The performance of traditional techniques is reduced when it comes under huge processing of tasks. Most scheduling problems are NP-hard in nature. Many of the complex problems are recently solved by the GPU programming. GPU scheduling is another complex issue as it runs thousands of threads in parallel and needs to be scheduled efficiently. For such large-scale scheduling problem, the performance of state of art algorithms is very poor. It is observed that Evolutionary and genetic-based algorithms exhibit better performance for large-scale combinatorial problems.

The last chapter will provide information about the use of wireless sensors in Biomedical Technology. The wireless sensor networking plays an important role in sensor signal communication and data transfer. The WSN is one of the trending fields in Medical Data Mining. WSN provides the connecting link between the real physical world and virtual Environment. In this study the various WSN network algorithm, Topologies, Architectures and its application towards to Medical Technology is discussed. This study will be useful for the readers to know about various communicative technology and its standards followed in Biomedical Technology.

Overall, we can conclude that this book will be beneficial for all those people who are directly or indirectly working in the area of IoT because this book covers all the applications based on FPGA with IoT. This also explains the different aspects of FPGA with its advantages and disadvantages. Book also shows the importance of FPGA in the field of induction motor, neuroscience, biomedical, etc. In this book we have covered the security parameters and processor scheduling related to IoT, including about the importance of CPU and GPU in the field of IoT.

Acknowledgment

We would like to express special thanks to management of Jagran Lakecity University and Bansal College of Engineering for their motivation and continuous support during the editing of the book. Also like to thank to IGI publication for giving the opportunity to write the book on this topic. We gratefully acknowledge the authors for their support and taking pain of writing book chapters. Finally, we would like to express our gratitude to our Parents family members and friends for their motivation. Last but not the least a special thanks to our beloved son Akshobhya Nair for giving us the time to complete this book.

Chapter 1
Challenges in FPGA Technology Paradigm for the Implementation ofIoT Applications

Arul Murugan C.
Karpagam College of Engineering, India

Banuselvasaraswathy B.
Sri Krishna College of Technology, India

ABSTRACT

Internet of things (IoT) is a recent technology, and it will become the next generation of internet that connects several physical objects to interact amongst themselves without the assistance of human beings. It plays a significant role in our day-to-day lives and is used in several applications. IoT is a boon to this modern world, but it lacks in security. It cannot protect the user data from assailants, hackers, and vulnerabilities. Field programmable gate arrays (FPGA) helps to achieve all these objectives by incorporating secured end-to-end layer into its architecture. In this chapter, ultralow power and reduced area AES architecture with energy efficient DSE-S box techniques and clock gating for IoT applications are introduced. The proposed AES architecture is implemented over different FPGA families such as Cyclone I, Cyclone II, Virtex 5, and Kintex 7, respectively. From the experimental results, it is observed that the Kintex 7 FPGA kit consumes less power than other FPGA families.

DOI: 10.4018/978-1-5225-9806-0.ch001

INTRODUCTION

IoT is a burst out from the wireless communication technology in 21st century. Its evolution is due to the emerging technologies, software embedded sensors, internet, and communication protocols. In the present globalized world, internet of things is generally used to access any data from anywhere with no limits. According to technology consulting firm Gartner, 2.1 billion devices are relied to be connected by 2020. Correspondingly, (Dave Evans, 2011) the Cisco Internet Business Solutions Group (IBSG) report clearly stated that the number internet connected devices is 500 Million in the year 2003. In future Cisco IBSG expects 50 billion devices to be connected to the internet by the year 2020.Therefore, IoT has a great impact to modernize the entire world in near future. IoT will systematically alter the way of living as the Internet strikes on education, health, homes, communications, transportation, cities, business, science etc in general because, daily life and interaction with every devices will connect to the internet in the upcoming decade.

The present IoT technology automates the process and ensures safety life of the individuals. The Automation and monitoring system demands mobility, fault tolerance and security features with the resource constrained inputs. Providing security and reliability within stipulated memory and processing capability confines the mobility of the user within a small Region of Interest, restricting their demands. In the advanced technology of connected devices, machines in addition to devices need to be secured in design and system levels. The use of FPGA benefits all the aforementioned objectives to be met.

The FPGA has reconfigurable hardware and it is a special purpose programmable processor. The term 'Field' indicates the operation changing capability within the field and 'Gate Array' means the construction of internal architecture of the device. It accepts the inputs from the input device, process it and sends the processed signals to the output device. IoT encloses an incredible number of small devices connected together. Therefore each device require end to end layered protection from the device level as shown in figure 1

In order to ensure security from the device layer to the network layer the FPGA system architecture should be designed with unique features The FPGA should protect all the data and hardware components from attackers. The Physically Un-clonable Function (PUF) technology was basically implemented in hardware to provide authentication by generating private and public keys for cryptographic methods. In order to carry out PUF technology in FPGA, the device should be well equipped with hardware components to support several cryptographic techniques like for AES, SHA, Elliptic Curve Cryptography etc. By using this provision, the user can design their own public key. So that, every hardware and their data communication are protected, secured and confidently used in IoT applications.

Figure 1. End to end layer connected system

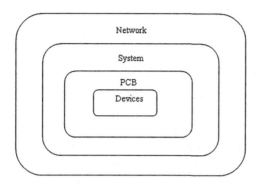

RELATED WORKS

Yasir et al (2014) introduced PRINCE algorithm. The proposed algorithm was implemented in virtex 4 and virtex 6 FPGA boards. The experimental results are compared and it is observed that virtex 6 has high efficiency, throughput, and low power consumption compared to virtex 4. It also proved that PRINCE algorithm gives better performance compared to the already proposed ICEBERG and SEA algorithm. Soheil Feizi et al (2014) presented a hardware implementation on Simon algorithm, It has different block size such as 32,48,64,96,148), word size (16,24,32,48,64) and key size (64,72/96,96/128,96/144,128/192/156). The Simon algorithm was demonstrated on FPGA model Virtex-5 XC5VFX200T. From the observed results, it is concluded that the Simon Algorithm was powerful when compared to X-TEA algorithm and Humming bird. Nascimento FM et al (2015) carried out HIGHT (Highest Security and Light Weight) algorithm in Finite State Machine (FSM) abstraction using VHDL. It uses 64 bit block size and 128 bits key size. The algorithm was implemented using Altera Quartus II version 11 and version 13. The simulation results showed that the version 13 exhibits low latency and high speed compared to version 11. Chatterjee S R et.al (2014) implemented pipelined architecture for Blowfish Algorithm on FPGA. In this approach, the text size is 64 bit and key size is 32 bit. The security is enhanced by using 16 rounds. The observation made from the result obtained, it is observed that the pipelined architecture has a minimum delay and high throughput than the non-pipelined architecture. Marzouqi H et.al (2015) proposed pipelined architecture with Redundant Signed Digit (RSD) based Elliptic curve cryptography (ECC) processor on high-speed FPGA. To optimize the multiplication process, karatsubaofman multiplication method was introduced to maximize throughput and minimize area. Dhanuka et al (2015) brings out a humming bird algorithm with 256 bit key size, 16 bit block and 16 bit Linear Feedback Shift Register (LFSR).In this method, two S box substitution techniques such as Boolean function representation method (BFR) and Look Up table method (LUT) are used for S box implementation. The results showed that the Four (4) - S box is better compared to one (1) - S box because of decreased cycle time and power consumption. Mahmood S S et.al (2014) proposed OLBCA Algorithm and implemented using FPGA. It has 64 bit plain text, 80 bit key size and 22 rounds. It comprises of three layers namely layer 1, layer 2 and layer 3. OLBCA take 2112 steps to complete all rounds while PRESENT takes 2976 steps to complete. Bansod et al (2015) demonstrated a PRESENT Algorithm which depends on bit permutation instruction Group operations (GRP). It utilizes 64 and 128 bit block size. PRESENT algorithm has one confusion property and diffusion property. The results are examined by comparing GRP rules for PRESENT Algorithm, SEA algorithm and ICEBERG algorithm and it was discerned that GRP rules for PRESENT algorithm are more applicable. Zhang et al (2014) designed a light weight block cipher known as RECTANGLE. In this design, bit slice techniques are handled to scale down the hardware cost as well as to carry out efficient software implementation with high speed. It has 64 bit block size and 80 or 12 bit key size for 25 rounds. The design offer great adaptability in both hardware and software environment. Poonam Poonam Jindal & Brahmjit Singh, (2015) modified the existing RC6 algorithm to Maximum Column - Rivest Cipher (MC-RC) 6 with enriched architecture for better performance. It has 128-bit block size and variable key size 128/192/256 bits. It was noticed that MC-RC6 has less avalanche effect compared to RC5 and RC6 algorithm. Farashahi et al (2014) proposed 128-bit Advance Encryption Standard (AES) algorithm based on 2 slow retiming techniques on FPGA. Pipelining, sub stage pipelining and rolling concept are used to embellish the architecture with reduced execution time. The multiplication process was introduced in the third transformation process of AES algorithm to decrease the count of registers used in the design. The feedback loop was integrated into the 2 slow retiming technique balance the register in design. Sood et al (2010) proposed a scheme for eliminating all those limitations of password based authentication scheme described above. This scheme gives shielding to various attacks and anonymity for the users. Sunil VK Gaddam et.al (2011) have generated acryptography 256 bit key using finger print cancellable template. They used three phase for key generation from finger print. Shriya et al. (2015) presents various existing distributed techniques for node clone detection. Zhijun Li et al. (2013) suggests two distributed protocols for clone detection. Siba et al. (2011) introduced a detection scheme for node clone detection and use zero knowledge protocol. A 128-bit key with compact FPGA architecture was suggested by Pawe Chodowiec *et.al (2003)* using AES algorithm with FPGA implementation. Sumio Morioka et.al (2003)proposed a low power AES architecture to yield a low power S-Box. Manoj B C et.al (2013) introduced a trusted system with the aim of safety as a demand to increase security. V. Bradshaw (2006) striving to save energy in today's world many buildings are constructed with sensors. Alireza Hodjat et. Al (2004) proposed various pipelining techniques and pipeline registersto reduce the delay at the time of implementation. Chi-Wu Huang et.al (2007)introduced data path implementation with 32 bit in small Xilinx FPGA chip by the usage of BRAMs. Liu Zhenglin et.al (2007)realized the S-Box functions using XOR operations. M. Benabdellah et. Al (2011) a new method of hybrid approach was proposed in AES encryption algorithm and compares the designed FMT methos with other methods. T. Good et, al (2007) proposed pipelined concept in AES with two different designs to achieve the operations of sub bytes. Xinmiao Zhang et. Al (2004) uses non feedback modes to achieve high speed for AES Implementation. T Morkel, et.al (0002) uses filters in quantum encryption techniques to provide a platform for hardware implementation. Yao-Jen Chang, Wende, et.al (2004)generated a cryptographic key for various attacks. C. E., et.al (1948) used the properties of bio-chaotic algorithm for varous analysis purpose. J. Daugman et.al(1993) proposed a method for identifying human face structure. Shenglin Yang, et.al (2004) offers invariant features with greater security in emerging technology.

Table 1. Comparison of different existing cryptographic algorithms

S.No	Author	Block Size	Algorithm	Key Size	Rounds
1	Amer et al	64	PRINCE	128	12
2	SoheilFeizi et al	32,48, 64,96, 128	SIMON	Variable	32,36, 42,44, 52,54
3	Nascimento FM et al	64	HIGHT	128	32
4	Chatterjee S R et.al	64	BLOW FISH	32	16
5	Marzouqi H et.al	N/A	RSD	N/A	N/A
6	Dhanuka et al	16	HUMMING BIRD	256	N/A
7	Mahmood S S et.al	64	OLBCA	80	22
8	Bansod et al	64	PRESENT	128	32
9	Zhang et al	N/A	RECTANLGE	80	N/A
11	Poonam Jindal et.al	128	MC-RC6	128, 192, 256	20
13	Farashahi et al	128	AES	128/192/ 256	10/12 /14

From the table 1, it is clear that the symmetric algorithm is faster than asymmetric algorithm and efficiency in hardware is also high compared to software. So, in this paper, hardware optimization design for AES algorithm operating at ultralow-power and high speed is presented.

AES ALGORITHM

AES algorithm can be implemented in both software and hardware. The proposed design uses variable key sizes to achieve multiple security levels. In addition, power and energy used for both data path and key expansion are also optimized. AES is a symmetric key algorithm (Umeer Farooq & M.Faisal Aslam, 2017) uses a single key for both encryption and decryption. It has 128 bit block size and variable key sizes: 128/192/256 bits respectively. AES is an iterative algorithm and each iteration is called as rounds. The number of rounds for variable key size is listed in table 2.

Table 2. Comparison of advanced encryption standard algorithm of different key size

Parameters	AES 128	AES 192	AES 256
Block Length	4	4	4
Key Length	4	4	4
No of Rounds	10	12	14

In AES architecture, the encryption and decryption data path consist of the individual block. The transformation involved in encryption and decryption process is Sub Byte /Inv-Sub Byte, Shift Row/Inv- Shift Row, Mix Column/Inv-Mix Column and Add Round Key.

AES Encryption Process

AES works on an array of 4x4 matrix known as state. All encryption process are performed through state. The result of each and every information is stored as state and this state become input for the next transformation process. All transformations of encryption process are performed only on a state. After each transformation values are stored in a state, this state is the input for the next transformation process. It consists of following four transformation processes namely:

1.   Substitute bytes (or) Sub-bytes

2.   Shift rows
3.   Mix Columns
4.   Add Round Key

The algorithm starts with add round key. It consists of 10 rounds. In first nine rounds, it performs with all four process. But, in the ninth round it removes mix column stage and proceeds with the remaining three stages.

Sub-Bytes

This process performs non-linear transformation on individual byte of input state independently. Here, each byte of each stage is replaced by substituting each byte from substitution box using Look Up Table (LUT) method. LUT lessens the latency, computation time and hardware complexity. S box is the only non-linear transformation process in AES algorithm. The s box has two transformations process. In the first transformation, the multiplicative inverse is performed over finite field Galois Field (GF (2^8)), where all input zero bits are mapped to itself. In the second transformation, affine transformation is performed over finite field GF (2). The same process is used for decryption without invertible operation.

Shift Rows

The function of shift rows is to carry out the circular shift over the individual bits. The circular shift is performed only over the last three rows. It is similar to diffusion property where the first row of the state does not perform any shift, but the 2,3 and 4 rows are rotated by one, two or three bytes respectively.

Mix Column

Here, individual column is treated separately as a fourth polynomial. These polynomials are considered over GF (2^8) and modulo x^4+1 is multiplied by a fixed polynomial m(x). The m(x) is defined as follows

m(x) = {03} x^3 + {01}x^2 + {01}x + {02}

Add Round Key

This is the final stage of the encryption process. It is used to mix the key transformations with the data being operated on. In this process, the outputs are obtained by performing xor operation over the bytes of current state matrix with the bytes of round key.

Add Round Key= current State Matrix $\oplus$ Round Key

Key Expansion Module

The key expansion module module (Umeer Farooq & M.Faisal Aslam, 2017) estimates a round key to determine the number of rounds to be accomplished by cipher. The number of rounds is calculated based on the original key size. It consists of three modules namely rot word, round const and sub word. The function of rot word is to perform cyclic permutation over input word. Sub word takes four input byte and applies s box over input and produces output. Round const performs bit wise XOR operation. It can be further implanted by using on chip memory and computing resources.

AES Decryption Process

Decryption process is the reversal process of encryption. The original message are recovered from cipher text and given to the output of decryption block. The cipher block of encryption and decryption differs but the key expansion scheduling remains same for both the process. It consists of following four transformations. They are

Inverse Sub Bytes

In this transformation, the bytes are transformed by the non-linear values form the inverse S-box.

Inverse Shift Rows

This function carry over the inverse operation of shift rows in encryption process where cyclic shifting operation is performed.

Inverse Add Round Key

This process is similar to add round key of encryption process where inverse operation is carried out in decryption process.

Inverse Mix Columns

This process is alike mix column in encryption process but performs inverse operation in decryption process.

There exist 10 rounds in decryption process as similar to encryption process. The first 9 rounds of decryption process consider all four stage of transformation. At the last round, the inverse mix column stage is exempted and continues with the other three stages.

S BOX TECHNIQUES

S box is the most powerful component in symmetric key algorithm and performs substitution. According to Shannon property of confusion (Shannon.C.E,1949), S box provides the connectivity between the cipher text and key. The strength of ciphers can be increased by incorporating permutation and substitution circuits alternatively. Recently, non-linear transformation should be added to algorithm to enhance the functionality and remain strong besides differential and linear cryptographic attacks (Hosseinkhani & Javadi, 2012).

Properties of S Box

S box is widely used and plentiful methods are introduced to make S box most efficient and difficult to attack. The robustness and of s box depends on properties. Still researcher finds difficult to analyse the properties of s box due to lack of proper guideline. As a result, more importance should be given while designing s box for efficient AES algorithm. This section deals with some s box properties (Kamsiah et.al, 2014) as following

Algebraic Complexity

It is required to withstand against algebraic attacks and other interpolation attacks.

Bit Independence Condition

In this condition, the independence between bits should be maintained low. If the independence between the bits increases then it becomes tedious to assume the design of system.

Balancing

If S:$\{0,1\}n \rightarrow \{0,1\}m$ is balanced, then HW(f) = 2n-1. The balancing of s box is dependent of the higher magnitude of ^{imbalance} functionality which results in increased probability linear approximation.

Differential Uniformity

The value of differential uniformity should be controlled and kept low to safeguard the s box from different cryptanalysis.

Opposite Fixed (OFp) and Fixed Points (Fp)

The value of the fixed points and opposite fixed points of the s box should be kept as small as possible in order to reduce leakage in cryptanalysis.

Nonlinearity

For all non – zero linear combinations of x Boolean functions fi: $\{0,1\} \rightarrow \{0,1\}$, i= x-1,…,1,0. The value of S:$\{0,1\}x \rightarrow \{0,1\}y$ is should be defined as the minimum value to repel against linear and differential cryptanalysis attacks.

Strict Avalanche Criterion (SAC)

Whenever there occurs a change in one bit of input, it affects the fraction of the output bits. Then the cryptographic function is to meet the avalanche criterion. It becomes tedious process to analyse the cipher text when it is exposed to external attack.

Linear Approximation

In order to protect the s box from linear and differential cryptanalysis linear approximation value should be kept minimum.

Robustness

Consider F = (f1, f2,...,fn) . Let F be an n × n S-box and fi is a component function of S-box mapping fi: {0, 1}n →{0, 1}.F should repel to bear against cryptanalysis attack.

An efficient s box should satisfy maximum properties to become strong and resist against several external and internal attacks. In this DSE-S box is utilized

Comparison of Previous S Box Techniques

(Banik, 2015) compared energy consumption of LUT, Canright and DSE S box Techniques shown in table 3.

Table 3. Comparison of several existing S box techniques for AES 128 algorithm

S Box	Mix Column	Energy (in PJ)
Canright	108 gates	708.5
LUT	108 gates	755.3
DSE	108 gates	350.7

From the table 3, it is inferred that DSE S box techniques consume less energy than LUT and Canright S box. Hence, DSE S box technique is preferred for architecture design but it has main drawback of high area .This work, focus on to reduce the area of DSE S box by using following techniques.

Proposed S Box Design

The S box has great impact on power consumption and area of AES design. In this design most energy efficient is DSE S-box is utilized. DSE S box consumes less energy but occupies more space. The power consumption of DSE S box is minimized by decreasing the number of operation within the S box. To lessen the storage area of DSE S box shift registers are introduced. In addition, several optimization techniques are incorporated into the introduced design to result in energy efficient and reduced area DSE-S box. The flip flops and control logic in the data path are minimized by using shift registers to reduce the power consumption and area in the data path. However, reducing the usage of flip-flop in turn decreases the number of clock buffers and power consumed by the clock tree because the clock buffers consumes major amount of power in the clock tree. The main advantage of using shift register in this design simplifies the number of steps in loading of data and key. Moreover, original message and key are loaded into the state register simultaneously with the help of shift operations in the shift register. In key expansion module several mechanism are introduced to save power. It comprises of two 4*4 shifter registers, key transform module with four S boxes and XOR gate (Duy-Hieu Bui, 2017). In 128 key bits only one shift register is used. The clock signal of other shift registers is disabled to save power. Moreover, clock gating techniques are applied to save power in key expansion mechanism. It consists of AND gate with enable signal and clock signal as inputs. The output of enable signal is connected to the inverter. It consists of global clock signal which is being controlled by separate AND gate. In this clock gating structure, if enable signal is low and clock signal is high, the AND gate output becomes high. During positive edge of global clock signal and based on the availability of new data the switching activity is performed. During negative edge, switching activity is not carried out to save power. The clock gating structure is applied in each and every round of encryption and decryption process in AES algorithm.

FPGA ARCHITECTURE

The FPGA architecture includes I/O blocks, configurable logic blocks (CLB) and switch matrix. It is two dimensional and helps in providing interconnection between the logic blocks. The main function of CLB is to implement the user logic. It comprises of inputs, outputs and digital logic. I/O pads are very much useful for the external world to communicate with different operations. Switch matrix are used to connect two logic blocks. CLB are the main block in FPGA for implementing AES transformation operations like Add round key, Mix columns and shift rows. S box can be implemented in memory or CLB. The implementation of both cipher module and key expansion module using CLB in AES algorithm results in improved delay. There exists different FPGA family architecture. In this article, Cyclone I, Cyclone II, Virtex 5 and Kintex 7 FPGA family kits are used for design implementation.

RESULTS AND DISCUSSION

In this work, AES architecture is implemented on different FPGA families and power consumed in each FPGA family is being analysed clearly. For configuring FPGA, Xilinx ISE software are used to generate bit stream file and for further enhanced development.

Figure 2. Proposed S box structure with clock gating and shift register

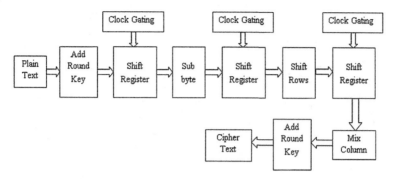

Figure 3. Simulation result of shift row transformation

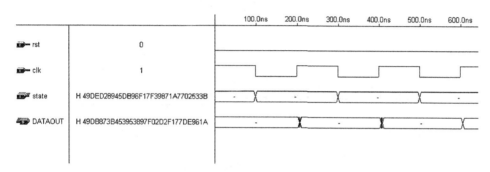

Figure 4. Simulation result of Key Schedule Generation

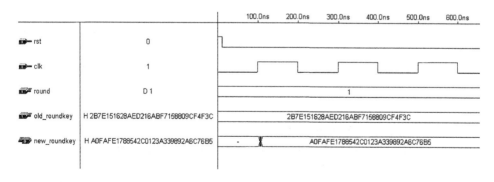

Figure 5. Simulation result of Inverse Byte Substitution.

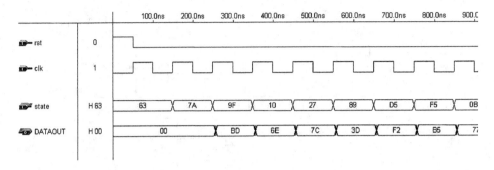

Figure 6. Simulation result of Inverse shift row transformation

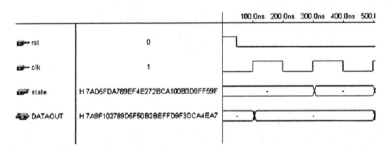

Figure 7. Simulation results of Inverse mix column Transformation

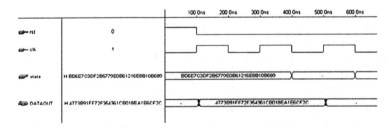

The ultralow power AES algorithm is implemented in cyclone II, Cyclone IV E, Virtex 5, Kintex 7 FPGA kits. The powers consumed by AES Architecture in each different family are tabulated.

From the figure 14, it is analysed that the AES algorithm implemented in Kintex 7 FPGA kit consumes less power compared to other FPGA families.

Figure 8. Simulation result of encryption process

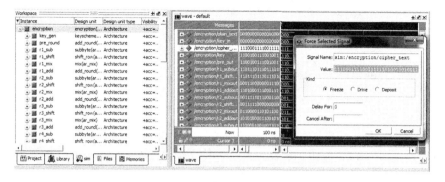

Figure 9. Simulation result of decryption process

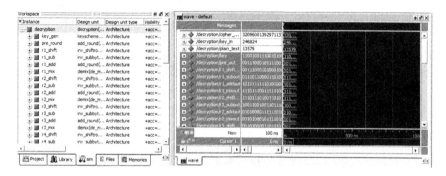

Table 4. Comparison of power consumption by different FPGA families

S.NO	Family	Device	Power(mw)
1	Cyclone II	EP2C35F672C6	156.80
2	Cyclone IV E	EP4CE115F29C8	231.45
3	Virtex 5	Xc5vlx50t	584
4	Kintex 7	Xc7K160t	148

Figure 10. Design summary of Cyclone II family FPGA kit

Top-level Entity Name	full_encryption
Family	Cyclone II
Device	EP2C35F672C6
Power Models	Final
Total Thermal Power Dissipation	156.80 mW
Core Dynamic Thermal Power Dissipation	0.00 mW
Core Static Thermal Power Dissipation	80.08 mW
I/O Thermal Power Dissipation	76.72 mW
Power Estimation Confidence	Low: user provided insufficient toggle rate data

Figure 11. Design summary of Cyclone IV E family FPGA kit

Top-level Entity Name	full_encryption
Family	Cyclone IV E
Device	EP4CE115F29C8
Power Models	Final
Total Thermal Power Dissipation	231.45 mW
Core Dynamic Thermal Power Dissipation	0.00 mW
Core Static Thermal Power Dissipation	98.97 mW
I/O Thermal Power Dissipation	132.48 mW
Power Estimation Confidence	Low: user provided insufficient toggle rate data

Figure 12. Design summary of Virtex 5 family FPGA kit

Device	
Family	Virtex5
Part	xc5vlx50t
Package	ff1136
Grade	Commercial
Process	Typical
Speed Grade	-2

On-Chip	Power (W)	Used	Available	Utilization (%)
Clocks	0.024	1	---	---
Logic	0.000	2243	28800	8
Signals	0.000	2722	---	---
IOs	0.000	386	480	80
Leakage	0.560			
Total	0.584			

Environment	
Ambient Temp (C)	50.0
Use custom TJA?	No
Custom TJA (C/W)	NA
Airflow (LFM)	250
Heat Sink	Medium Profile

	Effective TJA (C/W)	Max Ambient (C)	Junction Temp (C)
Thermal Properties	1.5	84.1	50.9

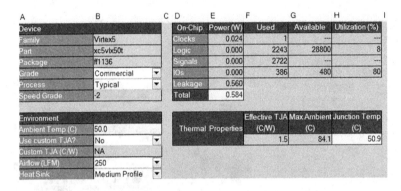

Figure 13. Design summary of Kintex 7 family FPGA kit

Device	
Family	Kintex7
Part	xc7k160t
Package	fbg676
Grade	Commercial
Process	Typical
Speed Grade	-3

On-Chip	Power (W)	Used	Available	Utilization (%)
Clocks	0.000	1	---	---
Logic	0.000	2255	101400	2
Signals	0.000	2860	---	---
IOs	0.000	386	400	97
Leakage	0.148			
Total	0.148			

Environment	
Ambient Temp (C)	25.0
Use custom TJA?	No
Custom TJA (C/W)	NA
Airflow (LFM)	250
Heat Sink	Medium Profile

	Effective TJA (C/W)	Max Ambient (C)	Junction Temp (C)
Thermal Properties	1.9	84.7	25.3

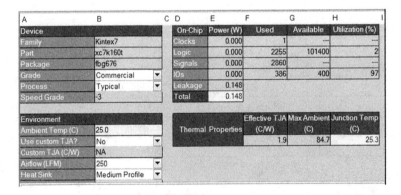

Figure 14. Comparison of power consumed by AES algorithm in different FPGA kit

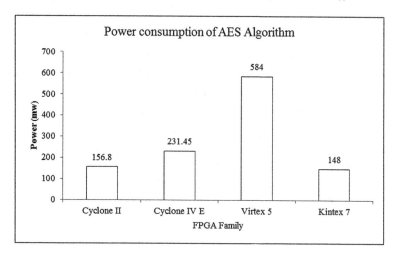

FPGA CHALLENGES

The challenges in FPGA comprises of unauthorized access, denial of service, privacy, malicious control and security. A hardware-first strategy has been interrelated historically to improve upon protection of the system on chip (SoC) possible to implement fully securing devices namely, tablets, FPGAs, intelligent appliances, smartphones and wearables. For these motives, IOT devices should leverage hardware primarily based security and isolation mechanisms that offer sturdy safety towards numerous sorts of attack., Drone helicopters, thermostats and smart appliances are the presence of entire control systems. IOT encounters with the appearance of complete systems, actuators and sensors at the edge of the network. These solutions paved to encounter with extensive variety of technologies that interact in IOT.The features are provided with dramatic flexible interface in long periods of sleep, low power access controls and short bursts of activity with wireless interfaces. To interface with the real world it is directly involved with a great variety of possessions. Those traits necessitate a new form of device which is simplified between the following layer of IOT features and capillary community. There are many improvements in the transmission of data such as electronic mail, commercial activity on the internet etc. Many online transactions and many internet entries are happening now a day. Some of those include sensitive personal and confidential informations like bank account details, Passwords for bank transaction and military instruction etc. This leads to the necessity for secured communication. After all, the amalgamation of platforms and numerous IOT devices create intensification among new digital infrastructure in ever-widening bandwidth.

CONCLUSION

In this paper, new AES architecture was designed with energy efficient DSE S box. However, this S box consumes less power but occupies larger area. Thus shift registers are introduced to minimize area. In addition clock gating techniques are introduced by minimizing the usage of flip-flop to optimize power. The proposed architecture is implemented over different FPGA families such as cyclone I, cyclone II, Virtex 5 and Kintex 7. The experimental results showed that the power consumed by the kintex 7 FPGA family is less when compared to other families. Moreover, for configuring FPGA, Xilinx ISE software is used to generate bit stream file and for further enhanced development. The designed AES architecture results in ultralow power and reduced area. Hence it can be well suited for IoT applications.

ABBREVIATIONS AND ACRONYMS

AES - Advance Encryption Standard
BFR - Boolean function representation method
CLB - Configurable Logic Blocks
DSE-Decoder Switch Encoder
ECC - Elliptic curve cryptography
FPGA - Field Programmable Gate Arrays
GF - Galois Field
GRP - Group operations
IBSG - Internet Business Solutions Group
IoT - Internet of things
LFSR - Linear Feedback Shift Register
LUT - Look Up table method
MC-RC - Maximum Column - Rivest Cipher
PUF - Physically Un-clonable Function
RSD - Redundant Signed Digit
S - Substitute bytes (or) Sub-bytes

REFERENCES

Abbas, Y. A., Jidin, R., Jamil, N., Z'aba, M. R., Rusli, M. E., & Tariq, B. (2014). Implementation of PRINCE Algorithm in FPGA. *International Conference on Information Technology and Multimedia (ICIMU)*. 10.1109/ICIMU.2014.7066593

Autkar, Dhage, & Bholane. (2015). A Survey on Distributed Techniques for Detection of Node Clones in Wireless Sensor Networks. IEEE.

Banik, S. (2015). Selected Areas in Cryptography (SAC). *22nd International Conference*.

Bansod, G., Raval, N., & Pisharoty, N. (2015). *Implementation of a New Lightweight Encryption Design for Embedded Security. IEEE Transaction.* doi:10.1109/TIFS.2014.2365734

Benabdellah, M., Regragui, F., & Bouyakhf, E. H. (2011). Hybrid Methods of Image Compression-Encryption. *J. of Commun. & Comput, 1*(1-2).

Bradshaw, V. (2006). *The Building Environment: Active and Passive Control Systems*. River Street, NJ: John Wiley & Sons, Inc.

Bui, D.-H., Puschini, D., Bacles-Min, S., & Tran, X.-T. (2017). *AES Datapath Optimization Strategies for Low-Power Low-Energy Multisecurity-Level Internet-of-Thing Applications. IEEE Transactions on Very Large Scale Integration (VLSI) Systems*.

Chang', Y.-J., Zhung, W., & Chen, T. (2004). Biometrics-Based Cryptographic Key Generation *IEEE International Conference on Multimedia and Expo (ICME)*.

Chatterjee, S. R., Majumder, S., Pramanik, B., & Chakraborty, M. (2014). FPGA implementation of pipelined blowfish algorithm. *5th International Symposium*.

Chodowiec & Gaj. (2003). Very Compact FPGA Implementation of the AES Algorithm. *LNCS, 2779,* 319–333.

Daugman, J. (1993). High Confidence visual recognition of persons by a test of statistical independence. *IEEE Transactions on Pattern Analysis and Machine Intelligence, 15*(11), 1148–1161. doi:10.1109/34.244676

Evans, D. (2011). *The Internet of Things - How the Next Evolution of the Internet is Changing Everything*. Cisco Internet Business Solutions Group.

Farashahi, Rashidi, & Saye. (2014). *FPGA based fast and high-throughput 2-slow retiming 128bit AES encryption algorithm*. Elsevier.

Farooq & Aslam. (2017). Comparative analysis of different AES implementation techniques for efficient resource usage and better performance on FPGA. *Journal of King Saud University-Computer and Information Science,* 295-302.

Feizi, S., Ahmadi, A., & Nemati, A. (2014). *A Hardware Implementation of Simon Cryptography Algorithm*. ICCKE. doi:10.1109/ICCKE.2014.6993386

Gaddam & Lal. (2011). Development of Bio-Crypto Key From Fingerprints Using Cancelable Templates. *International Journal on Computer Science and Engineering, 3*(2), 775-783.

Good, T., & Benaissa, M. (2007). Pipelined AES on FPGA with support for feedback modes (in a multi-channel environment. *IET, VOL, 1*(1), 1–10. doi:10.1049/iet-ifs:20060059

Hodjat, A., & Verbauwhede, I. (2004). A 21.54 Gbits/s Fully Pipelined AES Processor on FPGA *Proceedings of the 12th Annual IEEE Symposium on Field-Programmable Custom Computing Machines.* 10.1109/FCCM.2004.1

Hosseinkhani & Javadi. (2012). Using Cipher Key to Generate Dynamic S-Box in AES Cipher Syst. *International Journal of Computer Science and Security, 6*(1).

Huang, Chang, Lin, & Tai. (2007). Compact FPGA Implementation of 32-bits AES Algorithm Using Block RAM. IEEE.

Jindal & Singh. (2015). *Analyzing the Security Performance Tradeoff in Block Ciphers.* ICCCA.

Kdhanuka, Sachdeva, & Sheikhnitk. (2015). Cryptographic algorithm optimization. *IEEE-IACC.*

Li, Z., & Gong, G. (2013). *On the Node Clone Detection in Wireless Sensor Networks.* IEEE. doi:10.1109/TNET.2012.2233750

Manoj, B. C. (2013). A Trust System for Broadcast Communications in SCADA. *International Journal of Engineering and Computer Science, 2*(12), 3534-3537.

Marzouqi, Al-Qutayri, Salah, Schinianakis, & Stouraitis. (2015). A HighSpeed FPGA Implementation of an RSD-Based ECC Processor. *IEEE Transaction.*

Morioka & Satoh. (2003). An Optimized S-Box Circuit Architecture for Low Power AES Design. Springer-Verlag.

Morkel & Eloff. (2002). *Encryption Techniques: A Timeline Approach.* Information and Computer Security Architecture (ICSA) Research Group Department of Computer Science University of Pretoria.

Nascimento, dos Santos, & Moreno. (2015). A VHDL implementation of the Lightweight Cryptographic Algorithm. *HIGHT.*

Nazran, Pauzi & Ali. (2014). Study of S-box properties in block cipher. *International Conference on Computer, Communications and Control Technology.*

Salim, S., AlDabbagh, M., & Shaikhli, I. F. T. A. (2014). *OLBCA: A New Lightweight Block Cipher Algorithm*. ICACSAT.

Shannon, C. E. (1948). A Mathematical Theory of Communication. *The Bell System Technical Journal, 27*(4), 623–656. doi:10.1002/j.1538-7305.1948.tb00917.x

Shannon, C. E. (1949). Communication Theory of Secrecy Systems. *Bell Sysit. Tech, 5*(28), 656–715.

Sood, S. K., Sarje, A. K., & Singh, K. (2010). An Improvement of Liou et al.'s Authentication Scheme Using Smart Cards. *International Journal of Computers and Applications, 1*(8), 16–23.

Udgata, S. K., Mubeen, A., & Sabat, S. L. (2011). *Wireless Sensor Network Security model using Zero Knowledge Protocol*. IEEE. doi:10.1109/icc.2011.5963368

Yang, S., & Verbauwhede, I. M. (2004). *Secure Fuzzy Vault Based Fingerprint Verification System*. IEEE.

Zhang, Bao, Lin, Rijmen, Yang, & Verbauwhede. (2014). *RECTANGLE: A Bit-slice Ultra-Lightweight Block Cipher Suitable for Multiple Platforms*. Academic Press.

Zhang & Parhi. (n.d.). High-Speed VLSI Architectures for the AES Algorithm. *IEEE Transactions on Very Large Scale Integration Systems, 12*(9).

KEY TERMS AND DEFINITIONS

Advance Encryption Standard (AES): It is a symmetric key algorithm and the plain text is processed in blocks. A similar key is utilized for both encryption and decryption.

Cryptography: It is used to protect the information. Cryptography is the study of secret writing or art of solving codes.

Decryption: It is the way of recovering ciphertext from plaintext.

Encryption: It is the way of converting plaintext to ciphertext.

Field Programmable Gate Array (FPGA): FPGA is basically a silicon chip that has reprogrammable digital circuitry.

Internet of Things (IoT): IoT is a convergence platform which enables anything unconnected to connect with any device.

Key: Group of bits which plays a vital role in decryption and encryption. It is information stored in cipher which is known only to sender/receiver.

S-Box: A substitution-box is a primary component of symmetric key algorithm. S-boxes are composed of highly nonlinear Boolean function. It performs substitution process in symmetric key algorithm.

Chapter 2
Use of FPGAs for Enabling Security and Privacy in the IoT:
Features and Case Studies

Arturo Diaz-Perez
*Centro de Investigación y de Estudios Avanzados del Instituto Politécnico
Nacional, Guadalajara, Mexico*

Miguel Morales-Sandoval
*Centro de Investigación y de Estudios Avanzados del Instituto Politécnico
Nacional, Tamaulipas, Mexico*

Carlos Andres Lara-Nino
iD https://orcid.org/0000-0003-0333-2564
*Centro de Investigación y de Estudios Avanzados del Instituto Politécnico
Nacional, Tamaulipas, Mexico*

ABSTRACT

*In this chapter, the authors discuss the utilization of FPGA technology in providing
the internet of things (IoT) with security and privacy services through means of
cryptographic realizations. The first part of the chapter focuses on the practical
aspects of using FPGAs for providing the IoT with security and privacy. The authors
explore the feasibility of using these devices in constrained environments and
the features attractive for their use in security applications. The second part is a
revision of case studies reported in the literature where FPGAs have been employed
for security applications in the context of IoT and related technologies. The main
goal of this chapter is to present a general perspective of the role played by FPGA
technologies in protecting the IoT.*

DOI: 10.4018/978-1-5225-9806-0.ch002

INTRODUCTION

The Internet of Things is an emerging technology of rapid development. In this paradigm, every-day objects are connected to the internet in aims to increase the volume of information that can be gathered from the environment. With this data, developers can offer improved services for the user. Manufacturing, military, transportation, healthcare, urban development, first response, and domestic appliances are some of its most popular applications. The IoT ecosystem is shown in Figure 1. It is estimated that by 2020 the number of IoT devices installed will reach 31B, with this amount growing more than twice by 2025 up to 75B (Columbus, 2017).

Some of the information harvested by IoT devices is inherently sensitive, and in other cases the massive volume of shared information can be used for inferring user's behaviors. These data ought to be protected from malicious actors to ensure that only authorized entities have access to them, that they are not altered during the transmission, that they come from an authentic source, and that they are being transmitted to an authentic collector. Security services of confidentiality, integrity, and authentication are required for mitigating these risks. Multiple protocols have been designed for providing these services and ensuring that IoT messages are secured against these threats by means of cryptography.

Figure 1. The IoT ecosystem

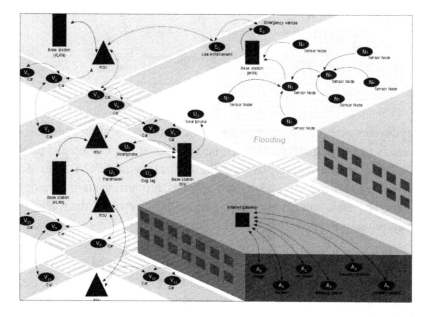

Everyday objects are provided with internet connection which enables querying information in real time. The depicted scenario shows multiple technologies which are present in our lives.

Deploying practical cryptography in the IoT paradigm is not an easy task. Multiple IoT devices suffer from constraints in their processing power, physical size, communications bandwidth, or energy allowance. Designing and implementing cryptographic algorithms tailored for the application constraints is the goal of Lightweight Cryptography (Buchanan, Li, & Asif, 2017).

Typical IoT devices are equipped with small processors for performing their regular tasks: sensing and processing of data. Security services require running cryptographic algorithms which represent an overhead to their regular operations. Figure 2 illustrates an architecture of such devices.

Figure 2. Composition of an IoT mote

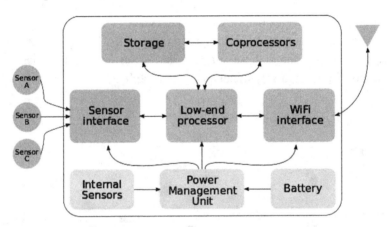

These devices are equipped with processors and communication interfaces which gather data from the in-platform sensors, perform some processing, and publish it.

In this chapter, the authors discuss the utilization of FPGA technology in providing the IoT with security and privacy services through means of cryptographic realizations. The main aim is to present a general perspective of the role played by FPGA technologies in protecting the IoT. Our goals can be summarized as:

- Discussing the needs of providing security for constrained environments and how these can be solved with the use of FPGAs.
- Presenting the advantages and challenges in the use of FPGAs for security applications.

- Reviewing case studies where FPGAs have been successfully used in security applications.

To the best of our knowledge this is the first chapter that addresses these matters in a comprehensive manner. Additionally, our review of case studies which back up our claims is a significant improvement over less detailed descriptive texts.

BACKGROUND

In this section the authors provide notations and concepts which are fundamental for the understanding of this chapter. Readers familiar with these concepts might choose to head for the next section.

Three key points are discussed. First, the operational scope and composition of the IoT paradigm are explained. Then, we provide brief notions regarding to provide security services through means of cryptography. Lastly, we explore a particular branch of cryptography which has been associated with the IoT and other constrained technologies.

The Internet of Things Paradigm

Imagine yourself shopping at the supermarket, and somehow you forgot to check if there is enough milk in the fridge. If you get more, some of it might spoil. But if there is not enough, the children will not be able to enjoy their cereal bowl. Then you remember that your new fridge has smart capabilities. A quick look at the fridge app in your smartphone and the doubt is solved!

This scenario is a trivial application of the IoT but represents just one of the several possibilities which appear once you have constant feedback from *the things*. In our hypothetical case, the fridge has some sensor which allows it to monitor its contents. This data is then gathered by some collector and probably published through the internet. When the remote app is launched, the user has access to the information published by the fridge in real time. The user can then take better decisions based on these data. In theory it would be possible to replace the fridge with any other object and obtain some information from it. The sensors would be different, but the communications dynamic can be identical.

There are different possibilities for sensing physical magnitudes. In the case of the fridge, it might be equipped with some vision system. Such images can be processed by the *IoT node* installed in the appliance in order to extract information: for this example, an inventory of its contents. When the node performs computing over the data sensed, it is called *Edge Computing* (Shi & Dustdar, 2016; Shi, Cao,

Zhang, Li, & Xu, 2016). Another alternative is that the items placed in the fridge have some computing capabilities as well. R*adio-frequency identification (RFID)* is a technology already in deployment for inventory control and security in commerce as well as other applications (Want, Nath, & Reynolds, 2006). These RFID devices, denominated *tags*, are said to be *passive*. This means that they do not require to be equipped with a power source. They are usually rather simple, which reduces their production costs. If the milk box placed in the fridge has an RFID tag adhered to it, the fridge can read this tag and verify that a milk box is inside. Figure 3 shows the classical components of an RFID ecosystem.

Figure 3. Components of an RFID system

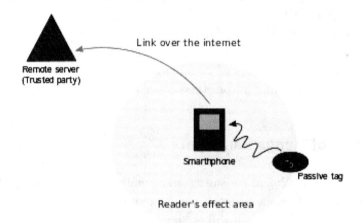

The passive tags must receive a stimulus from the reader which are mobile platforms requiring intervention from a trusted party for tag authentication.

When the thing of interest is restricted to a physical space, the IoT model is simplified. We assume that the power and network availability are constants. This simplifies the design of the IoT nodes and the algorithms that run in them. But there are instances where this is not the case such as *Vehicular ad-hoc networks (VANETs)* and *Wireless Sensor Networks (WSN)*. In Figure 4 we show the composition of these networks.

These networks have a topology neither deterministic nor static. They are deployed on non-controlled environments and exposed to security risks. WSN motes exhibit limited processing capabilities.

Figure 4. Composition of a VANET (left) and a WSN (right)

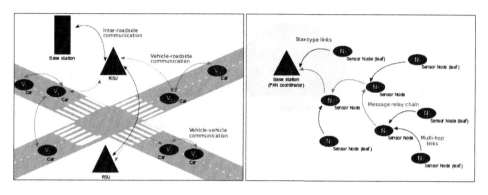

All the technologies described in the previous examples form part of the IoT ecosystem. In the near future it is very likely that our lifestyle will be influenced directly by some of these systems. The volume of information collected and transmitted will grow as the number of physical devices increases. Some of this information is bound to be sensitive and must be protected. But even if the information is not inherently sensitive, its sheer volume can provide insights on the user's behavior. Therefore, it is necessary to provide IoT devices with security services for protecting these data. Nonetheless, such protections must be aware of the application scope and its inherent constraints.

Security Services and Cryptography

Information security rests on three cornerstones denominated security services: *Confidentiality*, *Integrity*, and *Availability (CIA)*. There are additional security services created for ensuring distinct security features, but the *CIA triad* is the basis.

Data confidentiality implies that only *authorized parties* have access to the information. When an *attacker* gains access to the data, its confidentiality is being broken as the privacy of the information cannot be guaranteed. If the attacker's goal is to modify a piece of information, this represents an attack on the information's *integrity*. *Authentication* is a particular case of integrity where the data origin is also verified. The third fundamental service ensures that the information is always available for authorized parties. These security services rely on cryptographic constructions.

Data *encryption* ensures that the information has confidentiality and remains private. In a basic encryption scheme, the authorized parties must share a common *secret* or *key*. This piece of information is used by the sending party to *encrypt* the data. The encryption procedure implies transforming the plaintext from the message space M to an encryption space C by using simple operations over the data and the secret key. The shared key is obtained from the key space K, it is used for instantiating a particular encryption transformation and must be disclosed to the receiver party so that it can *decrypt* the message. The receiver party applies the inverse procedure, called *decryption*, in order to retrieve the message. Under this system, for the inverse transformation to successfully recover the plaintext, the key used in the decryption must be identical to the one used in encryption. The cryptographic construct which has an encryption procedure and its corresponding decryption algorithms is called *cipher*. When the key used for encryption is the same as the one used for decryption the cipher is said to be *symmetric*.

Preserving integrity and authentication usually requires exchanging multiple messages between the main parties, and often times a *trusted actor*. These message exchanges with aims of providing some security service are called *cryptographic protocols*. These are critical for RFID applications. In a restricted way, however, authentication and integrity can be provided by adding a cryptographic tag to the message which is generally called *Message Authentication Codes (MAC)* and can be created by a *MAC function*. Symmetric ciphers can be used as MAC functions under certain *operational modes*. That is, a particular configuration or connection the cipher's input/output and some other logic for constructing a different algorithm. The idea is to compress the entirety of the message into a tag, so that if the contents of the message are modified, when a new tag is computed over the altered message it will not match the original tag. Furthermore, the attacker ought not be able to regenerate the tag since it is also protected by a secret key. *Keyed hash functions* are another alternative for creating MACs. A cryptographic hash function can create a tag or *digest* of given length for a message of any length by compressing the data while ensuring that an identical tag cannot be generated easily. When this tag is also protected by a shared key, the attacker cannot modify the message and the tag without leaving traces. In this case the goal is not to prevent the attacker from tampering with the message, but to make such alterations evident for the authorized parties.

Basic hash functions differ from ciphers in that the original message cannot be reconstructed from the digest. Such operations are called *one-way transformations*. The existence of different one-way functions has enabled the development of a second branch of cryptography. Up to this point we have considered that the key used for data encryption is the same used for decryption. However, this is not the case in *public-key cryptography (PKC)*.

A public-key algorithm has a *key pair*, in which one of the keys is kept secret (private key) whereas the other is generally published (public key). Taking the case of encryption as an example, under these schemes the sender encrypts the data using the public key of the receiver; the receiver then decrypts the message using its secret key. The key pair is related in a way such that the public key can be computed from the secret key, but the inverse procedure is computationally inviable. This is where one-way functions come into play.

Integer factorization over finite fields and *computing discrete logarithms over multiplicative groups* are the most-common one-way functions for creating public-key cryptographic systems. The popular cryptosystem RSA is part of this family of algorithms. *Computing discrete logarithms over Elliptic Curve groups* has also been used for enabling public-key cryptography. The latter is the basis of *Elliptic Curve Cryptography (ECC)*. Recently, *linear codes* and *hard lattice problems* have also been explored for constructing secure public-key cryptosystems.

The main advantage of public-key systems is that it is not necessary to have a common secret shared among the parties. On the contrary, these algorithms are orders of magnitude costlier than their symmetric counterparts restricting their use in constrained applications.

Key establishment contributes to protect the data availability. In a restricted networked environment, such as in WSN, the ability of only authentic devices for joining the network is critical. Messages sent by the motes must be confidential and authentic. This can be achieved using symmetric algorithms, but a shared key is required for any pair of motes wishing to communicate. A naive solution is to preload all the devices with a single master key; but once one of the motes is compromised the security of the WSN crumbles. If a node is forced to store a key pair for every other node in the network, the storage required will grow quadratically. Assigning group keys to the motes provides some probabilistic estimation of network formation, but in the worst case the WSN will be crippled if some groups are left isolated. Key establishment mechanisms based on public-key cryptography ensure that any pair of nodes can establish a shared secret without significant risks.

Lightweight Cryptography

When cryptographic algorithms are used for providing security services to constrained environments, their realization ought to be aware of the underlying system restrictions. The design of such implementation can be stratified in abstraction levels in which it is possible to take implementation decisions according to the application. A possible division of these abstraction levels is system, protocol, algorithm, and realization.

At the top level of System, the designer should consider the application constraints and characteristics. The standards governing the technology can also provide insights on the operational bounds for the device which can be used for delimiting the design space or exploring more acute tradeoffs.

Protocols are more related with the security services required by the system. Depending on the attacks feasibility the designer might choose to implement a simple protocol considering the network infrastructure available. It is commonplace to consider that a trusted party can act as an authenticator in the protocol, but this is not always the case.

The protocols rely on cryptographic *algorithms*. The security strength of the realization usually depends on the parameters selected for these algorithms. The designer should choose the parameter set that provides security strength *ad hoc* to the application requirements.

The *realization* of the cryptographic solution can be performed through software or hardware. For the former, the processor in the target platform must be capable of bearing the processing overhead associated with the computational tasks. A hardware realization can offer attractive advantages for the device. In any case, the selected algorithms should improve the performance, reduce the physical size, and reduce the energy footprint.

FPGAS FOR PROTECTING THE IOT

The use of FPGAs for providing IoT with security services offers attractive advantages and challenges for security applications. Several examples of using FPGAs for security services in the IoT context are reported in the literature. In this section we discuss some of these challenges, advantages, and case studies.

There exists a trend in using FPGAs whiting the context of IoT in security-related areas. We queried the SCOPUS database with the terms "FPGA + IoT" and then further filtered the results using the keywords "Security, Cryptography, Authentication, Encryption." Figure 5 shows the quantitative obtained results.

The tendency shows a growing interest on the use of FPGAs for IoT-related applications. The security-related works amount for approximately 50% of all the publications.

Challenges

Different challenges must be overcome for deploying cryptographic algorithms on the constrained devices used in IoT. In contrast with traditional networks, IoT systems have wider attack surfaces, must comply with specific security standards, and are prone to suffer from different constraints.

Attack Models

The attack vectors which might be exploited for compromising an IoT system can broadly be divided into *cybernetic attacks* (over the internet), *network attacks* (over the air), and *physical attacks* (over the devices).

Figure 5. Trends in the use of FPGAs for the IoT

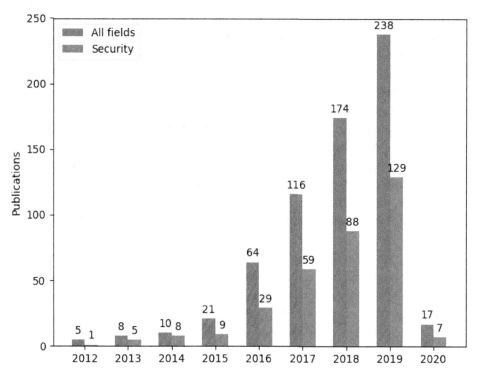

In a cybernetic attack the service provider can be targeted compromising the confidentiality and availability of data. Internet security mechanisms built in the *IPv6* protocol (Deering & Hinden, 2017), as well as additional protections such as DoS/DDoS mitigation (Mirkovic & Reiher, 2004; Peng, Leckie, & Ramamohanarao, 2007) are the main countermeasures against these attacks. However, in most of the cases, the human factor is easier to exploit for attackers than breaking the security protections (Wood & Banks, 1993; Whitman, 2003). Either due to bugs generated by faulty implementations or due to stolen credentials. These kinds of attacks can be carried out remotely and are not much different from conventional breaches of storage systems.

Over-the-air attacks usually have as goal gaining access to the network or disrupting its operations. In the first scenario the information being transmitted can be stolen or altered, effectively violating the data confidentiality or integrity. The attacker might also choose to impersonate legitimate devices and disrupt the flow of messages, which represents an attack against the data availability and authentication. In the second scenario, the attacker might deploy jamming devices in the vicinity of the network for disrupting the operations of the system; in this case, although the attacker does not gain access to the data, its availability is compromised. Network access mechanisms can effectively thwart network infiltration attacks, device's authentication is widely used for this reason.

The physical-attack approach is in certain instances the most difficult to counteract. When the IoT devices are deployed, it is often the case that there are not physical barriers restricting their access. The ubiquitous nature of this technology makes monitoring the status of each device in real-time an impossible task. Evidently, malicious actors can also have access to the devices (Becher, Benenson, & Dornseif, 2006). The goal of a physical attack can be either removing the node, crippling it, hijacking it, or stealing security materials from it for compromising the network. It is almost impossible to prevent the attacks which intend to damage the network infrastructure, most of the times it can be due to simple vandalism. However, more sophisticated attacks aimed at infringing the network as a whole must be taken into account.

Hijacking an IoT node implies that the attacker now has control over the messages received and transmitted by the device. Whereas a single compromised device might not represent a major threat, it might be possible to clone it and then disrupt the network operation. *Physical Unclonable Functions (PUF)* have been created as countermeasures for node cloning (Maes & Verbauwhede, 2010). These unique signatures generated by some hardware of the device can be employed in the cryptosystems mounted in the platform. When the intent is to retrieve cryptographic materials from the node the attacker might choose different alternatives (Maletsky, 2015; Micali & Reyzin, 2004; Genkin, Pipman, & Tromer, 2014). The goal of the latter is to study the information leaked by the node as it might provide insights on the cryptographic algorithms running on it. Computers, be it a general processor or a specific core, in their operation tend to leave physical traces which can be correlated with the data being processed. The energy consumption, power dissipation, heat, electromagnetic signature, among others, are called side channels and can be exploited by an attacker to break the security of the device, or in the worst case of the network. Multiple side-channel countermeasures have been developed aiming at reducing the amount of information leaked by a device. Using constant-time algorithms and hardware masking are the most common ones.

FPGAs for providing security to the IoT must consider common attack strategies and appropriate countermeasures. Note that up to this point we have not described any actual security solution nor discussed cryptographic attacks over the algorithms.

Standardization

Standardization is important for any technology since it enables interoperability. Standard-compliant IoT devices must follow specific design guidelines that ensure it will be able to communicate with other platforms. In the context of security, standards allow for reducing the number of algorithms that must be implemented since it is understood that all standardized implementations can interoperate. It also ensures that the algorithms selected are secure since these were reviewed detailed by experts. In addition, it allows to shorten development times since it is common for researchers to develop optimized implementations of standardized technology for posterior use. An optimized implementation of the standard can therefore be used in a wide range of devices effectively reducing the design costs.

Developing standards is a lengthy task and novel technologies usually lack of widely accepted guidelines and standards. Early prototypes will have to be deprecated rather quickly or risky deviating from the main development trends. An even final releases tend to be amended, when vulnerabilities are detected the standard must adapt to the new challenges.

IoT is an emerging technology that takes advantage of technologies developed during the past 15 years. Some standards have been published specifically for the IoT, whereas others cover some of its underlying technologies. In the same vein, the study of security for constrained applications has gained increasing interest over the past decade. Probably in part due to the rapid development of its application scope, standardization efforts for lightweight cryptography have progressed smoothly. Some of the standards available in these two areas are briefly reviewed in the following.

In august of 2018, the International Organization for Standardization (ISO) and the International Electrotechnical Commission (IEC) jointly published the standard ISO/IEC 30141:2018 which describes a reference architecture for the IoT. This document approaches the security of IoT from the perspective of trustworthiness with emphasis on safety, information security, privacy, protection of personally identifiable information, reliability, and resilience. These organizations have also released standards concerning use cases (ISO/IEC TR 22417:2017) and nomenclature (ISO/IEC 20924:2018) for the IoT, with several more related standards under development (ISO/IEC NP 30147, ISO/IEC PDTR 30148, ISO/IEC NP 30149, ISO/IEC NP 30160 - ISO/IEC NP 30163, ISO/IEC NP TR 30164, ISO/IEC NP 30165). In regards of security solutions applicable for constrained environments, the ISO/IEC institutions have published a series of standards on lightweight cryptography (ISO/IEC 29192-1:2012) for different algorithms such as block ciphers (ISO/IEC 29192-2:2012), stream ciphers (ISO/IEC 29192-3:2012), asymmetric cryptography (ISO/IEC 29192-4:2012), hash functions (ISO/IEC 29192-5:2012), MAC functions (ISO/IEC 29192-6) and broadcast authentication protocols (ISO/IEC 29192-7). The latter two continue under development at the time of writing.

The National Institute of Standards and Technology (NIST) has also addressed the relevancy of IoT and the security concerns associated with this technology. For this end, the "NIST Cybersecurity for IoT Program" was created. The program identifies "fostering cybersecurity for devices and data in the IoT ecosystem, across industry sectors and at scale" as its main challenge, with the declared mission of cultivating trust in the IoT. The institute has released reports on managing the cybersecurity and privacy risks of the IoT (Boeckl et al., 2018) as well as the trust concerns regarding IoT (Voas, Kuhn, Laplante, & Applebaum, 2018). In late 2018, an interagency report on the status of International Cybersecurity Standardization for the IoT (Interagency International Cybersecurity Standardization Working Group, 2018) was released as well. The document analyzes the scope of standardization for 12 core areas of security in regard to five main IoT applications: vehicles, consumer, healthcare, construction, and manufacturing. In the scope of lightweight cryptography, in 2017 NIST published a report detailing the state of the art for this field (McKay, Bassham, Turan, & Mouha, 2017) with aims at launching a standardization process for lightweight cryptographic algorithms. Is in this way that in august of 2018, NIST initiated the process to "solicit, evaluate, and standardize lightweight cryptographic algorithms that are suitable for use in constrained environments where the performance of current NIST cryptographic standards is not acceptable." This process is expected to span for a couple years and deliver a set of algorithms which can be used for the IoT and similar technologies.

The Institute of Electrical and Electronics Engineers (IEEE) is another organization that has created standards in the context of the IoT and constrained applications. IEEE 802.15.4-2011 is perhaps the standard with wider adoption reviewed thus far. This standard concerns local and metropolitan area networks, and in particular *Low-Rate Wireless Personal Area Networks (LR-WPANs)* which include several of the IoT's underlying technologies such as WSN. Amendments to the standard include considerations for RFID (IEEE 802.15.4f-2012), *Smart Metering Utility Networks* (IEEE 802.15.4g-2012), and *Medical Body Area Network (MBAN)* (IEEE 802.15.4j-2012). In regard to security, this standard considers the use of the *Advanced Encryption Standard (AES)* for providing LR-WPANs with security services of confidentiality, integrity, and authentication.

In regard to general aspects of the IoT, the Internet Engineering Task Force (IETF) is the body that has pushed further in aims to provide "standards and guidance." Through several *working groups* this organization has addressed methods for adapting IPv6 to IEEE 802.15.4 (RFC 4919, RFC 6606, RFC 6568, RFC 6282, RFC 6775, RFC 8025, RFC 8066, RFC 8505), obtained routing protocols of IPv6 for low-power and lossy networks (RFC 6550), created the *Constrained Application Protocol (CoAP)* (RFC 7252), and produced a TLS/DTLS profile that is suitable for constrained IoT devices (RFC 7925). Related to security, the group has addressed authentication and authorization for constrained environments (RFC 7744, RFC 8392) as well as lightweight implementation of security solutions for the IoT (RFC 7228, RFC 7815, RFC 8352, RFC 8387). Beyond informational and standardization publications, the

IETF also releases reports such as the state of the art and challenges for IoT security (Garcia-Morchon, Kumar, & Sethi, 2018).

None of the reviewed groups considers that the standardization efforts are complete. Some of the works are progressing towards collaborating in aims of defining interoperation rules that allow for a more interconnected IoT. Since these standards are not definite, the designer must keep up to date with the changes brought up in each new version. This represents a paramount challenge.

System Constraints

The standards that govern IoT and its underlying technologies provide insights in bounds that must be covered for the device to be standard compliant. As an example, IEEE 802.15.4 states that WSN messages must be transmitted at a rate of 250kbps. In order to maintain a steady transmission and do not require additional storage, the messages must be processed at similar rates. This is can be considered a performance bound for certain WSN motes. Note that this does not account for sensing periods, which usually are determined by the application's real time. As another example, the same standard states the use of AES with 128-bit keys for providing security services; this algorithm has a security level of 128-bits. The designer of additional security modules might be compelled to employ the same security level: if anything, stronger is used, AES becomes the 'weak link'; if anything, weaker than AES is used, the system will not be as secure as the standard intends. These boundaries are system constraints that must be observed in aims to improve the efficiency of the system.

Other constraints obey design guidelines or principles. If the manufacturer decides that the cost of producing the device only allows for an 8-bit microcontroller, after all, chips with more elements are more difficult to design and create. The security solutions must adapt for the processing constraints generated due the lack of processing units. For battery-enabled platforms, manufacturing costs can also mean lower battery capacity. Draining too much power will render the device useless sooner, therefore the energy footprint of the algorithms running on the device must be reduced. Manufacturing costs should obey market studies to determine if the end user is willing to absorb the additional costs to obtain additional features. However, doing more with less is always a welcomed approach.

In a simplified way, we can look at these constraints independently. But that is not the case for real applications. Reducing the performance might lead to consuming more energy. Increased the security implies performance sacrifices. Mounting more hardware elements to improve performance will also imply increasing the energy expenditures. Performance, area, energy, and security are, in some cases, the four corners of a triangular pyramid: getting closer to one of the corners means that one is departing from the others. The IoT designer is the one in charge of balancing the tradeoff between the device's constraints.

FPGA Advantages for Security Applications

The realization of cryptography, in particular of Public-key algorithms, represents processing costs which might be too high for the processor of an IoT device. This computational cost motivates the developers of these technologies to employ hardware acceleration in order to offload the security tasks from the constrained processor. Generally, silicon implementations of *Application Specific Integrated Circuits (ASIC)* are preferred in such cases.

An ASIC implementation has the characteristics that the physical size and energy profile are much lower than those of a processor. The critical path delay and latencies of ASIC are also shorter, which allows for faster realizations. But these advantages come with multiple drawbacks. First, restricted flexibility: once the ASIC is created it will perform the same task in perpetuity. If the algorithm implemented is found to be unsecure, all the circuits produced and deployed ought to be scrapped. Second, the development time from design to construction of a prototype is considerable. If the prototype fails it can cause catastrophic delays. Third, for cost reasons, manufacturing these components often needs to be done in foreign plants; this opens the door to possible tampering of the product done by the manufacturer or third parties.

FPGAs are attractive platforms since they represent a middle point between the ASIC efficiency and the processor's generality. Some of their advantages for security applications are detailed in the following.

Reconfigurability

This is a characteristic of FPGAs which enables modifying the behavior of the platform when the device is inactive (*static reconfiguration*) or running (*dynamic reconfiguration*). Effectively, it allows for modifying whichever algorithm is implemented in the hardware. Even remotely, creating a new firmware and distributing it over the internet can be used for updating deployed devices without the need of recalling the product. This is a key advantage for cryptographic applications, since algorithms and protocols are being patched constantly.

Rapid Development and Prototyping

In FPGAs, the development process is longer than software development, but shorter than ASIC's. The most efficient design tools are hard to use and have slow learning curves, not to mention they are vendor-locked and require costly licenses. Nowadays a trend for high-level synthesis (HLS) aims at closing the development gap between FPGAs and software by enabling high-level software descriptions to be synthesized.

With HLS the designer does not require specialized knowledge about hardware design. It is desirable for improving the automatically generated output, however. Using HLS, a program written in C language can be ported to a hardware description, which is then configured in the FPGA. The tools used for this process are still technology-dependent and costly, but they can allow for speeding up the design process to some degree.

In-House Security

Manufacturing integrated circuits is usually performed in foreign countries for reducing the production costs. This implies that third parties might have access to the design during the manufacturing process. These parties might seek different goals: to copy the design, to sabotage the product, or even to add spyware or malicious elements. The latter are called *hardware trojans* in the literature (Tehranipoor & Koushanfar, 2010; Liu, Jin, & Makris, 2013). The ASIC designer can certainly set protections against tampering, obfuscate the design to prevent copying, and even choose to scramble parts of the circuit rendering the manufactured part useless until some key is entered (Chakraborty & Bhunia, 2011). But all these countermeasures are difficult to create and add into the final product, increasing the design complexity. The alternative is to allow the design to be stolen, which can affect the invention profits, and to seek for these trojans by analyzing effectively all the manufactured devices through some efficient method. This also represents increased production costs.

On the other hand, the FPGA fabric is generic and regular. These devices are generally structured as a 2D array of logic blocks. The main components in these units are *Lookup tables (LUT)* and *Flip-Flops (FF)* plus some connection circuitry such as logic shifts and multiplexers. Surrounding this array there are rows of programmable IO pins which serve as source, clocking and logic inputs/outputs. Each logic block is generally identical, and they are interconnected by programmable gates. The gates are *opened* or *closed* during configuration so that the fabric is capable of carrying out some computation. These regular structures make easy to verify if a device has been modified during production.

The manufacturer does not have access to the actual algorithm realizations, only the designer does. When the device is created, any test file can be used to verify that the FPGA works as intended. After the FPGA has been manufactured and inspected the user can load the actual architectural design to be deployed. The new firmware will change the state of the gates in the FPGA fabric for performing the new computation.

Side-Channel Attacks Resilience

The implementation of IoT devices does not follow defined topologies nor has any physical barrier. This implies that attackers can gain direct access to the network. With physical access to the device a more complex attack vector becomes feasible: exploiting side-channel vulnerabilities. *Masking* is the term used to define the techniques which aim at suppressing these side-channel footprints. But designing and validating a mask is not trivial as the actual prototype is required to verify that the masking is actually working. The short development time in FPGA-based implementation and prototyping reduces the complexity of designing and applying masks for protecting IoT against side-channel attacks.

The critics of FPGA use in constrained devices always float around the efficiency of the prototyping board. However, if the IoT device includes a reconfigurable core it is evident that it will be of reduced cost, size, and energy profile. Even if it is not as efficient as the ASIC alternative, as explained in this section, it offers significant advantages for security applications.

Case Studies

Use in Symmetric Cryptography

FPGAs can be used for prototyping realizations of block ciphers, hash functions, or MAC functions. In these cases, the designers benefit from the rapid prototyping and testing of FPGAs. These platforms allow for evaluating different algorithms under fair conditions. For this, the designers only need to exchange the hardware description of the design and any synthesis configurations.

It is less common to find instances where complete security solutions are implemented in hardware. Mainly due to the complexity in the control design. In (Lara-Nino, Diaz-Perez, & Morales-Sandoval, 2018) the authors created a sensor node prototype for WSN with security services of confidentiality, integrity, and authentication. The goal of the work was to explore the impact of different cryptographic functions, both standardized and lightweight, on the lifetime of the sensor node. For providing confidentiality the authors explored the use of the symmetric ciphers AES and PRESENT (Bogdanov et al., 2007). In the case of integrity and authentication they used MAC functions based on symmetric ciphers (AES and PRESENT) and the hash functions SHA (National Institute of Standards and Technology, 2015) and SPONGENT (Bogdanov et al., 2011). The algorithms PRESENT and SPONGENT are lightweight functions that were designed for use in constrained environments.

The authors report two main findings in their work:

1. **On the use of Lightweight Functions:** These allow for reducing the energy consumption, which translates into longer lifetimes of the node.
2. **On the use of Symmetric Ciphers:** Cipher-based MACs are generally more efficient than hash functions, which also contributes to reduce the energy footprint of the system.

This study provides experimental results to back up the claims made. For that end, the energy consumption of the FPGA was measured using a digital oscilloscope and a shunt resistor connected in series with the power supply of the board. In their experiment, the lifetime of the sensor node ranged from 10 to 12 hours which is evidently too short for WSN applications. However, the authors employed prototyping FPGA boards powered by rechargeable batteries. In a practical scenario, the FPGA and its power supply would observe different specifications.

Use in Asymmetric Cryptography

Public-key algorithms are generally costlier than symmetric constructions. They are useful for providing security services that are difficult to achieve in other ways. One of such services is key establishment. Standards which define security mechanisms for constrained applications such as IEEE 802.15.4 leave the key establishment outside of their scope. In others, such as the RFC series, key establishment is proposed to be obtained through generic solutions (Struik, 2018). Realizations of key establishment systems in the context of lightweight cryptography for hardware platforms are limited.

ECC is one of the most efficient alternatives for constructing key establishment solutions. These algorithms rely on a group operation dubbed *scalar multiplication*, which is expensive in terms of latency cycles. Some works have addressed the design and implementation of accelerators for this procedure in FPGA (Varchola, Guneysu, & Mischke, 2011; Trujillo-Olaya, Sherwood, & Koc, 2012; Driessen et al., 2012; Schramm & Grzemba, 2013; Wenger, Korak, & Kirschbaum, 2013; Roy, Das, & Mukhopadhyay, 2016; Yalcin, 2016; Salman et al., 2017). In most of the cases the main design goal is to increase performance. However, constrained applications might benefit from area or energy reductions.

The work in (Lara-Nino, Diaz-Perez, & Morales-Sandoval, 2019) explores the design of scalar multiplication accelerators for the IoT in FPGA. The authors present the design of a scalar multiplication architecture with a special class of elliptic curves selected due their efficiency. Their area-oriented design only requires a bit-serial multiplier, an XOR layer, a register set, and a few multiplexers. By improving the inversion algorithm used, the multiplier, and adding a squaring module they generate an energy-oriented design. This second architecture is reported to achieve reductions in the energy cost superior to 90% with a 20% hardware increment.

If the manufacturer decides to include a reconfigurable core in the device, the key establishment module can be mounted during network formation. Once the key has been established, the core can be reconfigured with a different accelerator to contribute in other tasks. This reconfiguration can be static, but the main processor would be required to load the different configuration file from some storage unit.

Use of Dynamic Reconfiguration

In recent years, the reconfigurability of FPGAS has attracted the interest of security developers. For the IoT, this enables the possibility of modifying the device "in field" in a non-invasive way (Johnson, Chakraborty, & Mukhopadhyay 2015). In particular, (Johnson et al., 2015) propose to use *dynamic partial reconfiguration* for implementing a "lightweight cryptographic security protocol." To this end, the authors describe a "modified DPR methodology that does not require any paid-on utility." As main contribution, the authors claim to demonstrate the feasibility of implementation of two different low overhead secure DPR architectures targeted for IoT applications.

Other Cryptographic Uses of FPGAs

In hardware, it is possible to observe measurements of certain magnitudes that differ from platform to platform, even when the systems are in theory identical. The 'blank' state of a memory, the time required for a signal to travel over a wire, and the frequency offset of the system are some of such magnitudes. These differences can be used for creating *signatures* that are specific for each platform. PUFs employ these variations for delivering a digital representation of the measurement which is constant with high probability.

In cryptography, the values generated by PUFs can be employed for obtaining cryptographic keys through *key derivation functions (KDF)*. In this way, the cryptographic materials are not stored explicitly in the device and thus cannot be read when the system is offline. If the attacker compromises the integrity of the platform, there is a possibility that the PUF will not generate the same result. This strategy reduces the attacker possibilities of success.

The work of (Ovilla-Martinez, 2015) explores the use of FPGA-based PUFs for providing security services to WSN. In that work, the authors study five PUF constructions using *reliability, uniformity, diffusivity,* and *unicity* as metrics and describe four communication protocols for key-establishment based on one of them.

The authors report that their experimental results show "that using PUFs in key-establishment protocols, without storing the key in memory, is feasible."

An application of (Ovilla-Martinez, 2015) is reported in (Ovilla-Martinez, Diaz-Perez, & Garza-Saldaña, 2013). In that instance the authors describe a key establishment protocol for a patient monitoring system using *body sensor networks (BSN)*. Over the years, healthcare has become one of the main application areas for IoT.

FUTURE RESEARCH DIRECTIONS

Much research is still required in exploring the unique features of FPGAs and their advantage for security applications. In particular, in how these platforms can be used in restricted devices.

The manufacturing process of FPGAs has improved significantly over recent years. Nowadays, FPGAs in minimal boards are commonplace. Some recent designs do not include signature elements in the traditional FPGA architecture such as BRAMs and DSPs. Miniaturization of the electronics world is key. Novel strategies for reducing the energy consumption of FPGAs have also been introduced to the market.

Offering additional services for the end user is always an attractive selling point. Reconfigurability can contribute with this. Updating the hardware in the platform allows for obtaining adaptive designs. These even can have applications beyond security.

Hardware description using high-level languages has been introduced recently but commercial solutions are already available. The complexity on the hardware design pushes for investing in creating tools capable of porting the software designs automatically rather than designing each new circuit. It is expected that the efficiency of the available tools will increase and that as the practice is accepted, more vendors and organizations will offer alternative solutions that are not locked or free of cost.

Modern requirements for outsourcing production to reduce costs clash with the need to maintain certain technologies secret. With FPGAs only the generic fabric needs to ever leave the manufacturing operation, effectively protecting the design and easing the device verification and testing.

Preventing the physical device from leaking information has been described by some as "an art." With FPGAs, it would be possible to design generic protections which can be implemented while creating the device. This could enable to shield all the platforms with a single protection design. Thus, all the circuits implemented in such devices would also be protected. This requires further work, but the fact that IoT is becoming a ubiquitous reality can speed this process up.

CONCLUSION

In this chapter we have discussed the features and use of FPGAs in providing security for the IoT. We have provided a detailed background for the reader and then studied each one of these features. We also revised case studies where FPGAs have been used in this context.

Several characteristics of FPGAs make these systems an attractive choice for implementing security cores in constrained applications. Reconfigurability goes hand in hand with the ever-changing nature of security and cryptography applications. When new threats are discovered, the hardware systems can be updated remotely. New architectural versions can also be introduced, or the design can be changed altogether for different ends. This, while offering greater performance than software-based realizations. The rapid development and testing of prototypes offer significant advantages for applications where it is critical to assess the physical behavior of the device, such as in the design of PUFs and SCA countermeasures. Reconfigurable cores are not vulnerable to IP infringements since the final complete design is released until the device is deployed. Moreover, the regular design of the FPGA fabric eases the design and testing of the boards. All in all, exploring the use of FPGAs for the IoT and other emerging technologies is an emerging field of opportunities.

ACKNOWLEDGMENT

This research was supported by CONACyT [grant number 336750]; by "Fondo Sectorial de Investigación para la Educación CONACyT" [project number 281565]; and by CINVESTAV.

REFERENCES

Becher, A., Benenson, Z., & Dornseif, M. (2006). Tampering with Motes: Real-World Physical Attacks on Wireless Sensor Networks. In J. A. Clark, R. F. Paige, F. A. C. Polack, & P. J. Brooke (Eds.), *Security in pervasive computing* (pp. 104–118). Berlin: Springer Berlin Heidelberg. doi:10.1007/11734666_9

Boeckl, K., Fagan, M., Fisher, W., Lefkovitz, N., Megas, K. N., Nadeau, E., . . . Scarfone, K. (2018). *Considerations for Managing Internet of Things (IoT) Cybersecurity and Privacy Risks*. National Institute of Standards and Technology. Retrieved from www.nist.gov

Bogdanov, A., Knezevic, M., Leander, G., Toz, D., Varici, K., & Verbauwhede, I. (2011). spongent: A Lightweight Hash Function. In B. Preneel & T. Takagi (Eds.), Cryptographic Hardware and Embedded Systems - CHES 2011 (pp. 312-325). Berlin: Springer Berlin Heidelberg.

Bogdanov, A., Knudsen, L. R., Leander, G., Paar, C., Poschmann, A., Robshaw, M. J. B., & Vikkelsoe, C. (2007). PRESENT: An Ultra-Lightweight Block Cipher. In P. Paillier & I. Verbauwhede (Eds.), *Cryptographic Hardware and Embedded Systems - CHES 2007* (pp. 450–466). Berlin: Springer Berlin Heidelberg. doi:10.1007/978-3-540-74735-2_31

Buchanan, W. J., Li, S., & Asif, R. (2017). Lightweight cryptography methods. *Journal of Cyber Security Technology, 1*(3-4), 187–201. doi:10.1080/23742917.2017.1384917

Chakraborty, R. S., & Bhunia, S. (2011, December). Security Against Hardware Trojan Attacks Using Key-Based Design Obfuscation. *Journal of Electronic Testing, 27*(6), 767–785. doi:10.100710836-011-5255-2

Columbus, L. (2017). 2017 Roundup of Internet of Things Forecasts. *Forbes.* Retrieved from www.forbes.com

Deering, S. E., & Hinden, B. (2017, July). *Internet Protocol, Version 6 (IPv6) Specification.* RFC 8200. RFC Editor. Retrieved from rfc-editor.org

Driessen, B., Guneysu, T., Kavun, E. B., Mischke, O., Paar, C., & Poppelmann, T. (2012, December). IPSecco: A lightweight and reconfigurable IPSec core. In *2012 International Conference on Reconfigurable Computing and FPGAs (ReConFig)* (pp. 1-7). 10.1109/ReConFig.2012.6416757

Garcia-Morchon, O., Kumar, S., & Sethi, M. (2018, December). *State-of-the-Art and Challenges for the Internet of Things Security.* Internet Engineering Task Force. Retrieved from www.ietf.org

Genkin, D., Pipman, I., & Tromer, E. (2014). Get Your Hands Off My Laptop: Physical Side-Channel Key-Extraction Attacks on PCs. In L. Batina & M. Robshaw (Eds.), *Cryptographic Hardware and Embedded Systems - CHES 2014* (pp. 242–260). Berlin: Springer Berlin Heidelberg. doi:10.1007/978-3-662-44709-3_14

Interagency International Cybersecurity Standardization Working Group. (2018). *Interagency Report on the Status of International Cybersecurity Standardization for the Internet of Things (IoT).* National Institute of Standards and Technology. Retrieved from www.nist.gov

Johnson, A. P., Chakraborty, R. S., & Mukhopadhyay, D. (2015, April). A PUF-Enabled Secure Architecture for FPGA-Based IoT Applications. *IEEE Transactions on Multi-Scale Computing Systems*, *1*(2), 110–122. doi:10.1109/TMSCS.2015.2494014

Lara-Nino, C. A., Diaz-Perez, A., & Morales-Sandoval, M. (2018, September). Energy and Area Costs of Lightweight Cryptographic Algorithms for Authenticated Encryption in WSN. *Security and Communication Networks*, *2018*, 1–14. doi:10.1155/2018/5087065

Lara-Nino, C. A., Diaz-Perez, A., & Morales-Sandoval, M. (2019). Energy/Area-Efficient Scalar Multiplication with Binary Edwards Curves for the IoT. *Sensors (Basel)*, *19*(3), 720. doi:10.339019030720 PMID:30744202

Liu, Y., Jin, Y., & Makris, Y. (2013, November). Hardware Trojans in wireless cryptographic ICs: Silicon demonstration & detection method evaluation. In *2013 IEEE/ACM International Conference on Computer-Aided Design (ICCAD)* (pp. 399-404). 10.1109/ICCAD.2013.6691149

Maes, R., & Verbauwhede, I. (2010). P*hysically Unclonable Functions: A Study on the State of the Art and Future Research Directions*. In A.-R. Sadeghi & D. Naccache (Eds.), *Towards Hardware-Intrinsic Security: Foundations and Practice* (pp. 3–37). Berlin: Springer Berlin Heidelberg. doi:10.1007/978-3-642-14452-3_1

Maletsky, K. (2015). *Attack Methods to Steal Digital Secrets*. Atmel Corporation. Retrieved from www.microchip.com

McKay, K. A., Bassham, L., Turan, M. S., & Mouha, N. (2017). *Report on Lightweight Cryptography*. National Institute of Standards and Technology. Retrieved from www.nist.gov

Micali, S., & Reyzin, L. (2004). Physically Observable Cryptography. In M. Naor (Ed.), *Theory of Cryptography* (pp. 278–296). Berlin: Springer Berlin Heidelberg. doi:10.1007/978-3-540-24638-1_16

Mirkovic, J., & Reiher, P. (2004, April). A Taxonomy of DDoS Attack and DDoS Defense Mechanisms. *Computer Communication Review*, *34*(2), 39–53. doi:10.1145/997150.997156

National Institute of Standards and Technology. (2015). *FIPS PUB 202: SHA-3 Standard: Permutation-Based Hash and Extendable-Output Functions*. Gaithersburg, MD: National Institute of Standards and Technology. Retrieved from www.nist.gov

Ovilla-Martinez, B. (2015). *Seguridad en Redes de Sensores Inalambricos Basada en Funciones Fisicamente No-Clonables* (Unpublished doctoral dissertation). CINVESTAV Tamaulipas.

Ovilla-Martinez, B., Diaz-Perez, A., & Garza-Saldaña, J. J. (2013, October). Key establishment protocol for a patient monitoring system based on PUF and PKG. In *2013 10th International Conference and Expo on Emerging Technologies for a Smarter World (CEWIT)* (pp. 1-6). 10.1109/CEWIT.2013.6713752

Peng, T., Leckie, C., & Ramamohanarao, K. (2007, April). Survey of Network-based Defense Mechanisms Countering the DoS and DDoS Problems. *ACM Computing Surveys*, *39*(1), 3. doi:10.1145/1216370.1216373

Roy, D. B., Das, P., & Mukhopadhyay, D. (2016). ECC on Your Fingertips: A Single Instruction Approach for Lightweight ECC Design in GF(p). In O. Dunkelman & L. Keliher (Eds.), *Selected Areas in Cryptography - SAC 2015* (pp. 161–177). Cham: Springer International Publishing. doi:10.1007/978-3-319-31301-6_9

Salman, A., Ferozpuri, A., Homsirikamol, E., Yalla, P., Kaps, J., & Gaj, K. (2017, December). A scalable ECC processor implementation for high-speed and lightweight with side-channel countermeasures. In *2017 International Conference on Reconfigurable Computing and FPGAs (ReConFig)* (pp. 1-8). 10.1109/RECONFIG.2017.8279769

Schramm, M., & Grzemba, A. (2013, September). On the implementation of a lightweight generic FPGA ECC crypto-core over GF(p). In *2013 international Conference on Applied Electronics* (pp. 1-4). Academic Press.

Shi, W., Cao, J., Zhang, Q., Li, Y., & Xu, L. (2016, October). Edge Computing: Vision and Challenges. *IEEE Internet of Things Journal*, *3*(5), 637–646. doi:10.1109/JIOT.2016.2579198

Shi, W., & Dustdar, S. (2016, May). The Promise of Edge Computing. *Computer*, *49*(5), 78–81. doi:10.1109/MC.2016.145

Struik, R. (2018, November). *Alternative Elliptic Curve Representations*. Internet Engineering Task Force. Retrieved from www.ietf.org

Tehranipoor, M., & Koushanfar, F. (2010, January). A Survey of Hardware Trojan Taxonomy and Detection. *IEEE Design & Test of Computers*, *27*(1), 10–25. doi:10.1109/MDT.2010.7

Trujillo-Olaya, V., Sherwood, T., & Koc, C. K. (2012). Analysis of performance versus security in hardware realizations of small elliptic curves for lightweight applications. *Journal of Cryptographic Engineering, 2*(3), 179–188. doi:10.100713389-012-0039-x

Varchola, M., Guneysu, T., & Mischke, O. (2011, November). MicroECC: A Lightweight Reconfigurable Elliptic Curve Cryptoprocessor. In *2011 International Conference on Reconfigurable Computing and FPGAs* (pp. 204-210). 10.1109/ReConFig.2011.61

Voas, J., Kuhn, R., Laplante, P., & Applebaum, S. (2018). *Internet of Things (IoT) Trust Concerns*. National Institute of Standards and Technology. Retrieved from www.nist.gov

Want, R., Nath, B., & Reynolds, F. (2006, January). RFID Technology and Applications. *IEEE Pervasive Computing, 5*(1), 22–24. doi:10.1109/MPRV.2006.13

Wenger, E., Korak, T., & Kirschbaum, M. (2013). Analyzing Side-Channel Leakage of RFID-Suitable Lightweight ECC Hardware. In M. Hutter & J.-M. Schmidt (Eds.), *Radio Frequency Identification: Security and Privacy Issues - RFIDsec 2013* (pp. 128–144). Berlin: Springer Berlin Heidelberg. doi:10.1007/978-3-642-41332-2_9

Whitman, M. E. (2003, August). Enemy at the Gate: Threats to Information Security. *Communications of the ACM, 46*(8), 91–95. doi:10.1145/859670.859675

Wood, C. C., & Banks, W. W. Jr. (1993). Human error: An overlooked but significant information security problem. *Computers & Security, 12*(1), 51–60. doi:10.1016/0167-4048(93)90012-T

Yalcin, T. (2016). Compact ECDSA engine for IoT applications. *Electronics Letters, 52*(15), 1310–1312. doi:10.1049/el.2016.0760

Zeadally, S., Hunt, R., Chen, Y.-S., Irwin, A., & Hassan, A. (2012, August). Vehicular ad hoc networks (VANETS): Status, results, and challenges. *Telecommunication Systems, 50*(4), 217–241. doi:10.100711235-010-9400-5

ADDITIONAL READING

Biryukov, A., & Perrin, L. (2017). *State of the Art in Lightweight Symmetric Cryptography*. Cryptology ePrint Archive. Retrieved from eprint.iacr.org

Blodget, B., James-Roxby, P., Keller, E., McMillan, S., & Sundararajan, P. (2003). A Self-reconfiguring Platform. In P. Y. K. Cheung & G. A. Constantinides (Eds.), *Field Programmable Logic and Application* (pp. 565–574). Berlin, Heidelberg: Springer Berlin Heidelberg. doi:10.1007/978-3-540-45234-8_55

Kuon, I., & Rose, J. (2007, February). Measuring the Gap Between FPGAs and ASICs. *IEEE Transactions on Computer-Aided Design of Integrated Circuits and Systems*, 26(2), 203–215. doi:10.1109/TCAD.2006.884574

Lara-Nino, C. A., Diaz-Perez, A., & Morales-Sandoval, M. (2018). Elliptic Curve Lightweight Cryptography: A Survey. *IEEE Access: Practical Innovations, Open Solutions*, 6, 72514–72550. doi:10.1109/ACCESS.2018.2881444

Mangard, S., Oswald, E., & Popp, T. (2007). *Power Analysis Attacks, Revealing the Secrets of Smart Cards*. Boston, MA: Springer.

Menezes, A. J., Vanstone, S. A., & Oorschot, P. C. V. (1996). *Handbook of Applied Cryptography*. Boca Raton, FL, USA: CRC Press, Inc.

Moore, W. R., & Luk, W. (1994). More FPGAs. 49 Five Mile Drive, Oxford, United Kingdom: Abingdon EE&CS Books.

Paar, C., & Pelzl, J. (2010). *Understanding Cryptography, A Textbook for Students and Practitioners*. Berlin, Heidelberg: Springer. doi:10.1007/978-3-642-04101-3

Rashidi, B. (2017). *A Survey on Hardware Implementations of Elliptic Curve Cryptosystems*. Retrieved from arxiv.org

Sklavos, N. (2010). *On the Hardware Implementation Cost of Crypto-Processors Architectures*. Information Security Journal: A Global Perspective, 19(2), 53-60.

Tuan, T., Kao, S., Rahman, A., Das, S., & Trimberger, S. (2006). A *90Nm Low-power FPGA for Battery-powered Applications*. In Proceedings of the 2006 ACM/SIGDA 14th International Symposium on Field Programmable Gate Arrays (pp. 3-11). New York, NY, USA: ACM.

KEY TERMS AND DEFINITIONS

Advanced Encryption Standard (AES): Symmetric block cipher algorithm standardized by NIST in 2001.

Attacker: Unauthorized party that seeks to obtain or manipulate digital information.

Authentication: Certainty that the digital information comes from the declared source. Applied to devices, that these hold authorized credentials.

Authorized Party: The information producer or its intended receiver.

Availability: Certainty that the digital information can be accessed at the discretion of the authorized user.

Block Cipher: Cryptographic tool that encapsulates encryption and decryption mechanisms for processing plain data in blocks of determined size.

Cipher: Cryptographic tool that encapsulates encryption and decryption mechanisms for processing plain data.

Ciphertext: Piece of digital information that has been obfuscated by means of encryption.

Confidentiality: Certainty that the digital information is disclosed only to authorized parties.

Cybernetic Attack: Attack on a digital information system over the internet.

Decryption: Transformation applied to a ciphertext in order to retrieve the original plaintext.

Discrete Logarithms Over Elliptic Curve Groups: Given an elliptic curve group with generator P, an additive group operation, and the scalar multiplication procedure $kP = P + P + ... + P$, solve for k.

Discrete Logarithms Over Multiplicative Groups: Given a multiplicative group with generator G, a multiplicative group operation, and the modular exponentiation procedure $G^k = G \times G \times ... \times G$, solve for k.

Dynamic Partial Reconfiguration: Feature of an FPGA that allows for reconfiguring part of the fabric while the device is running.

Dynamic Reconfiguration: An FPGA is dynamically reconfigurable if it can be partially reconfigured while active.

Encryption: Transformation applied to a plaintext in order to obfuscate the information enclosed by means of data confusion and diffusion.

Hardware Trojan: Hardware design introduced in a chip by an unauthorized party during the manufacturing of the device.

Hash Function: Cryptographic tool capable of compressing an input text of arbitrary length of a string of defined length.

In-House Security: The final hardware design is always in control of the authorized parties prior to deployment.

Information Security: Area of research concerning with providing digital information systems with security services.

Integer Factorization Over Finite Fields: Let F be a finite field defined by a primer generator P, (A, B) two big numbers in F, and the modular multiplication procedure $C = A \times B$. Given C, find (A, B).

Integrity: Certainty that the digital information has not been modified by an unauthorized party.

Internet of Things (IoT): Ecosystem of coexisting technologies centered around the precept that everything has something to say and that some user has a use for this information.

Key Derivation Function: Cryptographic deterministic tool that allows for obtaining pieces of digital information of determined size employing a seed and some tweak value.

Key Establishment Mechanism: Information exchange system that allows two parties to communicate each other in a networked environment. It can be static (key pre-distribution) or dynamic.

Lightweight Cryptography: Branch of cryptography that deals with protocols and algorithms tailored for use in constrained environments.

Low-Rate Wireless Personal Area Networks (LR-WPANs): Data communication devices using low-data-rate, low-power, and low-complexity short-range radio frequency (RF) transmissions in a wireless personal area network (WPAN).

MAC Function: Cryptographic tool capable of generating a MAC tag of determined length from a message of arbitrary length. It must exhibit resistance against collisions and forgery.

Medical Body Area Network (MBAN): Network of devices deployed over the body of the patient.

Network Attack: Security attack against the network services.

One-Way Transform/Function: Mathematical function considered to be a computationally hard problem of high complexity. It is designed so that evaluating result while knowing all the inputs it is easy; but given the output and not all the inputs, finding the missing value is difficult.

Physical Attack: Attack against the physical infrastructure of the network.

Physically Unclonable Function: Hardware design that exploits irregularities in the manufacturing of devices for producing digital information in a deterministic way.

Plaintext: Piece of digital information whose contents are discernible to everyone.

Privacy: Certainty that only the authorized parties have access and control over the digital information.

Public-Key Cryptography: Set of cryptographic algorithms with operate using a key pair, as well as the protocols that employ these algorithms.

Public-Key Encryption Scheme: System that allows for the sender of the message to encrypt the plaintext using the public key of the receiver. The receiver shall use its public key to decrypt the ciphertext.

Reconfigurability: Feature of FPGAs that allows for modifying partially or totally the configuration of the fabric.

RFID Tag: Passive device that operates with radio-frequency impulses for providing information regarding on demand.

Secure Hash Algorithm (SHA): Family of hash functions standardized by NIST for their use in cryptographic applications.

Security Service: Precept of information security upheld by means of cryptography.

Side-Channel Attack: Analysis of the physical footprints observed on a device resulting from its natural operation with aims of retrieving cryptographic materials or data.

Side-Channel Attack Countermeasures: Mechanisms designed to reduce the physical influence of a device on its medium and the traces associated with the information being processed on it.

Smart Metering Utility Network: Network of utility meters which are equipped with 'smart' features.

Static Reconfiguration: Feature of an FPGA that allows for modifying the configuration of the fabric while the device is inactive.

Symmetric Cryptography: Set of cryptographic algorithms with operate using symmetric key, as well as the protocols that employ these algorithms.

Symmetric Key: Piece of information that must be kept secret by the user.

Vehicular Ad-Hoc Networks (VANETs): Mobile networks created by vehicles on the road.

WSN: Network of wireless devices without a defined topology, distributed in a wide geographical area for monitoring some physical phenomenon.

WSN Mote: Each one of the leaf devices on a WSN. These are equipped with sensing and network capabilities.

Chapter 3
FPGA Memory Optimization in High-Level Synthesis

Mingjie Lin
University of Central Florida, USA

Juan Escobedo
University of Central Florida, USA

ABSTRACT

High-level synthesis (HLS) with FPGA can achieve significant performance improvements through effective memory partitioning and meticulous data reuse. In this chapter, the authors will first explore techniques that have been adopted directly from systems that possess a fixed memory subsystem such as CPUs and GPUs (Section 2). Section 3 will focus on techniques that have been developed specifically for reconfigurable architectures which generate custom memory subsystems to take advantage of the peculiarities of a family of affine code called stencil code. The authors will focus on techniques that exploit memory banking to allow for parallel, conflict-free memory accesses in Section 3.1 and techniques that generate an optimal memory micro-architecture for data reuse in Section 3.2. Finally, Section 4 will explore the technique handling code still belonging to the affine family but the relative distance between the addresses.

INTRODUCTION

Despite all the attention processing power gets, the fact is it can be wasted if the processor does not have enough data to crunch. If the memory system cannot provide data fast enough to the processing cores to keep them busy, then most of the time

DOI: 10.4018/978-1-5225-9806-0.ch003

those extremely powerful units will be idle which translates to underutilization of resources and energy waste.

Because of that reason memory subsystems have been the focus of extensive research trying to find smarter ways to take advantage of the available bandwidth and avoid problems related to the latency of the accesses which are the most common reasons for the bottlenecks in modern computer systems. The roof-line model (Williams et al, 2009) seeks to describe the behavior of a system with a particular memory bandwidth under certain computational load.

Figure 1. Roofline model. O_1 is a computation bounded by the available bandwidth while O_2 is bounded by processing power.

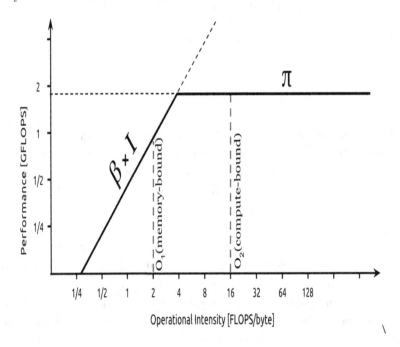

The model shown in figure 1, is a graph where the X axis measures the operational intensity, in operations per byte. This is, how many arithmetic operations, usually floating-point operations or FLOPS, can be performed per byte of. On the Y axis we see the bandwidth of the system, measured in bytes/sec or a multiple of it. We A say the system is memory bounded when increasing the available bandwidth will increase the number of arithmetic operations completed per second. On the other hand, more complex operations such as square root require several clock cycles to complete after we have fetched the data it needs. In that case, we say have an operation that is computationally bounded because an increase in bandwidth does not change the number of arithmetic operations we can complete per second. This is the desired point of operation since processing powers is orders of magnitude faster than memory accesses. A modern Intel Core i7 processor can demand up to 409.6 GB/s while even most modern DDR4 based system can only provide ≈9% of the maximum bandwidth that a processor demands (Gaur et al, 2017).

Adapting the roofline model to reconfigurable architectures and High -Level Synthesis to take advantage of its expressiveness and determine the source of the bottleneck has proven difficult because unlike in traditional architectures, one can instantiate more processing elements, effectively increasing the computational power of the device for the specific task. One proposed model also includes a measurement of how many resources would additional processing elements would utilize over the total available and include that into the Computational Performance (da Silva et al, 2013).

Solutions to overcome the memory bandwidth problem usually involve taking advantage of size-speed trade off some types of memories. One of the most widely implemented techniques is known as caching. Caching uses a type of memory called cache, and takes advantage of the fact most code reuses data that either has been used recently or is "free" to access since it is already on cache because it was brought on a recent batch. Once data is brought on the cache memory, not only does it sit physically closer to the processing unit, but the memory itself is constructed in such a way that acceding it is orders of magnitude faster than accessing RAM. Computing units or cores can have several levels of this type of memory, each one being slower than the one above, but with more capacity. To fully take advantage of this architecture, complex prediction algorithms are implemented to determine which data is the best to be evicted from cache to make room to newer one as the code executes. Modern prediction schemes can determine with effectiveness of over 90% (Hennessy et al, 2012) what the best eviction policy for certain program is. But even with this, the bandwidth gap is too wide to solve the problem at hand. Some researchers have even considered taking advantage of the comparatively smaller, but available, bandwidth of RAM memory to create a compound channel that takes advantage of all the available bandwidth instead of relying on the fast cache memory alone (Gaur et al, 2017).

In this chapter we will first explore techniques that have been adopted directly from systems that possess a fixed memory subsystem such as CPU's and GPU's (section 2). These techniques offer a lot of flexibility and can handle most types of code with minimum modification at the cost of sub-optimal performance. Section 3 will focus on techniques that have been developed specifically for reconfigurable architectures which generate custom memory subsystems to take advantage of the peculiarities of a family of affine code called stencil code. We will focus on techniques that exploit memory banking to allow for parallel, conflict-free memory accesses in section 3.1 and techniques that generate an optimal memory micro-architecture for data reuse in section 3.2. Section 4 will explore the technique handling code still belonging to the affine family but the geometry of the memory access changes with time but still has enough structure such that through some smart analysis and transformations the HLS software is able to generate efficient memory subsystems with better performance than general purposes one.

TECHNIQUES BASED ON TRADITIONAL MEMORY ARCHITECTURE

Programmers with expertise in traditional C-like languages might find very attractive to use HLS software to gain a performance boost by implementing their code in a custom hardware accelerator. Unfortunately, the nature of some code does not allow for the synthesis of optimal hardware. For the more complex cases, HLS software will borrow concepts from the compiler world aimed at traditional memory architectures that are general enough that can handle most kind of computing kernels and still give a performance boost. In this section we explore techniques such as Tiling, Loop Unrolling and Pipelining, and Scratchpad memories.

Figure 2. Hierarchy of memory optimization methods

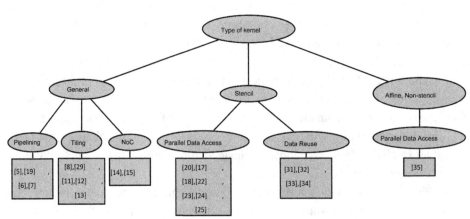

Loop Unrolling and Pipelining

Loop unrolling is one of the main and most straightforward optimizations done by HLS tools. Unrolling the loop and synthesizing parallel execution units that perform the computations in parallel is a low effort transformation that can be easily implemented in reconfigurable logic. Work in (Cilardo et al, 2015) studies the effects of loop unrolling when combined with another of the most popular transformations in the HLS community: memory partitioning. Particularly, the work in (Cilardo et al, 2015) explores the relationship between loop unrolling and the complexity of the interconnect.

Figure 3 shows how given a stencil code (a) and a cyclic partitioning of the data domain with 4 banks, without any unrolling (b), all the accesses in the stencil need to access all the banks at some point. Creating the need for 4 5-to-1 multiplexers and 5 4-to-1 muxes. On the other hand, unrolling the innermost loop by a factor of 1 (d) yields the 8-point stencil from (e). Note that now the stride size is 2 because of the unrolling and during each iteration, all the points in the augmented stencil always access the same bank, this reducing switching time. This allows for the use of 4 4-to-1 and 10 2-to-1 muxes (f). Using power of 2 logic and reducing the number of inputs greatly reduces complexity of the muxes (and thus the interconnect). The fact that the same bank will need to be accessed twice (meaning serialized access) is compensated by the fact that we have enough data to finish 2 stencils, thus unitary throughput is maintained. For this work however the authors do not provide an algorithm way to determine the best unroll factor in any of the dimensions but rather provide a metric that can be used to select the most appropriate unrolling from the test cases. They do not take into consideration data dependencies and they do the analysis blindly assuming no dependencies are broken for any case. The work also does not consider the minimum number of banks needed to allow for a conflict-free parallel memory access.

Another of the challenges faced by HLS software is bridging the gap between the data structures defined in the system-level specification and what is synthesizable given the available on-chip resources or even the available IP. This is the focus of the work in (Pilato et al, 2014). The approach is based on automatically finding Pareto-optimal design points that balance resource utilization, area, and latency. These design points will determine the requirements in terms of bandwidth which will in turn translate to the memory port requirements to allow access to the desired date without stalls. To control the access to the memory subsystem, the algorithm generates what is called a Flexible Memory Controller, seen in figure 4, that handles the arbitrary requirements of the data structures used by the processes being accelerated and takes care of the address translation and access to the lower level of memories. One limitation of this work is the simple banking scheme does

Figure 3. (a) Original code for a 5-point stencil computation. (b) Data domain partitioning with 4 banks. Shown 3 different instances of the stencil for 3 distinct iterations. (c) Banking interconnect. All memory accesses are routed to all the memory banks. (d) Unrolled code by a factor of 1. (e) Data domain partitioning with 4 banks Shown 3 instances of the unrolled stencil during 3 distinct iterations. (f) Simplified banking. Each memory access is only routed to one bank.

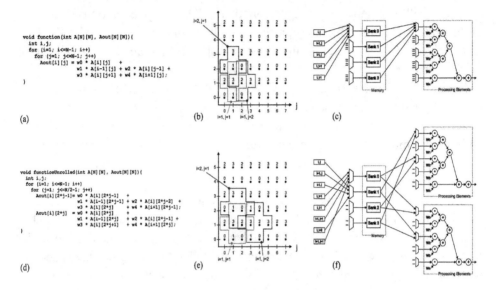

(a)   (b)   (c)

(d)   (e)   (f)

not grantee conflict-free access, meaning ensuring no two memory reads will try to access the same bank at the same time during the whole execution of the code. Handling this case is left unresolved in this work.

Pipelining is another popular technique used to improve throughput. When data dependencies are defined and known at compile time HLS software can do a good job in determining what iterations can be pipelined. The problem is usually the tools take a conservative approach and if any of the iterations cannot be pipelined, then it does not pipeline any of iterations. The problem is augmented when the data dependency is not constant or not known at compile time such as seen in figure 5 (a), where m is not known at compile time. The work in (Liu et al, 2018) proposes a workaround this issue for HLS. The paper proposes taking a less conservative approach, allowing for the pipelining of iterations without data dependency between them, and changing the initiation interval or II of the pipeline at certain points of execution during runtime to delay the start of iterations that depend on the data currently being processed in the pipeline. This approach can be seen in figure 5 (b). In general, we can schedule m consecutive iterations to be started with an II of 1,

Figure 4. Sample architecture generated by the method in, colors represent data structures that have been grouped together
source: Pilato et al, 2014

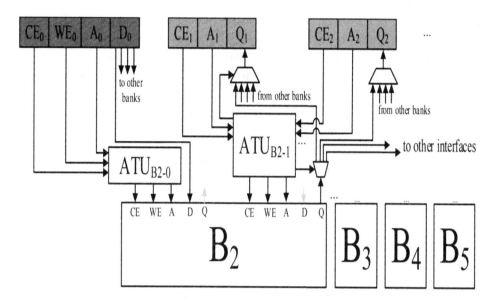

only scheduling the next set of m iterations to start after we have finished processing all the elements m iterations later.

The authors take advantage of the powerful and flexible polyhedral representation of the code to find a parametric representation of the data accessed on every iteration for every value of m and perform an automatic code transformation that inserts the necessary break in the execution of the pipeline to avoid data dependency violation.

Figure 5. (a) Sample code with unknown dependencies at compile time defined by m. (b) Proposed methodology with dynamic stalled pipeline operation.

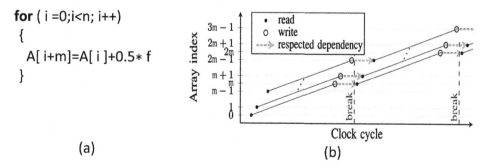

They can find near-optimal pipeline performance (in terms of cycles/iteration) for each value of m for the code shown in figure 5.

In (Cong et al, 2018) the authors propose an architecture they call a Composable Parallel Pipeline or CPP. The key idea is that by decoupling the kernel itself, which is the traditional synthesis target of HLS tools, from the memory interface, one can take better advantage of the available off-chip bandwidth on its entirety.

Another advantage of this approach is that now the load/compute/store stages can be pipelined under certain conditions. Furthermore, if there are no dependencies, the main loop of the kernel can be unrolled and implemented into separate computation engines that execute in parallel. This requires the input data to be partitioned in a number of banks equal to the unroll factor so that each of the engine can access the data it needs independently.

This approach has an extremely large design space and full exploration to determine design points such as unroll factor and memory interface width is not feasible even for relatively simple designs. To work around this, the authors propose to present the problem as a non-linear programming problem that can be solved in polynomial

Figure 6. (a) Traditional approach taken by HLS software. Accelerator is designed around the explicit declaration of the kernel I/O requirements leading to poor bandwidth utilization. (b) Decoupled approach proposed by (Cong et al, 2018). Computing kernel is decoupled from memory access to improve bandwidth utilization.

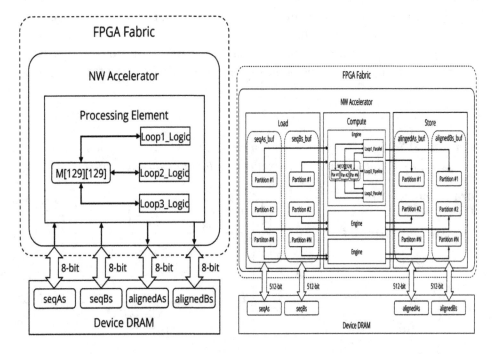

time. This non-linear problem incorporates information regarding resource utilization related to the previous design specs. For example, increasing the unroll factor allows for more parallelism but also requires more BRAM, which might also lead to more complicated routing that will degrade performance.

Tiling and Re-Scheduling

Due to the nature of the memory hierarchy in traditional processors, tiling has played a big role in optimizing the use of cache systems. In general, the data domain in partitioned in tiles that fit the desired level of cache. To maximize data reuse and avoid having to fetch new data constantly, iterations that use the data on the target level of cache are re-scheduled to be executed together when possible. It is this combination of tiling and iteration re-scheduling that gives the biggest performance improvement.

In (Cong et al, 2011), the authors include data reuse analysis to find a tiling that reduces communication cost while maintaining a size buffer within certain constraints. They use a polyhedral representation of the problem since it allows for the modeling of a sequence of simpler loop transformation into one single transform. They solve the joint problem of optimizing bandwidth use and minimizing resource utilization by using a combination of a branch-and-bound algorithm to prune sub-optimal solutions and a knapsack algorithm to model and maximize the reuse opportunities for every transformation. Unlike most of the previous work, their reuse analysis models not only read reuse opportunities but also includes information about writes, which saves having to read from lower levels of memory when the data is already on-chip as a product of a computation.

Another approach that tries to take advantage of the expressiveness of the polyhedral framework is explored in (Pouchet al, 2013). The authors use a scratchpad memory system and evaluate different arbitrary tile sizes by solving an optimization problem aiming to minimize bandwidth while adhering to a maximum buffer size while exploiting data reuse between iterations when possible. The main limitations of this method are that it relies on costly scratchpad memory systems as on-chip storage that have a high resource utilization due to its complexity. Although the authors claim the number of possible tile sizes to try is tractable this cannot be ensured for all cases. Their model also suffers from the general limitation that the possibilities are enumerated based on a model which if not defined properly might miss a better solution. They also mention this technique cannot guarantee correctness of behavior for the case of imperfectly nested loops.

In (Peemen et al, 2015) the authors face the problem of exploring the huge design space that is associated with reducing the amount of off-chip data transfers. This time the authors also explore a design that maximizes inter-tile reuse, which makes the solution space even larger. They achieve the reduction in communications mainly by exploring iteration reordering. Once a target volume of memory operations is achieved, extra optimizations seek to reduce the size of the buffers by means of additional transformations. The way this is done is by modeling the problem with two independent cost functions, one that tries to minimize inter-tile communication cost and another one that minimizes intra-tile communication costs by using reuse buffers.

Figure 7. (a) Naive implementation of a matrix multiplication kernel with 3x3 tiles with just intra-tile reuse. (b) Improved implementation with inter-tile reuse. (c) Optimized buffer sizes for a different tiling. Data transfer remains unchanged, but buffer size is nearly halved.

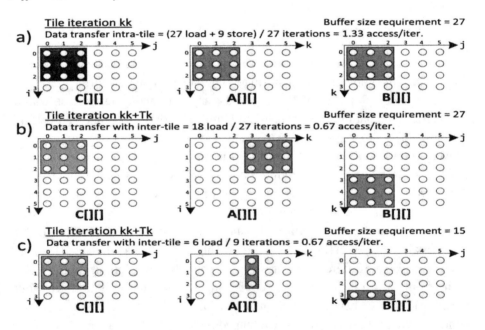

In figure 7 we see the communication reduction when inter-tile data reuse is considered. In a) we see an example of matrix multiplication. Without inter tile reuse, the host sends 27 values and receives 9. If we exploit the reuse between successive tiles, only the 18 values needed to be read are transferred each iteration after the first one (fig. 8 b). The authors make the key observation that the cost function they propose to model intra-tile reuse does not take inter-tile reuse into account and such tile factors and interchanges are sub optimal in terms of data transfer. Is this observation that allows them to find better tiling of the innermost loop without affecting inter-tile reuse. In c) we see how having a tile size of 1 (width) in the innermost loop allows for a smaller memory footprint, only needing 15 elements, while still maintaining the same amount of data transfer.

The massive difference between the bandwidth available for off-chip communication and on-chip resources is noted in the work in (Milford et al, 2016). In figure 8 (a) we see how access to off-chip memory is almost a million times slower than access to the much faster, but much scarce distributes RAM. In this work the authors take advantage of the cyclo-static representation that can be used to model perfectly nested, stencil code, to solve the problem of how to automatically determine the tile size and optimal buffer size. The authors divide the problem in two stages: finding a CSDF or Cyclo-Static Data Flow representation of C statements in the innermost loop level based on consumption of input data tokens and the corresponding output tokens. Once the size of the input tokens for the compute kernel are known, then their method analyzes the size of the data domain region accessed at every loop level. At each level, they consider the accessed data is a sliding window of the upper level loop. At the outermost loop the whole data domain is accessed. Based on the available bandwidth and the total amount of data each loop level requires to achieve a certain level of performance, they decide what levels of the loop hierarchy should be placed on-chip, if the bandwidth requires is higher than the off-chip bandwidth, or off-chip is the requirements are low enough, thus saving on-chip resources. An example of this can be seen in figure 8 (b) where for a given bandwidth and throughput, the algorithm automatically determent the best tiling, or division of the loop hierarchy, to be brought on chip at any given point. Based on the bandwidth and performance needed at a certain level, different resources are used. As more bandwidth is needed while approaching to the innermost level of the loop hierarchy, some of the data will be partitioned on-chip using BRAM or even

Figure 8. (a) Bandwidth available at different levels of the memory hierarchy for a typical FPGA system with on chip and on-board memory. (b) Sample memory hierarchy generated by (Milford et al, 2016).

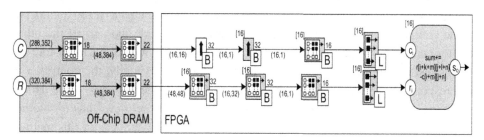

registers as long as there are enough sources. If resources are insufficient, as much of the data as possible is put on-chip.

In a similar manner, the work in (Liu et al, 2017) seeks to find optimal tile sizes that partition the data/iteration domain into chunks that can fit into size-constrained faster on-chip memory. While most work trying to solve this problem uses a partial solution enumeration approach, here the authors an analytical approach based in polyhedral parametric model to find the size for optimized data reuse.

Their parametric approach formulates a non-linear optimization problem takes into account on-chip memory constraints and finds the tile size for minimizing communication overhead. To test the validity of their approach and optimization model, they apply their method to three very popular computing kernels: matrix multiplication, a full search motion estimation, and Convolution

Neural Network. They compare their results with results for other methods that use random enumeration of tile sizes, a method where the tile sizes are selected through at random and then performance results are computed. On average, it takes this approach half the time to find a solution that meets the requirements in comparison to the random approach while also achieving a much better communication cost for a given tile size.

Network-on-a-Chip

Another approach that has been explores is to simply emulate the behavior of traditional software execution where the program running simply executes an instruction requesting data and the underlying hardware platform takes care of the actual memory access. The software only sees the data back with different timing depending on whether there was a cache miss/hit or even a page fault.

The approach taken in (Chung et al, 2011) consists in creating a series of distributed application specific computing kernels as well as an underlying network of connected RAM (thus the name of their approach: CoRAM) that takes care of manages and transport data to and from the compute kernels.

In figure 9 (a) we see the architecture of the underlying memory system. The computing kernels will request the data they need from their local memory controller. This controller will have the equivalent of a chase system that will be able to quickly provide the requested data if it has been used recently in the past. If the data is not in the controllers local memory, it will access the network and ask all the other memory controller on it if they have it, The routing logic will take care of touring the request and the data from one controller to the other. Finally, the controller is also responsible of accessing off-chip memory (called edge memory) if the data is not in the on-chip network. This way, the application kernel never has to interact with neither on-chip nor on-board memory. One of the advantages of this method

Figure 9. (a) Sample underlying NoC for the CoRAM architecture. (b) Division of programming paradigms. HDL for application (1) allows for high degree of control on the optimality of the synthesized hardware and high-level languages (2) for the control threads allow for high flexibility in the personality of the CoRAM memories.

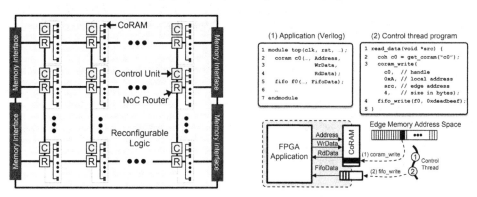

is that while the compute kernel can be specified using any HDL language, which provides great control over the performance allowing the implementation of very optimized computing architectures, the behavior of the memory controllers can be defined using higher level programming languages, allowing for a lot of flexibility (fig. 10 (b)). Every memory controller is controlled by a single thread, but a single thread can be used to control more than one memory controllers. These treads define what the authors call the "personality" of the memory system which in general can be defined as a FIFO, scratch pad, among others depending on the kernel. With this kind of flexibility one could even emulate multilevel-cache hierarchies in the CoRAm architecture. The limitation of this kind of of Network-on-Chip architecture is as with any network-based system the QoS of the network since the on-chip caching itself will depend on the nature of the code and code that often accesses off-chip memory would not see much advantage and actually supper form performance degradation.

The work in (Yang et al, 2017), backed by Intel and MIT, proposes feedback-driven network compiler that constructs an ad-hoc optimized memory network for a target program's memory access behavior. They use a newly designed network profiler to get the behaviors and extract the best architecture to handle the data access patter in order to minimize latency. This work is heavily based on previous developments from the same research group, namely: the concept of LEAP memories and a LEAP Memory Compiler.

LEAP private memories provide accelerators (called clients) running on the FPGA an additional layer of abstraction that allows them to use simple memory interface with the traditional read-request, read-response, and write APIs. These memories emulate the memory behavior that a traditional program running on software would see

Figure 10. (a) Sample memory hierarchy using a ring topology for inter-memory communication gendered by the LEAP framework. Clients can be assigned their own memory or placed on a shred memory structure. (b) Banking of client's private memory. Clients that require more bandwidth will be signed its own off-chip bank, while clients with lower bandwidth requirements share a DRAM bank and a memory controller. (c) Tree based topology for reduced latency. (d) Example of a tree based topology with banking.

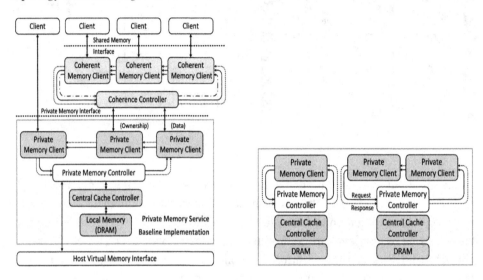

such as arbitrarily large data spaces and the ability to use any kind of data structure. LEAP memories can even be used to implement a shared-memory subsystem where each client possess its own LEAP memory but other clients can access the data from other memories, even being able to copy the data, avoiding costly trips to lower levels of memory. A coherence controller makes sure all the values of the data are kept up to date. This approach, separating the interface seen and used by the clients, and the actual memory architecture gives the compiler a great deal of freedom to determine what is the most appropriate hierarchy to implement without it affecting the client. An example of a possible solution the compiler might try based on the set of clients that need to be executed can be seen in fig. 11 (a).

To better utilize the available bandwidth of different board-level memories, the authors developed a LEAP Memory Controllers (LMC) which considers each memory as an independent cache managed by an separate controller instead of single unified memory. The idea is that the LMC keeps track of the incoming/outgoing traffic from each client and partitions them based on their bandwidth need. Low bandwidth clients can be place on the same network where ach one has its own LEAP memory, but they both access the same on-board memory module while a high-bandwidth module would be put on a different network and be assigned a single memory so it can access data at the full speed, without sharing. An example of the partitioned memory network LMC can create can be seen in figure 10 (b).

One important thing to note in figures 10 (a) and (b) is that the cases where we have LEAP memories at the same level of the hierarchy they are connected via ring-like network topology. The authors call this: LEAP rings. This ring-like topology was chosen due to its simplicity but the authors recognize that as the processing power increases and as more and more memories are placed on the same level of the hierarchy, the main flaw of this type of interconnect, namely latency, becomes more evident.

In (Yang et al, 2017) the authors seek to alleviate the latency problem of the ring topology of their interconnect with the constructions of tree-based networks instead (fig. 11 (c)). The authors test this new topology by implementing a reflect-tree, cryptosolver-filter, and a heat-filter algorithms and compare results in terms of area, resource utilization, and max operating frequency. They conclude depending on the application and constraints, the compiler should select one of the two topologies of interconnect: for cases when the program requires high-operating frequencies, the ring topology is preferred as it can achieve higher clock speeds; otherwise the compiler should construct a tree based networks due to its reduced latency and less area overhead. To determine the needs of the codes to be executed, they first run the clients individually to profile the memory accesses as well as latency sensitivity and determine which topology is preferred as well as if any partitioning of the on-board memory is required to ensure all the modules get the bandwidth they need.

One thing that is interesting to note between the two major NoC proposes is that they are complementary, meaning each one handles one side of the NoC problem. In (Yang et al, 2017) the authors go so far as to mention since CoRAM does not define the memory subsystem backing up the programmers interface one could use the LEAP architecture for their NoC.

TECHNIQUES FOR STENCIL CODE IN RECONFIGURABLE ARCHITECTURES

There are a certain kind of very popular computing kernels, particularly in scientific applications, called stencil computations. In this kind of applications, the relative distance of the memory locations accessed during the execution remains constant. This regularity allows for an in-depth analysis of the memory access's properties allows the automatic generation of ad-hoc optimal memory hierarchies that integrate certain techniques that provide a great degree of performance improvements. Among the two most common ones are conflict-free parallel data access, also called memory banking, and optimal micro-architectures for exploiting data reuse.

Parallel Data Access

Obtaining the smallest partition factor that allows for conflict-free, parallel memory access is very attractive due to the phenomena of bank-switching, which is explored in-depth in (Gallo et al, 2014). As the partition factor reduces, so does the complexity of the interconnect logic that connects banks with outputs. This directly translates to better performance due to being able to achieve reduced clock periods, and translates to resource utilization reduction which in many cases can also mean power savings.

In (Wang et al, 2013) the authors develop a method for obtaining an efficient memory partitioning scheme while also maintaining memory overhead to a minimum.

Figure 11. (a) Cyclic partitioning with a single family of hyperplanes using 5 banks for a 5-point stencil. (b) Intra-bank address calculation using a base and a offset polytope. Address is calculated by counting the number of integer points assigned to the same bank inside each of the polytopes

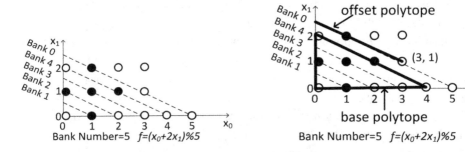

The method is based on finding a family of hyperplanes such that it can assign the memory access to different banks without conflicts as seen in figure 11 (a). Starting from an arbitrary partition factor, the method tries all unique combinations of hyperplanes families. If it is impossible to find one that gives conflict free partitioning, then the partition factor is increased, and the process repeats until a solution is found. Memory overhead, meaning the additional amount of memory needed to obtain a usable banking scheme, is reduced by using a polytope-based approach to calculate intra-bank memory offset. The data domain is partitioned into a base polytope and an offset polytope 12 (b). Depending on the polytope under considerations, different integer point counting algorithms are used to obtain the number of elements of the desired bank existing inside/on the polytope. The main

Figure 12. (a) Cyclic partitioning with a single family of hyperplanes using 5 banks for a 4-point stencil. (b) Block-cyclic partitioning with a single family of hyperplanes using 4 banks.

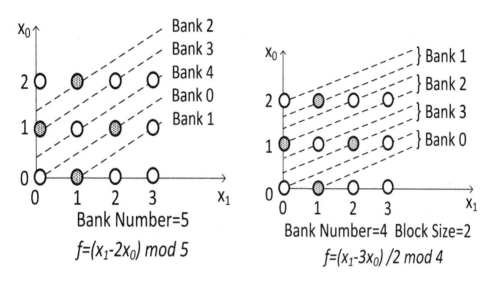

imitation of this technique is the heuristic search which. Also, as we will see, further reach has shown that using a single family of hyperplanes yields sub-optimal solutions for some cases. The advantage is in the simplicity of the implementation where the bank assignment is determined by a dot product between the vector normal to the direction of the family of hyperplanes and the memory location of interest and a modulo operation by the partition factor.

This work is further developed in (Wang et al, 2014), where the partition factor is improved by introducing the concept of block-cyclic partitioning, the idea of successive or contiguous memory locations belonging to the same partition.

Instead of having the linear partitioning scheme seen in 13 (a) where the next hyperplane assigns memory locations to a different bank, we rather have the scheme from (b). Now we have B times the number of hyperplanes before the assignment repeats, where B is the blocking factor. Having B consecutive hyperplanes assign memory locations allow for contiguousness memory locations in one dimension be assigned to the same bank which helps fill gaps in the memory access pattern without the need to add another bank. This idea is similar to the one presented in (Cilardo et al, 2015) where unrolling the loop can improve partitioning factors. They also improve on the intra bank memory offset calculation. Instead of using complicated integer point counting in arbitrarily shaped polytopes to calculate the address, they use padding to generate virtual memory locations with the goal of always being able to use rectangular polytopes at the cost of a bit more memory overhead. The

Figure 13. Multi-statement code (top left). Partitioning of the data domain for 4-bank scheme and location of the memory accesses for the first iteration they are executed (bottom left). Partition with conflicts using a single family of hyperplanes (right)

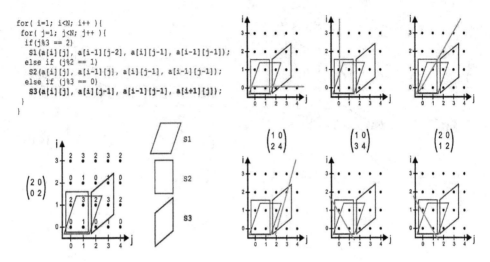

main limitation is that the block is still just 1D and the fact that not only using a single family of hyperplanes still means some better solutions are ignored but now the heuristic search has an additional parameter in the block size which adds to the time it takes to find a solution.

One work that tries to reduce the time to find a solution is the study performed in (Meng et al, 2015) which finds a solution using the geometric information of the stencil itself.

This work can find a closed form formula for the normal vector to the family of hyperplanes by taking into consideration the relative displacement of the memory vectors with one another. This avoids the problem of having to do a full search of the solution and gives a solution using much fewer arithmetic operations. The downside, as the solution space is smaller than in (Wang et al, 2014), they cannot ensure they have found the optimal solution. Their solution has a partition factor that is at least the same as the one in the (Wang et al, 2014). When their method finds a solution with the same partition factor, they can prove their memory overhead is no worse than in (Wang et al, 2014), but unfortunately, this is not always possible. On the other hand, they can find a banking scheme that while minimizing memory overhead and maintaining a balanced load on all the banks (they all contain the same number of elements) can ensure pipelined execution with the smallest Initiation Interval for a given partition factor.

Other works expand on the hyperplane idea and try to use more than one family of hyperplanes to find a solution. In (Cilardo et al, 2015) the authors introduce the concept of integer lattices to do memory partitioning. The main idea is to find a matrix of rank equal to the dimensionality of the problem space which determinant is equal to the number of available banks such that the total conflict count is reduced. They use multidimensional modulo mapping to assign the right bank to the right memory access by rewriting the code to explicitly assign a bank to a memory access for all the possible combinations of modulo values in all the dimensions.

Using more than one family of hyperplanes gives a much larger solution space, which in turn means we can now consider solutions previously inaccessible. Is in these solutions where we can find better partition factors than with previous methods. The main limitation is the quality of the solution, namely the number of conflicts, is based on the number of available banks and although an iterative version can be implemented to find the optimal partition factor, this is not the original goal of the algorithm. The algorithm presented by the authors focuses on reducing the number of conflicts for a given apportion factor instead. This method offers the advantage that one can achieve asymptotically small memory overhead at the cost of performing a multiplication and right shift instead of a division by an arbitrary number. This method can also be used to find a banking scheme that can be used by imperfectly nested loops or loops with multiple memory access patterns as seen in figure 13.

An extension of the method aiming to natively find the optimal solution for the banking problem using multiple families of hyperplanes can be found in (Juan et al, 2017). Here the authors use the stencil to tessellate the memory data domain, effectively generating N-dimensional integer lattices where N is the dimensionality of the problem, as seen in figure 14.

The key observation making this method implementable is that in a tessellation, there is a pattern repeating in all directions. One can find a rectangular region of space with a repeating banking pattern. The authors call this rectangle a Super-Tile. FPGA architectures allow for efficiently generating and accessing this kind of small, N-dimensional rectangular memories. The final address is calculated by counting how many tiles have occurred before the current one and adding an intra-tile offset calculated at compile time and stored in a similar N-dimensional memory. When the stencil cannot tessellate the data domain perfectly, extra virtual accesses are generated and added to it until the modified stencil tessellates the space perfectly. Similarly with previous heuristic techniques, the main drawback of this approach is the number and location of the extra "virtual accesses" to add in order to make the stencil tessellable is unknown and the authors perform an incremental exhaustive search until said stencil is found.

All the methods based in linear algebra an hyperplane partitioning have the limitation of their rigid structure which can cause "virtual conflicts". This is,

Figure 14. (a) 5-Point test stencil with arbitrarily assigned banks. (b) Tessellated data domain. Red rectangle indicates smallest region with a repeated bank assignment

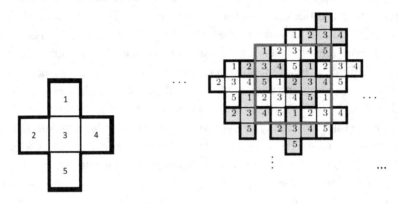

conflicts that arise from the banking function itself. In some cases, evens stencil code possesses certain geometric characteristics that cannot be easily represented using linear algebra. Recognizing this problem, some work has looked into more complex but flexible algorithms such as graph coloring, which can find the optimal partition factor, no matter if there are some non-linearities in the solution which would have made it impossible for linear algebra methods to find it, with the downside that they are NP-complete in complexity.

The graph-based approach presented in (Zhou et al, 2017) explores the entire memory trace of a computing kernel and by applying different masks, it generates a small family of addresses. Those addresses become nodes in a graph and the ones that appear together at any given iteration are joined by an edge. If the maximum clique of the graphs is not smaller or equal to the current estimate of the optimal partition factor, the algorithm proceeds to confirm the chromatic number by coloring the graph. If the chromatic number matches the expected minimum, the algorithm terminates. If no solution is found, another mask with the same number of active bits is tried. Once all permutations of masks for a given number of active bits are exhausted and no solutions is found, then another active bit is added to the mask, and the process repeated. The smallest solution for partition factor after coloring is stored, this way, once the algorithm terminates, the optimal solution is already computed. An overview of this process can be seen in figure 15.

The resulting coloring of the graph is stored is a multi-tiered lookup table and used to determine the bank. To do this, the requested address is masked and mapped to one of the nodes, and the color will correspond to the bank. One of the limitations of this method the exhaustive search required to find the final solution. For extensive data traces this could mean prohibitively long runtimes. The use of a heuristic coloring algorithm does not guarantee finding the true optimal portioning

Figure 15. Overview of the algorithm proposed in (Escobedo et al, 2018). Left to right: Trace generation and compression. Mask generation and evaluation with feedback. If target maximum clique size is exceeded, mask is updated: either try another permutation with the same number of active bits or increase number of active bits. Greedy coloring and multi-tier LUT generation for easy mapping.

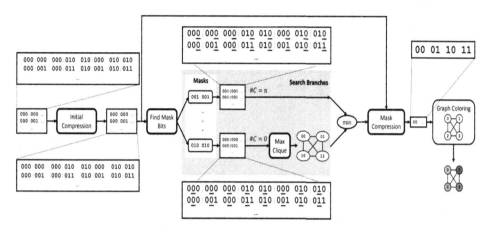

factor. Although one could use an optimal coloring algorithm, this would again mean solving an optimal coloring algorithm, which is an NP-complete problem, an indeterminate number of times.

When the true optimal partition factor is needed for any stencil kernel, the methodology from (Escobedo et al, 2018) can be used. Before this work no mathematical proof regarding optimality was given regarding the solution obtained by a partition method. In this work, the authors propose an algorithmic way of generating a graph they call the Extended Stencil Graph or ESG which is the smallest repeatable induced subgraph of the entire conflict graph such that it has all the information necessary to perform the conflict-free partition.

It algorithmically generates an induced subgraph of the entire conflict graph by convolving the stencil with itself around a pivot node. This graph is the smallest graph to the best of the author's knowledge that possesses enough information about the whole conflict graph such that when colored it can determine the chromatic number of the entire graph. The partition itself is done by applying an optimal coloring algorithm to this small graph, called ESG, whose size is only proportional to the size of the stencil, thus ensuring optimality of the solution and avoiding the problem of applying an NP-complete algorithm to an arbitrarily large problem. This process can be seen, from start to finish, in figure 16. Similarly to the work in (Cilardo et al, 2015), when the chromatic number of the ESG is the same as the number of memory accedes in the stencil, one can find a rectangular region with repeating

Figure 16. From left to right: Original 3-point stencil S. Extended Stencil obtained from convolving it with itself around pivot node (ES(S)). Graph representation of the Extended Stencil (ESG(S)). Optimal coloring of the ESG(S)

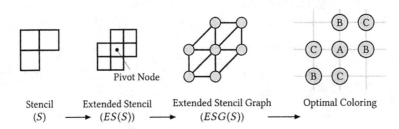

Stencil   Extended Stencil   Extended Stencil Graph   Optimal Coloring
(S) $\longrightarrow$ $(ES(S))$ $\longrightarrow$ $(ESG(S))$ $\longrightarrow$

coloring that can be used in an identical manner to compute bank assignments and intra-bank offset.

The main limitation of this work is the fact when the chromatic number of the ESG does not match the number of memory accesses (ESG is weakly perfect), the algorithm performs a heuristic search, adding up to as many "holes" from a tessellating pint of view lie within the ESG, to the original stencil in an incremental manner until the augmented ESG is weakly perfect. This mean performing an undefined number of iterations of an NP-complete optimal graph coloring algorithm.

One important limitation all the algorithms discussed in this section possess is that none of them included any kind of reuse analysis in the algorithm. How reusing data can affect the partition factor and improve not only performance, but memory overhead will be the focus of the next section.

Data Reuse

There has been a lot of effort by the HLS community to replicate the success of techniques in the compiler world to increase locality and reduce communication costs. While one could use the methods presented in section 2, they are far from optimal in many cases. For stencil code, one can perform compile-time analysis techniques that let the HLS software generate optimized memory micro-architectures that provide not only a reduced partition factor for conflict-free, parallel data access, but also give a performance boost in terms of reduced clock period.

In this section we will explore the two most recent approaches that automatically generate different kind of said micro-architectures.

Figure 17. (a) 5-point stencil "DENOISE" (black nodes) and exploration order of center memory access (dotted line). Problem dependent reuse distance between two memory accesses highlighted in red. (b) Micro-architecture with one bank . Buffers connecting memory accesses with problem dependent reuse distances implemented using BRAM.

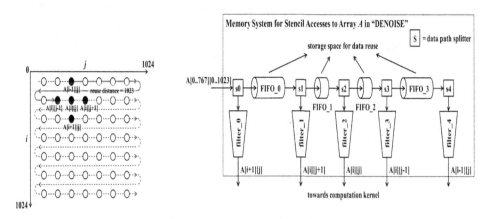

Micro-Architectures

An architecture first described in (Meeus et al, 2014) and then expanded on (Cong et al, 2016) is based on the construction of reuse chains built from FIFOs to perform data reuse and partitioning for stencil computations. Taking advantage of the constant geometry and regular exploration order of the data domain for most stencil kernels (18 (a)), the algorithm is capable of automatically generating a very simple structure of connected FIFOs of different depth, taking data from the connection points (b) to perform the parallel access.

In this approach the N-dimensional data space projected onto a line. The section of the data domain between the first and last memory accesses will be mapped to the reuse buffers. If the distance between two memory access in this linearized domain is larger a certain pre-defined threshold, the two are connected using a FIFO implemented using BRAM. Anything smaller is mapped to FIFOs built more efficient memory elements such as registers. The connection points between two of these buffers can be considered as fixed taping points in a single, larger FIFO comprised of all the reuse buffers. Because the FIFOS are of the right size, the correct data will always be available at the right time at these tapping points to complete the stencil which can easily be accessed in parallel.

Because our problem has been reduced to a 1-D domain, we will only need to access one new element per clock cycle to keep optimal throughput, thus requiring only one bank. Since the reuse buffers can be arbitrarily large, resource constraints

Figure 18. Sample stencils under consideration. Unrolled denoise (left), bicubic (center), Prewitt (right)

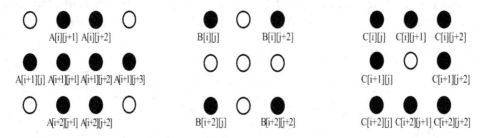

can become a limitation. One can replace the longer buffers with off-chip memory access at the cost of requiring more memory bandwidth to keep the same throughput.

Another approach first explored in (Yang et al, 2017) for stencil computations and then extended on (Li et al, 2018) for multi pattern accesses can be used to find a compromise between reuse opportunities, improved memory partition, and constrained buffer sizes. In this architecture, a stencil (such as the ones seen in figure 18) are divided in two parts: a reusable and a non-reusable section, based on the direction of exploration of the data domain. The idea is to let short reuse chains provide the data for the reusable portion of the stencil and just partition and access the non-reusable accesses every iteration as can be seen in figure 19. This approach does not consider implementing any data reuse when the reuse distance between two accesses is dependent on the problem size. This leads to higher partition factors than the previous 2 methods but circumvents some of its drawbacks while still maintaining good performance.

Unlike in (Cong et al, 2016; Su et al, 2017; Li et al, 2018) the authors project the stencil onto a space that is one dimension lower than the original space. The memory accesses in this "hidden dimension" are taken care off by the reuse buffers. It is in this dimensionality reduction where the reduced partition factor comes from. The main limitation of this method is that only taking advantage of reuse in one of the dimensions, the direction of exploration.

TECHNIQUES FOR AFFINE NON-STENCIL CODE IN RECONFIGURABLE ARCHITECTURES

Memory partitioning for non-stencil code however presents a very limited body of study, especially for FPGAs and the HLS community. General techniques as the ones presented in section 2 focus mainly on the use of tiling with scratchpad memories and lack the benefits in terms of optimal memory architectures such as the

Figure 19. (a) Reuse chains for the leftmost stencil in (b) Solution for the leftmost stencil in elements in blue are accessed in parallel every iteration. Elements in gray get data from tapping the reuse chain, (c) Solution for the middle stencil in, (d) Solution for the rightmost stencil in

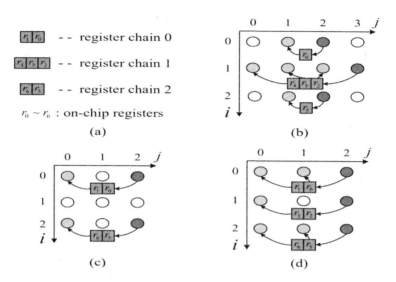

ones presented in 3. Particularly, one area that has rarely been explored is allowing parallel, conflict free memory access via data banking for non-stencil code.

The main difficulty lies in the fact that most analysis relies on the constant geometry of the stencil to do the memory banking. When the relative distances between the accesses changes during runtime, even if it is known at compile time, most methods break down or give a partition factor that is dependent on the problem size.

PARALLEL DATA ACCESS

Banking

One work that tries to tackle the problem of memory banking for affine, non-stencil code is (Li et al, 2018) where the author propose a best-effort approach that does not guarantees parallel conflict-free memory accesses but seeks to minimize the number of sequential reads or conflicts for a given partition factor.

Like some of the state-of-the-art methods for stencil memory partition, it uses a graph-based approach due to the flexibility it offers when dealing with problems that cannot be efficiently modeled using linear algebra. The method averages out the conflict graph to a manageable graph size by overlapping regions of a predefined size. Considering the data domain as an N-dimensional grid, memory locations with the same relative position (using modulo operations) in their own region are considered the same node in the overlapped graph. All edges between the memory locations that need to be accessed together are maintained and when overlapped, make the edges of the graph weighted. The weight represents the number of times a certain memory location needs to be accessed jointly with another during the same iteration which could translate to a memory conflict if both nodes are assigned to the same partition. If there are edged connecting two memory locations that will be overlapped into the same location the methods call this kind of edge a self-edge, while edges that when translated to the overlapped graph connect two different nodes, are simply called edges. The only way to change the weight of a self-edge is by changing the geometry of the area of the data domain considered, while traditional kind of edges are taken care of by the coloring algorithm used to generate the partitioning itself. The authors use a greedy coloring algorithm to avoid the problem of long runtime to find a solution given the NP-complete nature of the optimal graph coloring problem. The algorithm has an user defined maximum number of colors to use and tries to do proper coloring of nodes that are connected by the heaviest edges first with the goal of elimination as many conflicts as possible before proper coloring

Figure 20. (a) Memory accesses corresponding to 3 distinct iterations in blue, purple, and green in the original data domain. (b) Memory locations mapped to a 2x2 region with nodes mapped to the same relative position aligned vertically. (c) Weighted conflict graph generated by overlapping and collapsing all the tiles and adding the weight of the edges that connect the nodes in the same relative position

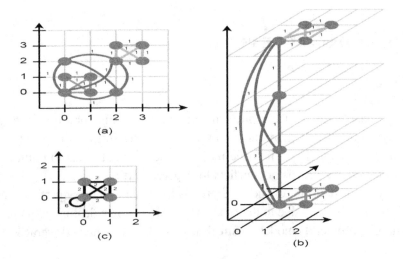

is not possible given the max partition factor constrain. Having a larger maximum for the partition factor means the greedy algorithm will be able to color more nodes properly and eliminate more conflicts.

The process of obtaining the overlapped graph with the weighted edges can be seen in figure 20. In (a) we see three different iterations and the corresponding memory accesses. Mapping the absolute address of the memory locations to a 2x2 tile using modulo logic they get the 4 tiles seen in (b). Finally, collapsing and overlapping the tiles onto a single one, where the weight of two edges connect the same two relative edges is added yields the 4-node graph from (c) with a self-edge and 6 edges.

Figure 21 shows how the greedy algorithm is used to color the graph with a given maximum number of colors allowed to reduce conflicts for a sample overlapped conflict graph. With the maximum partition factor being one, no proper coloring can be done, and all nodes are assigned to the same bank, needing to serialize the access every time. When 2 colors are allowed, the algorithm can eliminate 4 inter-node edges, namely the heaviest ones. With 3 colors we can remove an additional edge. Not that increasing the colors by 50% only eliminated 6 extra conflicts from the total. With 4 colors, we can have a proper coloring of the entire overlapped graph, meaning all inter-node conflicts are resolved, leaving only self-conflicts, which as stated before can only be modified by changing the geometry of the selected region.

Figure 21. a) Result of greedy coloring for sample weighted graph with 1 color. No edges are removed. (b) Result of greedy coloring for sample weighted graph with 2 colors. The 4 heaviest inter-node edges are removed. (c) Result of greedy coloring for sample weighted graph with 3 colors. The 5 heaviest inter-node edges are removed. (d) Result of greedy coloring for sample weighted graph with 4 colors. All inter-node edges are removed.

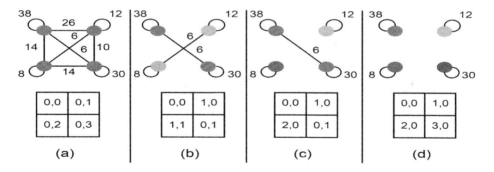

This approach has two main limitations: the first is no analysis of the optimal tile size is given. Instead, it just explores a set of predefined tile sizes, which are all power of 2 to simplify modulo logic, and selects the one that gives the best conflict resolution for a given maximum partition factor for the kernel under test. Although this method is general enough to be used for any kind of kernel code, this method does not offer conflict-free memory access for all cases and cannot provide the optimal partition factor for a given non-stencil code.

REFERENCES

Baradaran & Diniz. (2008). A compiler approach to managing storage and memory bandwidth in configurable architectures. *ACM Trans. Des. Autom. Electron. Syst.*, *13*, 61:1–61:26.

Chung, E. S., Hoe, J. C., & Mai, K. (2011). Coram: An in-fabric memory architecture for fpga-based computing. In *Proceedings of the 19th ACM/SIGDA International Symposium on Field Programmable Gate Arrays* (pp. 97–106). ACM. 10.1145/1950413.1950435

Cilardo & Gallo. (2015). Improving multibank memory access parallelism with lattice-based partitioning. *ACM Trans. Archit. Code Optim.*, *11*, 45:1–45:25.

Cilardo, A., & Gallo, L. (2015). Interplay of loop unrolling and multidimensional memory partitioning in hls. 2015 Design, Automation Test in Europe Conference Exhibition (DATE), 163–168. doi:10.7873/DATE.2015.0798

Cong, J., Li, P., Xiao, B., & Zhang, P. (2016). An optimal microarchitecture for stencil computation acceleration based on nonuniform partitioning of data reuse buffers. *IEEE Transactions on Computer-Aided Design of Integrated Circuits and Systems*, *35*(3), 407–418. doi:10.1109/TCAD.2015.2488491

Cong, J., Wei, P., Yu, C. H., & Zhang, P. (2018). Automated accelerator generation and optimization with composable, parallel and pipeline architecture. *Proceedings of the 55th Annual Design Automation Conference*, 154:1–154:6.

Cong, J., Zhang, P., & Zou, Y. (2012). Optimizing memory hierarchy allocation with loop transformations for high-level synthesis. *DAC Design Automation Conference 2012*, 1229–1234. 10.1145/2228360.2228586

Cong, J., Zhang, P., & Zou, Y. (2011). Combined loop transformation and hierarchy allocation for data reuse optimization. *2011 IEEE/ACM International Conference on Computer-Aided Design (ICCAD)*, 185–192. 10.1109/ICCAD.2011.6105324 da Silva, Braeken, D'Hollander, & Touhafi. (2013). Performance modeling for fpgas: Extending the roofline model with high-level synthesis tools. *Int. J. Reconfig. Comput.*, *2013*, 7:7–7:7.

Darte, A., Member, I. C. S., Schreiber, R., & Villard, G. (2005). *Lattice-based memory allocation* (Vol. 10). IEEE Transactions on Computers.

Escobedo, J., & Lin, M. (2018). Graph-theoretically optimal memory banking for stencil-based computing kernels. In *Proceedings of the 2018 ACM/SIGDA International Symposium on Field-Programmable Gate Arrays* (pp. 199–208). ACM. 10.1145/3174243.3174251

Escobedo, J., & Lin, M. (2018). Extracting data parallelism in non-stencil kernel computing by optimally coloring folded memory conflict graph. In *Proceedings of the 55th Annual Design Automation Conference* (pp. 156:1–156:6). ACM.

Gallo, L., Cilardo, A., Thomas, D., Bayliss, S., & Constantinides, G. A. (2014). Area implications of memory partitioning for high-level synthesis on fpgas. *2014 24th International Conference on Field Programmable Logic and Applications (FPL)*, 1–4. 10.1109/FPL.2014.6927417

Gaur, J., Chaudhuri, M., Ramachandran, P., & Subramoney, S. (2017). Nearoptimal access partitioning for memory hierarchies with multiple heterogeneous bandwidth sources. *2017 IEEE International Symposium on High Performance Computer Architecture (HPCA)*, 13–24. 10.1109/HPCA.2017.46

Han, H., & Tseng, C.-W. (2000). A comparison of locality transformations for irregular codes. In Languages, Compilers, and Run-Time Systems for Scalable Computers (pp. 70–84). Springer Berlin Heidelberg. doi:10.1007/3-540-40889-4_6

Hennessy, J. L., & Patterson, D. A. (2012). *Computer Architecture A Quantitative Approach* (5th ed.). Elsevier Inc.

Juan, E., & Lin, M. (2017). Tessellating memory space for parallel access. ASP-DAC.

Li, W., Yang, F., Zhu, H., Zeng, X., & Zhou, D. (2018). An efficient data reuse strategy for multi-pattern data access. In *Proceedings of the International Conference on Computer-Aided Design* (pp. 118:1–118:8). ACM. 10.1145/3240765.3240778

Liu, J., Wickerson, J., Bayliss, S., & Constantinides, G. A. (2018, September). Polyhedralbased dynamic loop pipelining for high-level synthesis. *IEEE Transactions on Computer-Aided Design of Integrated Circuits and Systems*, *37*(9), 1802–1815. doi:10.1109/TCAD.2017.2783363

Liu, J., Wickerson, J., & Constantinides, G. A. (2017). Tile size selection for optimized memory reuse in high-level synthesis. *2017 27th International Conference on Field Programmable Logic and Applications (FPL)*, 1–8. 10.23919/FPL.2017.8056810

Liu, Q., Constantinides, G. A., Masselos, K., & Cheung, P. Y. K. (2009, March). Combining data reuse with data-level parallelization for fpga-targeted hardware compilation: A geometric programming framework. *IEEE Transactions on Computer-Aided Design of Integrated Circuits and Systems, 28*(3), 305–315. doi:10.1109/TCAD.2009.2013541

Liu, Q., Constantinides, G. A., Masselos, K., & Cheung, P. Y. K. (2007). Automatic on-chip memory minimization for data reuse. *15th Annual IEEE Symposium on Field-Programmable Custom Computing Machines (FCCM 2007)*, 251–260. 10.1109/FCCM.2007.18

Meeus, W., & Stroobandt, D. (2014). Automating data reuse in high-level synthesis. 2014 Design, Automation Test in Europe Conference Exhibition (DATE), 1–4.

Meng, C., Yin, S., Ouyang, P., Liu, L., & Wei, S. (2015). Efficient memory partitioning for parallel data access in multidimensional arrays. *Proceedings of the 52Nd Annual Design Automation Conference*. 10.1145/2744769.2744831

Milford, M., & McAllister, J. (2016, August). Constructive synthesis of memory-intensive accelerators for fpga from nested loop kernels. *IEEE Transactions on Signal Processing, 64*(16), 4152–4165. doi:10.1109/TSP.2016.2566608

Peemen, M., Mesman, B., & Corporaal, H. (2015). Inter-tile reuse optimization applied to bandwidth constrained embedded accelerators. 2015 Design, Automation Test in Europe Conference Exhibition (DATE), 169–174. doi:10.7873/DATE.2015.1033

Pilato, C., Mantovani, P., Di Guglielmo, G., & Carloni, L. P. (2014). System-level memory optimization for high-level synthesis of component-based socs. *2014 International Conference on Hardware/Software Codesign and System Synthesis (CODES+ISSS)*, 1–10. 10.1145/2656075.2656098

Pouchet, L.-N., Bondhugula, U., Bastoul, C., Cohen, A., Ramanujam, J., Sadayappan, P., & Vasilache, N. (2011, January). Loop transformations: Convexity, pruning and optimization. *SIGPLAN Notices, 46*(1), 549–562. doi:10.1145/1925844.1926449

Pouchet, L.-N., Zhang, P., Sadayappan, P., & Cong, J. (2013). Polyhedral-based data reuse optimization for configurable computing. In *Proceedings of the ACM/SIGDA International Symposium on Field Programmable Gate Arrays* (pp. 29–38). ACM. 10.1145/2435264.2435273

Su, J., Yang, F., Zeng, X., Zhou, D., & Chen, J. (2017, October). Efficient memory partitioning for parallel data access in fpga via data reuse. *IEEE Transactions on Computer-Aided Design of Integrated Circuits and Systems, 36*(10), 1674–1687. doi:10.1109/TCAD.2017.2648838

Wang, Y., Li, P., & Cong, J. (2014). Theory and algorithm for generalized memory partitioning in high-level synthesis. *Proceedings of the 2014 ACM/SIGDA International Symposium on Field-programmable Gate Arrays*, 199–208. 10.1145/2554688.2554780

Wang, Y., Li, P., Zhang, P., Zhang, C., & Cong, J. (2013). Memory partitioning for multidimensional arrays in high-level synthesis. In *Proceedings of the 50th Annual Design Automation Conference* (pp. 12:1–12:8). ACM. 10.1145/2463209.2488748

Williams, S., Waterman, A., & Patterson, D. (2009, April). Roofline: An insightful visual performance model for multicore architectures. *Communications of the ACM, 52*(4), 65–76. doi:10.1145/1498765.1498785

Yang, H.-J., Fleming, K., Winterstein, F., Chen, A. I., Adler, M., & Emer, J. (2017). Automatic construction of program-optimized fpga memory networks. In *Proceedings of the 2017 ACM/SIGDA International Symposium on FieldProgrammable Gate Arrays* (pp. 125–134). ACM. 10.1145/3020078.3021748

Zhou, Y., Al-Hawaj, K. M., & Zhang, Z. (2017). A new approach to automatic memory banking using trace-based address mining. In *Proceedings of the 2017 ACM/SIGDA International Symposium on Field-Programmable Gate Arrays* (pp. 179–188). ACM. 10.1145/3020078.3021734

Chapter 4

FPGA on Cyber–Physical Systems for the Implementation of Internet of Things

Rajit Nair

 https://orcid.org/0000-0002-4564-0920
Jagran Lakecity University, India

Preeti Nair
Bansal College of Engineering, India

Vidya Kant Dwivedi
Bansal College of Engineering, India

ABSTRACT

Today, in cyber-physical systems, there is a transformation in which processing has been done on distributed mode rather than performing on centralized manner. Usually this type of approach is known as Edge computing, which demands hardware time to time when requirements in computing performance get increased. Considering this situation, we must remain energy efficient and adaptable. So, to meet the above requirements, SRAM-based FPGAs and their inherent run-time reconfigurability are integrated with smart power management strategies. Sometimes this approach fails in the case of user accessibility and easy development. This chapter presents an integrated framework to develop FPGA-based high-performance embedded systems for Edge computing in cyber-physical systems. The processing architecture will be based on hardware that helps us to manage reconfigurable systems from high level systems without any human intervention.

DOI: 10.4018/978-1-5225-9806-0.ch004

INTRODUCTION

It is well known that traditional wireless networks (Elson & Romer, 2003) are based on centralized processing of data even though they are based on distributed sensing scheme but these types of networks will not work efficiently due to requirement of high performance with huge amount of data. So to overcome from this situation there is transformation from centralized approach to distributive approach which keeps the processing unit in a distributive manner. Few years before one more area is also included in Wireless sensor network i.e. Cyber- Physical Systems (CPS) (J. Lee, Bagheri, & Kao, 2015), in which Wireless Sensor Network act as a bridge between physical and the cyber worlds. By 2020 it has been predicted that there will be as many as 50 billion devices which will be connected through internet. Today we can see there are many areas in which Cyber- Physical systems are developed which are like smart or self driving cars without drivers moving around the cities (Daily, Medasani, Behringer, & Trivedi, 2017), making decisions during dealing with number of difficult situations which appears during each route, sensing and understanding the environment deeply. Smart grids consist of millions of consumers which are connected to energy production centers, this has to make decisions during run time inorder to increase the operational efficiency of different distributors and generators that allows to make consumer flexible during making choices (Li et al., 2010). Industry 4.0 has revolutionalized many machines that are interconnected, provides intelligent, self adaptable, resilient and many more features which are cost effective and efficient also (Zezulka, Marcon, Vesely, & Sajdl, 2016). The advantages of using this methodology are as follows:

- A dynamic reconfigurable system based on hardware accelerated edge computing that manages the computing performance, energy consumption and resilient at execution phase.
- On-chip technology has been optimized for DMA powered memory transaction (Management, 2005).
- Parallel execution during run time for exploiting parallelism.
- Customized FPGA based edge computing system (Yu et al., 2017).
- **People and Process:** This is the last phase of IoT can be termed as end user or process, that is using the services provided by IoT devices through different applications.
- **Application:** An application can be software or hardware which acts as medium between user and the edge.
- **Data Storage and Accumulation:** It is well known that IoT needs a storage device or an accumulator for storing the data and that can be retrieved or analyzed later whenever it is needed.

Figure 1. IoT edge computing framework

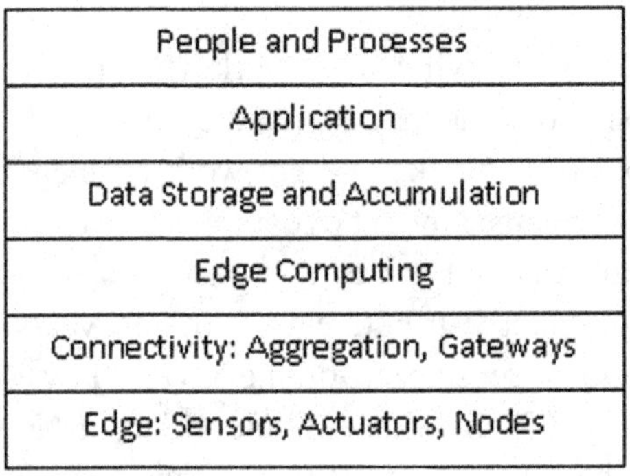

People and Processes
Application
Data Storage and Accumulation
Edge Computing
Connectivity: Aggregation, Gateways
Edge: Sensors, Actuators, Nodes

- **Edge Computing:** Edge computing is a term which is of great importance in IoT, though edge computing one can allow data produced by IoT devices to be processed near to that where it is created instead of sending them across far networks or some other cloud services. The benefit in edge computing is that data is processed very fast due to its computing closer to the edge of the network, so that organizations can analyzed and take quick decisions. This is very much important real time systems across various industries which includes, finance, manufacturing, health care, finance and telecommunication. It is considered as a mesh network with micro data centers that can store or process critical data locally and push all data to a cloud storage or central data center, which is in a limited range of 100 square feet.

- **Connectivity:** We can separate IoT into two broad categories one is Industrial IoT and the other one is Commercial IoT. In case of Industrial IoT, devices are connected to an IP network for global connectivity. In case of Commercial IoT devices are connected to Bluetooth or Ethernet. IoT devices are connected with local devices many times. The Local Network, can include a gateway, which translates proprietary communication protocols to Internet Protocol. In IoT communication, connectivity consist of many wireless sensor nodes with wireless sensor networks, routers, gateways, low power devices, IEEE 802.15.4 radio standard, etc.

- **Edge:** Edges devices are the device which can generate data. These could be sensors, attenuators, industrial machines that could produce or collect data. What type of edge will be used that depends on the use case. In case of telecommunication the edge may be cell phone or cell tower. In an IT enterprise it could be laptop, in an automotive the edges may be the car and in case of machine edges will be like machines or other devices that perform operation.

DISCUSSION OF WORK IN THIS CHAPTER

The work is divided in to two sections, first one is about the description of FPGA technology with its importance especially in the field of Cyber-Physical Systems and second one describes the processing architecture based on FPGA technology which also includes design tools with run time management techniques

Connecting Cyber Physical Systems with FPGA

In this section we will establish the relation between Internet of things and Cyber-Physical systems with the help of FPGA. FPGA based Cyber- Physical systems are built around IoT technology, which includes smart watches, smart cars and many health care applications. FPGA based devices provides much better results than Neural Networks after especially in case of power consumption rates, FPGA based devices are enabling to very low power consumption requirement in some applications on the edge. Another example based on FPGA is to deploy IoT where there is resource constraint is observed.

FPGA Based Architecture and Tools

Reconfigurable technology brings new challenges with already designed multi processor system. The challenges includes in the following phases like architecture, design tools, space exploration, infrastructure, simulation and implementation with operating system for execution. All the challenges description will be elaborated later.

What Is FPGA?

FPGA stands for "Field Programmable Gate Array", which contains huge array of gates that can be programmed and reconfigured at anytime and anywhere. FPGA is indeed much more complex than a simple array of gates. Due to large number of gates which are connected together inside the FPGA enables to make circuit of our own choice. Some of the FPGA have built-in hard blocks like memory controllers (Ipek, Mutlu, Martínez, & Caruana, 2008), PCIe Endpoints (Carvalho et al., 2015), high speed communications (Wang, 2010) etc. Companies that manufacture FPGAs are Altera (Altera, 2014), Xilinx (Xilinx, 2009), Microsemi (Cash et al., 2018) etc. In many application areas embedded systems (E. A. Lee & Seshia, 2011) are equipped with FPGA technology in the form of circuitry board that is design to solve very complex problems. It provides flexible structure that can fulfill several tasks like collection of nodes from base station, advanced sensor nodes, packet routing for security and robustness purposes, even different types of configuration can be applied. This chapter describes the use of FPGA which can be potentially applied on Cyber-Physical systems that help in increasing the performance, network robustness, flexibility and security. FPGA provide sensor nodes with dynamically configuring the features. Many times it is used as hardware accelerator which enables us to manipulate the working frequency on demand. Parallelism can be achieved by using pipelined version of FPGA. FPGA also provides security mechanism that helps to overcome from the attacks. There are many other contribution of FPGA which we will discuss in the later section, it can be like substituting the faulty components that can improve robustness, algorithms speed can be improved by using specialized cryptographic co-processors. Adhoc network can be also established by FPGA using suitable transceivers (Bai & Helmy, 2006). FPGA can be configured to transform into other nodes so that it can collect data or to get oversample.

Figure 2. Benefits of FPGA in IoT

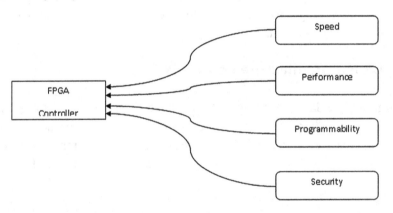

Now the discussion will be on the four important factors which can be achieved by FPGA in IoT are as follows:

1. **Speed:** FPGA system have several major benefits like performance, ease-of-use, lower cost, etc. Speed is one of the most important benefit because many times it achieves high order of speed than contemporary CPU and GPU due to its customization behavior. The working principles of FPGA are systolic array and pipelining that speed up data processing through parallelism. Recent FPGA contains combination of Static Random Access Memory (SRAM) (Guo et al., 2009), logical blocks (Zhang, Park, Parisi-Presicce, & Sandhu, 2004), high speed input/output pins and routing protocols (Bhushan & Sahoo, 2019). Field Programmable Gate Array (FPGA) is also selected as a Very Large Scale

Integration (VLSI) (Leung, 2011) platform device because they can provides certain computation at very high frequencies. Wide range of applications can be built on a programmable chip. It is very much cost effective than other multi core digital signal processing system. It performs parallel operations which help to make complicated operations into simpler ones. Comparing FPGA with microprocessor, FPGA works in smart and optimize way but microprocessor consumes more energy and time for performing any simple task. Suppose a simple task is given for multiplication in that case multiprocessor load the instruction from memory, decode it, load the numbers as input, multiply it and finally stores the result. Each of these steps will take time and energy. Unlike microprocessor, FPGA perform smart operation by reducing multiplication to addition because multiplication takes more power and slow execution time than addition. They are using hardware which performs logical processing and does not have operating system. Due to parallel processing, different operations need not to be competing for the same processing resource. FPGA don't have a fixed instruction, and its speed can also be increased by running multiple control loops on a single FPGA device at different rates.

2. **Performance:** FPGA in IoT increase the performance in many aspects which are as follows:

   a. It is characterize for high performance ratio, real time systems and robustness.
   b. It offers higher power efficiency and faster processing speed while achieving excellent durability against radiation and high temperature.
   c. It offers a high degree of flexibility and powerful processing capability.
   d. FPGA has been verified for applications in devices with limited usable power.
   e. Cost is less as compared to other micro controllers.
   f. Reusability can be done by using one hardware platform for different systems with similar basic design.
   g. Adaptable to industry standards and protocols.

3. **Programmability:** The third important aspect of FPGA in IoT is programmability, which provides reconfigurability and flexibility. By reconfigurability we can change the functionality of design whenever needed. Dynamic reconfiguration is also possible through which hardware can be changed. It can fix, update and enhance the code. By flexibility it allows us to get adaptable to industries in flux, immature specification and evolving protocols. FPGA supports different types of software that carries out complex conversion of hardware design into programming bits. Let's see the programming technologies in FPGA which are given below:

a. **Fuse and Anti-Fuse:** Connecting and breaking between two wires are known as fuse and anti fuse respectively. These connections are typically of 50-300 ohms and it is single time programmable.

b. **EPROM and EEPROM:** High consumption of power with connection of 2k– 4k ohm. They have low density.

c. **RAM Based:** It is most used programming technology because switch that connects or disconnects wires is controlled by a memory bit. Connections are of .5K-1K ohm. It can be programmed and re-programmed easily.

4. **Security:** An IoT consist of large number of logic gates with multiple electronic networks which needs end-end security from the starting level. To meet these requirements FPGA has to include some inbuilt security features with protection capability. Security is the most important concern in every field. FPGA must protect all data that includes application data which is to be processed. Protection includes hardware also because it has to be kept safe from channel attacks like differential power analysis. Differential power analyses are used to extract the secret keys through power consumption during different types of cryptographic operations take place (Bucci, Guglielmo, Luzzi, & Trifiletti, 2010). Machine or hardware authentication are done through Physical Unclonable Function (PUF) (Helfmeier, Boit, Nedospasov, & Seifert, 2013), this generates public-private key pair. In this PUF acts as a unique identifier for each device similar to human impression and these are considered unclonable. SRAM based PUF are considered one of the best and most reliable types of memory PU (Selimis et al., 2011). These can be implemented on the smartcard chip (Abrial, Bouvier, Renaudin, Senn, & Vivet, 2001), different IC's or FPGA and starts working by measuring the bits of the random start up state in the block of SRAM (Holcomb, Burleson, & Fu, 2009). Each bit of SRAM consists of cross-coupled inverters that are not completely equal or identical. When power is applied to IC, these bits may be in 1 or 0 state that is based on preference determined during the manufacture of IC.

Basically SRAM based PUF are designed for generating perfect key all over the environments and its validity is for lifetime with exceptionally with minimum error; it can be like one per billion. These PUF's gives us strong protection through secret key (Suh & Devadas, 2007), additionally this secret key disappears as soon as when the device power is turned off. Even if the activation code is erased there is no way of reconstructing the secret key. For the implementation of PUC in FPGA technology, it is required that the devices must have built in cryptographic capabilities like hardware accelerator for HMAC (Krawczyk, Bellare, & Canetti, 1997), AES (Gullasch et al., 2001), SHA (Group, 2006) and elliptic curve cryptography (Overill, 2005). In addition to this it must contain cryptographic grade true random bit generator.

Though these capabilities we can establish user public key infrastructure (Ellison, 2010) with user own certificate authority for each legal system in a network. In IoT by using FPGA every machine and their communication are protected and can be securely used in machine to machine.

Cyber-Physical System

In Cyber – Physical System (CPS), there is strong interaction between physical system and cyber system. Physical layer are considered as physical system and monitoring systems are considered as cyber systems. In IoT there are many devices and infrastructure which are based on these two systems. Cyber systems can be collection of heterogeneous nodes that can implement active or passive smart monitoring sensors.

Let's see some of the important application areas of Cyber-Physical System which are as follows:

1. Automotive electronics (Willis, 2014)
    a. **ABS:** Anti –lock braking system
    b. ESP- Electronic Stability Control
    c. Airbags
    d. Efficient automatic gearboxes
    e. Theft prevention with smart keys
    f. Blind-angle alert system and many more
2. Aviation System (D. S. Lee et al., 2009)
    a. Flight control system
    b. Anti collision system
    c. Pilot information system
    d. Power supply system
    e. Flap control system
    f. Entertainment System and many more
3. Medical Systems (I. Lee & Sokolsky, 2010)
    a. Artificial Eye
    b. Translation into sound
    c. Pattern recognition
    d. MRI image segmentation and many more

The applications are not limited to above three, there are many other applications like Banking sector, Railway System, Agriculture system, Satellite system, etc. The chapter will also covers a wide range of discussing on FPGA with related to securing Cyber-Physical Systems.

Cyber Physical System must possess some of the important characteristics which are as follows:

1. **Dependability:** CP's must be dependable, so that it can cover the following aspects
   a. **Reliability R(t):** If the system is working at probability t=0 means it is performing correctly.
   b. Maintainability M(t) - If the system is working correctly for d units after the occurrence of the error.
   c. **Availability A(t):** If the system is working at probability time t.
   d. Safety – No harm to be caused.
   e. Security – Confidential and Authentic communication.
2. Efficiency- CP's must be efficient
   a. Code size efficient.
   b. Run-time efficient
   c. Weight efficient
   d. Cost efficient
   e. Energy efficient
3. **Real Time Constraints:** CP's must meet real time constraints, real-time system must give instant response during instruction within the time interval. Time constraints are called soft and other constraint whose failure can lead us to catastrophe are considered as hard. Real time behavior is essential in CP's.
4. **Reactive and Hybrid Systems:** Reactive system are always in contact with the environment and they starts execution during pace generated by the environment. Behavior depends on the input and the current state. Hybrid systems are the combination of analog and digital parts.

Figure 3. Cyber physical system hardware loop

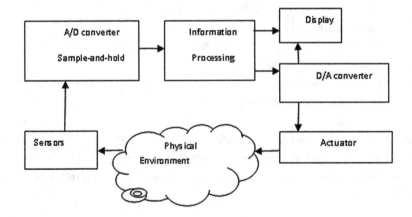

5. **Dedicated System:** These are the system that built towards a specific application. Behavior is already known during design phase, can be used to minimize resource and maximize robustness. For e.g. A system without mouse and have a keyboard and screen only.

As we have already discussed about the FPGA, Cyber Physical System, their applications areas and benefits of each other. Now next section will be discussed on the FPGA architecture and how they play a role in IoT.

Figure 4. Nodes in cyber-physical system

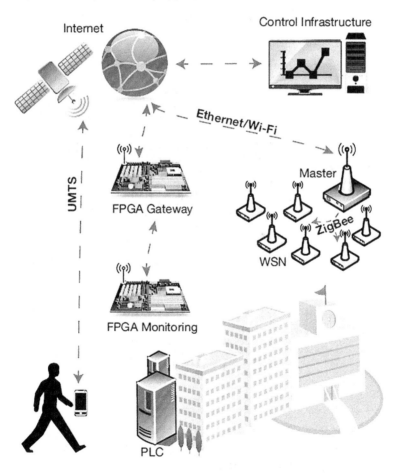

Most of the sensor nodes are battery powered with resource constraints, even their physical protection is also less, so they are more exposed to attack and it is not very much possible that we can provide complex security mechanism. In the past years FPGA is not used much due to their high power consumption and complex programming efforts, later on with advanced technology they are used widely in many areas of IoT. Microcontroller based programming and PLC has already done a lot of improvement in the design area of hardware (Hercog & Gergič, 2014). But nowadays FPGA has done a significant improvement in this area. In FPGA programming hardware's like sensors, communication networks, expansion ports, FPGA chips, etc. are configured. In physical layer, programmers write application independent of hardware's which give call to operating system to interact with hardware. Figure 4 shows the different nodes which plays a role in IoT.

Figure 5. Block diagram of FPGA

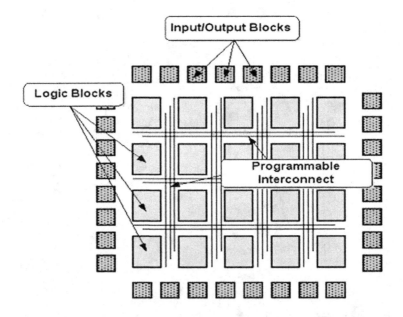

As it is clearly observed from the above figure that FPGA architecture consist of three important components that are logical block, Input-Output programmable block and the physical interconnection.

- **Logical Block**: The logical block consists of multiplexers, flip flops, look –up table (LUT), etc. LUT implements the combinational logical functions, multiplexers are used for selection of logic and flip flops are used for storing the output generated by LUT. Main purpose of logical block is to provide basic computation and storage elements used in digital system. It reduces area as well as delay cost by some fast logics. Most of the FPGA's contain heterogeneous mixture of varied block like multiplexers, dedicated memory block etc. A logical block enables configurable memory which is used to control the specific function of each block.

- **Input-Output Programmable Block**: These are the programmable I/O pads which act as an intermediate between the logic blocks and the external components. These I/O pads create cells that consume large area of FPGA's. The selection of standards is important in I/O architecture design. Supporting a large number of standards can increase the silicon chip area required for I/O cells. The selection of standards is important for I/O design and by supporting a more number of standards can increase the silicon chip required for I/O cells. Some of the functional blocks like ALUs block, multiplexers, RAM, etc. are added to the FPGA to fulfill the needs of such resources for different applications.
- **Physical Interconnection:** This interconnection is used to provide connection between logical blocks and I/O blocks to complete a FPGA design. It consists of multiplexers, pass transistors and tri-state buffers, which form the desired connection. Multiplexers and pass transistors are used in a logical cluster to connect the logical elements together, these components also provide global routing structures. Several global routing structures have been used in FPGAs as: island-style, cellular, bus-based and registered (pipelined) architectures.

CONCLUSION

This chapter present a high performance embedded system for edge computing in Cyber-Physical Systems. It shows a processing architecture based on hardware and the required tool for design and run time which eases the development of user defined applications. This also provides tradeoffs between computing performance, energy consumption and fault tolerance at run time. This approach basically provides users with support to get adapt dynamically with the available computing resources for finding the solution considering the factors like computing performance, energy consumption and fault tolerance.

REFERENCES

Abrial, A., Bouvier, J., Renaudin, M., Senn, P., & Vivet, P. (2001). A new contactless smart card IC using an on-chip antenna and an asynchronous microcontroller. *IEEE Journal of Solid-State Circuits*, *36*(7), 1101–1107. doi:10.1109/4.933467

Altera. (2014). *Altera SoC Embedded Design Suite User Guide*. Author.

Bai, F., & Helmy, A. (2006). *Wireless Adhoc Networks*. Wireless Ad Hoc and Sensor Networks.

Bhushan, B., & Sahoo, G. (2019). Routing protocols in wireless sensor networks. Studies in Computational Intelligence. doi:10.1007/978-3-662-57277-1_10

Bucci, M., Guglielmo, M., Luzzi, R., & Trifiletti, A. (2010). *A Power Consumption Randomization Countermeasure for DPA-Resistant Cryptographic Processors*. doi:10.1007/978-3-540-30205-6_50

Carvalho, P. F., Santos, B., Correia, M., Combo, Á. M., Rodrigues, A. P., Pereira, R. C., … Gonçalves, B. (2015). PCI express hotplug implementation for ATCA based instrumentation. Fusion Engineering and Design. doi:10.1016/j.fusengdes.2015.05.030

Cash, P., Krzewick, W., MacHado, P., Overstreet, K. R., Silveira, M., Stanczyk, M., … Zhang, X. (2018). Microsemi Chip Scale Atomic Clock (CSAC) technical status, applications, and future plans. *2018 European Frequency and Time Forum, EFTF 2018*. 10.1109/EFTF.2018.8408999

Daily, M., Medasani, S., Behringer, R., & Trivedi, M. (2017). Self-Driving Cars. *Computer*, *50*(12), 18–23. doi:10.1109/MC.2017.4451204

Ellison, C. (2010). Public key infrastructure. Handbook of Financial Cryptography and Security. doi:10.1201/9781420059823-c16

Elson, J., & Romer, K. (2003). *Wireless Sensor Networks: A New Regime for Time Synchronization. ACM SigComm Computer Communications Review*. doi:10.1145/774763.774787

Group, N. W. (2006). *US Secure Hash Algorithms (SHA and HMAC-SHA)*. Request for Comments. doi:10.1017/CBO9781107415324.004

Gullasch, D., Bangerter, E., Krenn, S., Liu, F., Lee, R. B., Wang, Z., … Fips, N. (2001). *197: Announcing the advanced encryption standard (AES)*. Technology Laboratory, National Institute of Standards. doi:10.1016/S1353-4858(10)70006-4

Guo, Z., Carlson, A., Pang, L. T., Duong, K. T., Liu, T. J. K., & Nikolić, B. (2009). Large-scale SRAM variability characterization in 45 nm CMOS. *IEEE Journal of Solid-State Circuits, 44*(11), 3174–3192. doi:10.1109/JSSC.2009.2032698

Helfmeier, C., Boit, C., Nedospasov, D., & Seifert, J. P. (2013). Cloning physically unclonable functions. *Proceedings of the 2013 IEEE International Symposium on Hardware-Oriented Security and Trust, HOST 2013.* 10.1109/HST.2013.6581556

Hercog, D., & Gergič, B. (2014). *A flexible microcontroller-based data acquisition device.* Sensors. doi:10.3390140609755

Holcomb, D. E., Burleson, W. P., & Fu, K. (2009). Power-Up SRAM state as an identifying fingerprint and source of true random numbers. *IEEE Transactions on Computers, 58*(9), 1198–1210. doi:10.1109/TC.2008.212

Ipek, E., Mutlu, O., Martínez, J. F., & Caruana, R. (2008). Self-optimizing memory controllers: A reinforcement learning approach. *Proceedings - International Symposium on Computer Architecture.* 10.1109/ISCA.2008.21

Krawczyk, H., Bellare, M., & Canetti, R. (1997). *HMAC: Keyed-Hashing for Message Authentication.* doi:10.17487/rfc2104

Lee, D. S., Fahey, D. W., Forster, P. M., Newton, P. J., Wit, R. C. N., & Lim, L. L. … Sausen, R. (2009). Aviation and global climate change in the 21st century. *Atmospheric Environment.* doi:10.1016/j.atmosenv.2009.04.024

Lee, E. A., & Seshia, S. a. (2011). *Introduction to Embedded Systems - A Cyber-Physical Systems Approach. LeeSeshia.org.* doi:10.1002/9781118557624.ch1

Lee, I., & Sokolsky, O. (2010). Medical cyber physical systems. *Proceedings of the 47th Design Automation Conference on - DAC '10.* 10.1145/1837274.1837463

Lee, J., Bagheri, B., & Kao, H. A. (2015). A Cyber-Physical Systems architecture for Industry 4.0-based manufacturing systems. *Manufacturing Letters, 3*, 18–23. doi:10.1016/j.mfglet.2014.12.001

Leung, B. (2011). *VLSI for Wireless Communication.* VLSI for Wireless Communication. doi:10.1007/978-1-4614-0986-1

Li, F., Qiao, W., Sun, H., Wan, H., Wang, J., & Xia, Y., … Zhang, P. (2010). Smart transmission grid: Vision and framework. *IEEE Transactions on Smart Grid.* doi:10.1109/TSG.2010.2053726

Management, M. (2005). 15. Memory Mapping and DMA. *Memory.*

Overill, R. E. (2005). Review: Advances in Elliptic Curve Cryptography. *Journal of Logic and Computation, 15*(5), 815. doi:10.1093/logcom/exi047

Selimis, G., Konijnenburg, M., Ashouei, M., Huisken, J., De Groot, H., Van Der Leest, V., ... Tuyls, P. (2011). Evaluation of 90nm 6T-SRAM as Physical Unclonable Function for secure key generation in wireless sensor nodes. *Proceedings - IEEE International Symposium on Circuits and Systems.* 10.1109/ISCAS.2011.5937628

Suh, G. E., & Devadas, S. (2007). Physical unclonable functions for device authentication and secret key generation. *Proceedings - Design Automation Conference.* 10.1109/DAC.2007.375043

Wang, J. (2010). *High-Speed Wireless Communications.* High-Speed Wireless Communications. doi:10.1017/cbo9780511754609

Willis, B. (2014). Understanding Automotive Electronics. *Microelectronics International.* doi:10.1108/mi.2004.21821aae.002

Xilinx. (2009). *Xilinx UG190 Virtex-5 FPGA User Guide. UG190.* Author.

Yu, W., Liang, F., He, X., Hatcher, W. G., Lu, C., Lin, J., & Yang, X. (2017). A Survey on the Edge Computing for the Internet of Things. *IEEE Access: Practical Innovations, Open Solutions.* doi:10.1109/ACCESS.2017.2778504

Zezulka, F., Marcon, P., Vesely, I., & Sajdl, O. (2016). Industry 4.0 – An Introduction in the phenomenon. *IFAC-PapersOnLine, 49*(25), 8–12. doi:10.1016/j.ifacol.2016.12.002

Zhang, X., Park, J., Parisi-Presicce, F., & Sandhu, R. (2004). *A logical specification for usage control.* doi:10.1145/990036.990038

Chapter 5
Neuroscience in FPGA and Application in IoT

Anjali Daisy

https://orcid.org/0000-0003-1207-5002

SASTRA University (Deemed), India

ABSTRACT

Neuroscience is a multidisciplinary science that is focused with the study of the structure and function of the nervous system. It contains the evolution, development, cellular and molecular biology, physiology, anatomy, and pharmacology of the nervous system, as well as computational, interactive, and cognitive neuroscience. A field-programmable gate array (FPGA) is an integrated circuit (IC) that can be programmed in the field after production. FPGAs are likely in principle to have vastly wider potential application than programmable read-only memory (PROM) chips. Internet of things (IoT) is an integrated part of future internet including existing and evolving internet and network developments and could be conceptually defined as a worldwide dynamic network infrastructure with self-configuring capabilities based on standard and interoperable protocols communication where physical and virtual "things" have identities, physical attributes, and virtual personalities.

INTRODUCTION

Neuroscience is a multidisciplinary science that is focused with the study of the structure and function of the nervous system. It contains the evolution, development, cellular and molecular biology, physiology, anatomy and pharmacology of the nervous system, as well as computational, interactive and cognitive neuroscience.

DOI: 10.4018/978-1-5225-9806-0.ch005

FPGA: Field Programmable Gate Array

A field-programmable gate array (**FPGA**) is an integrated circuit (IC) that can be programmed in the field after production. **FPGAs** are likely in principle to, but have vastly wider potential application than, programmable read-only memory (PROM) chips.

FPGA ALGORITHM APPLICATION

Internet of Things (IoT) is an integrated part of future internet including existing and evolving internet and network developments and could be conceptually defined as a worldwide dynamic network infrastructure with self configuring capabilities based on standard and interoperable protocols communication where physical and virtual "things" have identities, physical attributes, and virtual personalities, use intelligent interfaces, and are seamlessly integrated into the information network(). Internet of Things In the IoT, "smart things / objects" are expected to become active participants in business, data and social processes where they are enabled to interact and communicate among them-selves and with the environment by exchanging data and information "Sensed" about the environment, while reacting autonomously to the "real / physical world" events and influencing it by running processes that trigger actions and create services without direct human with or intervention.(1)The IERC definition AIMS to coin the IoT paradigm and concept by unifying the different statements and many visions referred to as a "Things," "Internet," "Semantics," "Object Identification" oriented definitions of Internet of Things promoted by individuals and organizations around the world (Burger & Schiele, 2018).

FPGA-based hardware web services have already been implemented and described. Their nature embedded allows developers to adapt easily those services to actively interact with their environment, e.g. Real-world to acquire measurement data or controlling various actuators. Such entities can be called environment-aware web services in contrast to classical web services that work on remote physical or virtual machines. Despite the fact that environment-aware web services may be implemented using much less expensive MCUs and sequential code, programmable hardware may perform better where very intensive computational tasks involved. At times of lower utilization they can be reconfigured to offer additional resources as spare their data-processing web services (Kapoor, Graves-Abe, & Pei, 2006). Whenever a task is more intensive processing to be performed, their resources can be employed back to the devices original provide functionality. This concept can be applied to regulate past that devices offer no web service compliance. In the latter case, however, we would lose some useful features: such as interoperability or the ability to use the management software tools available already etc. Important areas that use the IoT and web service concepts are the Smart Home and Smart Building. In order to provide IoT services in Smart Home / Smart Building environments, the authors propose a Web-of-Objects in the IoT platform service environment (Guinard, 2011). This platform has-been designed in order to create user-cantered services IoT. In Addition, complex services can be developed by combining elements of existing web services.

Artificial Intelligence (AI) will transform how we engage with the world and is already the fastest growing workload for data centres. **Field Programmable Gate Arrays** (FPGAs) can accelerate AI-related workloads. It makes perfect sense that Intel purchased Altera, a leading company specializing in FPGAs, in December 2015 (for $16.7 billion). Intel has integrated Altera's IP to improve performance and power efficiency and to enable reprogramming for custom chips that account for a more significant share of server chip shipments. Intel's Data Center Group is the most money-making group at Intel, driven by the growth in "big data" and cloud servers. AI is one of the fastest growth drivers for cloud services.

Artificial Intelligence and FPGAs

AI is driving demand for High-Performance Computing (HPC), especially since cloud services allow AI scientists and engineers to pay for only what they use. Gathering funding to install a supercomputer in the basement just is not necessary anymore for start-ups using AI. Data scientists can rent a high-performance computer (cloud) and use powerful computing resources to train a deep learning model (Rao, Newe, & Grout, 2014). Once training is complete, they export their model and get charged only for what they have used. For many researchers, the AI-tuned cloud platform is the only answer, as grants and other funding resources decrease to where universities and start-ups cannot afford the capital to establish HPC centres of their own. According to Tractica, a Market intelligence firm, revenue from AI, machine learning, deep learning, natural language processing, machine vision, machine reasoning, and other AI-related technologies will reach nearly $59.8 billion by 2025. Markets leading the adoption of AI include the aerospace, advertising, consumer, financial, and medical sectors, with many more seeking advantages in AI. Although global AI spending in 2016 was identified by Tractica at just $1.4 billion, the expectation is for exponential growth.

FPGAs Power Ideal Implementation

There is, however, an alternative to designing a different coprocessor for each application need: use an FPGA that can be configured as needed for each application.

The same semiconductor technology advances that have brought processors to their performance limits have turned FPGAs from simple glue logic collectors to highly capable programmable fabrics. FPGAs are fully capable of addressing the "four Ps" of the HPC market. Today's FPGAs offer tremendous performance potential. They can support pipeline structures of variable depth and provide parallel computing resources numbering in the thousands, allowing even highly complex functions to be implemented with single-clock execution. The programmability of FPGAs ensures that they can be tuned to meet the specific needs of an application without the cost or delay of designing a custom coprocessor. If the FPGA is also reprogrammable, it can provide highly customized co-processing for a wide range of applications in a single chip. The presence of on-board memory in an FPGA also has significant performance benefits (Wurz, Abplanalp, Tulej, & Lammer, 2012). For one, having memory on-chip means that the coprocessor logic's memory access bandwidth is not constrained by the number of I/O pins the device has. Further, the memory is closely coupled to the algorithm logic and reduces the need for an external high-speed memory cache. This, in turn, avoids power-consuming cache access and coherency problems. The use of internal memory also means that the coprocessor does not need additional I/O pins in order to increase its accessible memory size, simplifying design scaling. An FPGA with greater capacity can occupy the same board footprint as an older device, allowing performance upgrades without board changes. As a result of the structures and resources available in today's high-performance FPGAs (i.e., the Altera® Stratix® III family of FPGAs), they can serve as hardware acceleration coprocessors for a wide array of applications and provide significant performance boosts. Practical experience with FPGA-based coprocessors shows at least a ten-fold improvement in the execution speed of algorithms as compared to processors alone. Speeds more than 100 times faster are common (Musavi, Chowdhry, Kumar, Pandey, & Kumar, 2015)

NEUROSCIENCE IN IOT

1. Google home(max, mini)
2. Amazon alexa
3. Apple pod

All these internet of things uses neuroscience

NEUROSCIENCE IN FPGA AND APPLICATION IN IOT

There is no universal definition for the term IoT; different definitions are used by different parties, foundations, and groups to describe a specific view of what IoT means. IoT is defined as a system that permits the devices for communicating with each other directly without human intervention. In 2012, The International Telecommunication Union (ITU) published an overview of the Internet of Things and IoT is defined as a global infrastructure for society of information that enables interconnected things to communicate with each other and performs advance services based on existing and evolving interoperable information and communication technologies. Many definitions of different groups have been promoted. In a call for papers for a future topic issue of IEEE communication journal, IoT is defined as a framework wherein all things have a representation and existence in the internet. IoT goals for offering new applications and services bridge both physical and virtual worlds. A definition of IoT is offered by Oxford Dictionaries that defines IoT as: Internet of Things (noun), the interconnection via the internet of computing devices embedded in everyday objects, enabling them to send and receive data. For the purpose of this paper, IoT can be defined as a smart society consisting of smart devices that can communicate with each other through the cloud without human's intervention.

In recent years, the Internet-of-Things (IoT) has gained much attention from researchers, entrepreneurs, and tech giants around the globe. The IoT is an emerging technology that connects a variety of everyday devices and systems such as sensors, actuators, appliances, computers, and cellular phones, thus leading towards a highly distributed intelligent system capable of communicating with other devices and human being. The dramatic advancements in computing and communication technologies coupled with modern low-power, low-cost sensors, actuators and electronic components have unlocked the door of ample opportunities for the IoT applications. Smart home with integrated e-health and assisted living technology is an example of an IoT application in geron technology that can potentially play a pivotal role in revolutionizing the healthcare system for the elderly. As the world is rapidly moving towards the new era of the IoT, a fully functional smart home is closer to reality than ever before (Wilson, Hargreaves, & Hauxwell-Baldwin, 2015).

In a smart home, sensors and actuators are connected through a Personal Area Network (PAN) (Otto, Milenković, Sanders, & Jovanov, 2006) or Wireless Sensor Network (WSN) (Yick, Mukherjee, & Ghosal, 2008). Wearable biomedical sensors such as electrocardiogram (ECG) (Chen, 2017), electromyogram (EMG) (Merletti & Farina, 2009), electroencephalogram (EEG) (Thakor & Tong, 2004), body temperature and oxygen saturation (SpO2) .sensors can be connected in a Wireless Body Area Network (WBAN) (Latré, Braem, Moerman, Blondia, & Demeester, 2011) or Body Sensor Network (BSN) in order to obtain automated, continuous, and real-time measurement of physiological signals. The central BSN node collects all physiological data, performs limited data processing and functions as the gateway to the PAN/WSN. The actuators operate based on the feedback from the occupants or from the central computing system. The central computing system collects environmental, physiological and activity data through the PAN/WSN, analyzes them and can send feedback to the user or activate the actuators to control appliances such as humidifier, oxygen generator, oven and air conditioner. It also functions as the central home gateway, which sends measured data to the healthcare personnel/service providers over the internet or the cellular network (Catarinucci et al., 2015). In order to realize communication between all wireless sensors and actuators, standard protocols from Wireless Sensor Networks (WSNs) and ad-hoc networks are used. However, current protocols designed for WSNs are not always applicable to WBAN. Multiple sensors can be placed over clothes or directly on the body, or implanted in tissue, which can facilitate measurement of blood pressure, heart rate, blood glucose, EEG, ECG and respiration rate.

IOT REVOLUTION

In 1999, the term "Internet of Things" (IoT) was used for the first time by British technology pioneer Kevin Ashton to illustrate a system wherein physical world devices could be connected to the Internet via sensors (Ashton, 2011). Relatively, the term "Internet of Things" is new which is the concept of combination the computers and networks to monitor and control devices. This concept has been around for decades. For example, systems for monitoring meters remotely on the electrical grid via telephone lines were implemented at the late 1970s. In the 1990s, advanced wireless technology allowed machine-to-machine (M2M) enterprise and industrial solutions for monitoring equipment and operate to become widespread. Later the IP was used to connect devices to the internet like soda machine at Carnege Mellano University in US and a Coffee pot of the Trojan Room at the University of Cambridge in the UK which remained Internet connected until 2001. In the International Economic Forum (Davos), the head of Google Eric Schmidt in his speech he said: "There will be a lot of Internet addresses, which are a numerical addresses customized for each machine, and to a lot of smart devices, sensors and interactive tools to the degree that you will not feel the existence of the Internet on it, it will become like the air we breathe without feeling it. Then added: Imagine entering an interactive room, and be able to communicate with all smart devices in this room!" mentioning to the evolution of smart devices and devices to attire technology which are connected to the Internet.(yaqing,2013) The Internet of Things is still in its beginning and the possibilities are endless. By comparing the use of internet today to how the internet was envisioned just 25 years ago, the growth of the Internet of Things sensed as being potential inherent. By 2010 billions of devices are expected to be connected wirelessly.

IOT APPLICATIONS AND EXAMPLES

Today many products which we buy are Internet connectable. The following applications and examples are popular as IoT products.

1. **Wearable**: These are device-to device development. Many wearable products have been implemented, For example: wearable health care devices. One of the newest wearable items is Google Glass device which is enabled people to use numerous Internet applications on the go.
2. **Connect Vehicles**: For example the car navigation system or mapping applications of the smart phones that enabled the folks to find their way for unfamiliar places.
3. **Home Automation:** Usually, these systems use small data packets of information satisfy the communication between devices with relatively low data rate requirements. Smart thermostats, smart appliances, intelligent lighting, and many others smarted house devices are home automation scenarios.
4. **Location-Based Services**: Many useful services of location based can also provide by Internet of Things. Automate notifications, tracking children, eldercare, and location based marketing are examples of location- based services.

FPGA FOR IOT

Prototypes based FPGA, specifically geared to meet the design and verification constrains resulted by the complexity of IoT devices. FPGA is a device that was made of thousands or even millions of transistors which are connected to perform logic functions. FPGAs perform functions of simple addition and subtraction to complex digital filtering and error detection and correction. Aircraft, automobiles, radar, missiles, and computers are examples of FPGA based systems. Xilinx, Altera, and Quicklogic are just some companies that manufacturing FPGA kits. Using FPGA for IoT fills the gap between hardware and software and offer many advantages such as: Flexibility, Reliability, Low cost, Fast time-to-market, and Long term maintenance. IOT is implemented on various FPGA devices to project various devices for several applications. Many designs of FPGA based IoT systems are discussed by Microsemi Power Meter (Zheng, Gao, & Lin, 2013).

In present time, Intel FPGA (formerly Altera) provides many FPGAs based IoT systems. Smart city infrastructure and building automation, smart grid control, healthcare system infrastructure, car automotive systems, and machine vision systems can be seen at Altera website. Altera offered many advantages to the manufactures, which are: 1. Reduction of cost by avoiding ASICs' extensive. 2. Time to market advantage by avoiding the lengthy and risky development cycle. 3. Cost reduction and differentiation by integrating multiple ASSP functions into FPGAs. 4. Programmability during the design process and after equipment is in the field. 5. Reusability of one hardware platform for various systems with one basic design. 6. Adaptability to multiple industry standards and protocols. Xilinx for FPGA also has an FPGA for IoT. Many design examples can be seen on Xilinx website like: 1. Single-axis motor control which is supported by Xilinx Sparton-7 FPGA kit. 2. Multi-axis motor control which is designed with Zynq-7000s All Programmable Soc. 3. Motor control which can be designed with Xilinx Kinetex-7 FPGA or with Zynq7000s. All Programmable Soc. Xilinx provides hardware-accelerated torque control, speed control, and position control for single-motor and multi-motor applications for sensor and sensor less applications.

ADVANTAGES OF FPGA FOR IOT

A field programmable gate array (FPGA) consists of a matrix of reconfigurable gates arrays form logic circuitry. When the logic arrays configured, these gates connected with a way that builds a hardware implementation of a software application. Gradually more tools are enabling the designers of embedded control system to create adapt FPGA-based applications more quickly and more easily. FPGAs are unlike processors; FPGAs are using hardware which is dedicated for logic processing and do not have an operating system. Different operations do not have to compete for the same processing resources since the processing paths are parallel. So that speeds can be very fast, and multiple control loops can run on a single FPGA device at different rates (Nane et al., 2016).

The re-configurability of FPGAs provides the designers with unlimited flexibility. Christian Fritz, the product manager for motion control and mechatronics for National Instruments said: "Unlike hard-wired printed circuits board (PCB) designs that had fixed hardware resources, FPGA-based systems can literally rewire their internal circuitry to allow configuration after the control system is deployed to the field". FPGA-based platforms may use for IoT prototypes for two purposes: First, a designer could deploy a platform based on FPGA according to the purpose of the platform, or could target an FPGA to implement a full custom SoC application where the FPGA is used as a prototype of this application (Bellas, Chai, Dwyer, & Linzmeier, 2006). Using the SoC Prototyping allows real-time functional verification and timing verification. Second purpose is that FPGA-based prototype is perilous for producing an early validation of inexpensive platform design; automation of design is necessary for modelling, component selection, design space exploration, design entry and verification. Also, prototype of SoCs must consider that the achieved performance, power and size may not be as efficient as the final SoC. Automation in wholly of the design processes is essential to make prototype fast and efficient, and to simplify the prototype translation into a design of the final SoC.

CONCLUSION

IoT is still in its infancy and the possibilities are endless. In the near future, FPGA will drive the IoT. IoT will interface with electricity, pressure, temperature, acceleration, position, Analog to Digital convertor (ADC), Digital to Analog convertor (DAC), and many other systems; FPGA, Arduino, Raspberry Pi, and Orange Pi are suitable to implement IoT platforms. Using the FPGAs in IoT systems provided Flexibility, Reliability, Low cost, fast time-to-market, and long term maintenance. The popular FPGA manufactures like Altera and Xilinx have started working on IoT by designing many IoT systems like control systems, machine vision systems, Artificial Intelligence systems, and many other FPGAs based IoT systems while many prototypes are in their progress to be completed. FPGAs have flexibility to implement IoT extendable systems. There is an expectation that the whole world become IoT world by 2020.

REFERENCES

Ashton, K. (2011). *In the real world, things matter more than ideas*. RFID Journal.

Bellas, N., Chai, S. M., Dwyer, M., & Linzmeier, D. (2006). FPGA implementation of a license plate recognition SoC using automatically generated streaming accelerators. *20th International Parallel and Distributed Processing Symposium, IPDPS 2006*. 10.1109/IPDPS.2006.1639437

Burger, A., & Schiele, G. (2018). Demo Abstract: Deep Learning on an Elastic Node for the Internet of Things. *2018 IEEE International Conference on Pervasive Computing and Communications Workshops, PerCom Workshops 2018*. 10.1109/PERCOMW.2018.8480160

Catarinucci, L., De Donno, D., Mainetti, L., Palano, L., Patrono, L., Stefanizzi, M. L., & Tarricone, L. (2015). *An IoT-Aware Architecture for Smart Healthcare Systems*. IEEE Internet of Things Journal. doi:10.1109/JIOT.2015.2417684

Chen, W. (2017). Electrocardiogram. In *Seamless Healthcare Monitoring*. Advancements in Wearable, Attachable, and Invisible Devices; doi:10.1007/978-3-319-69362-0_1

Guinard, D. (2011). *A Web of Things Application Architecture - Integrating the Real-World into the Web (PhD Th.)*. ETH Zurich; doi:10.3929/ethz-a-006713673

Kapoor, C., Graves-Abe, T. L., & Pei, J.-S. (2006). A low-cost off-the-shelf FGPA-based smart wireless sensing unit. Health Monitoring and Smart Nondestructive Evaluation of Structural and Biological Systems V. doi:10.1117/12.658923

Latré, B., Braem, B., Moerman, I., Blondia, C., & Demeester, P. (2011). A survey on wireless body area networks. *Wireless Networks*, *17*(1), 1–18. doi:10.100711276-010-0252-4

Merletti, R., & Farina, A. (2009). Analysis of Intramuscular electromyogram signals. *Philosophical Transactions - Royal Society. Mathematical, Physical, and Engineering Sciences*, *367*(1887), 357–368. doi:10.1098/rsta.2008.0235 PMID:19008187

Musavi, S. H. A., Chowdhry, B. S., Kumar, T., Pandey, B., & Kumar, W. (2015). IoTs Enable Active Contour Modeling Based Energy Efficient and Thermal Aware Object Tracking on FPGA. *Wireless Personal Communications*, *85*(2), 529–543. doi:10.100711277-015-2753-z

Nane, R., Sima, V. M., Pilato, C., Choi, J., Fort, B., & Canis, A. ... Bertels, K. (2016). A Survey and Evaluation of FPGA High-Level Synthesis Tools. *IEEE Transactions on Computer-Aided Design of Integrated Circuits and Systems*. doi:10.1109/TCAD.2015.2513673

Otto, C., Milenković, A., Sanders, C., & Jovanov, E. (2006). System architecture of a wireless body area sensor network for ubiquitous health monitoring. *Journal of Mobile Multimedia*.

Rao, M., Newe, T., & Grout, I. (2014). Secure hash algorithm-3(SHA-3) implementation on Xilinx FPGAS, suitable for IoT applications. *Proceedings of the International Conference on Sensing Technology, ICST*. 10.21307/ijssis-2019-018

Thakor, N. V., & Tong, S. (2004). ELectroencephalogram aNalysis MEthods. *Review - Americas Society*. doi:10.1146/annurev.bioeng.5.040202.121601 PMID:15255777

Wilson, C., Hargreaves, T., & Hauxwell-Baldwin, R. (2015). Smart homes and their users: A systematic analysis and key challenges. *Personal and Ubiquitous Computing, 19*(2), 463–476. doi:10.100700779-014-0813-0

Wurz, P., Abplanalp, D., Tulej, M., & Lammer, H. (2012). A neutral gas mass spectrometer for the investigation of lunar volatiles. Planetary and Space Science. doi:10.1016/j.pss.2012.05.016

Yick, J., Mukherjee, B., & Ghosal, D. (2008). Wireless sensor network survey. *Computer Networks, 52*(12), 2292–2330. doi:10.1016/j.comnet.2008.04.002

Zheng, J., Gao, D. W., & Lin, L. (2013). Smart meters in smart grid: An overview. *IEEE Green Technologies Conference.* 10.1109/GreenTech.2013.17

Chapter 6

Smart Automotive Systems Supported by Configurable FPGA, IoT, and Artificial Intelligence Techniques

S. Saravanan
CMR Institute of Technology, India

ABSTRACT

Modern vehicles are very complex by incorporating various computational signals and critical information transactions. Electronic control units (ECUs) are embedded with various software functions, network information, sensor/actuator communication, and dedicated hardware. Altogether, the special hardware needs to be adaptable to the current needs of next-generation vehicles. This chapter will give a broad idea about modern automotive systems by considering various factors. Finding the best reconfigurable field programmable gate array (FPGA)-based hardware, intelligent assistance systems for drivers and various communication protocols are elaborated in this chapter. Moreover, it also provides the essential knowledge of IoT-based smart automotive systems along with its pros and cons. This chapter also gives the awareness and comparative study of artificial intelligence (AI) systems in the present smart automotive systems. The overall observation of this chapter will satisfy the audience by knowing the reconfigurable FPGA, IoT, and artificial intelligence-based automotive systems.

DOI: 10.4018/978-1-5225-9806-0.ch006

INTRODUCTION

A few decades ago, an automobile was a vehicle with extreme mechanical assembly along with few electrical parts. Gradually most of the mechanical assembly parts are controlled by for electrical and electronics components. Micro-controller based functions were implemented to control fuel injection system, spark plug systems and engine mechanism. Improved micro code utilized to control and manages sensors and actuator signals along with Engine Management Units (EMU). Later safety related mechanism also embedded (Felix, 2010; Insop, Keith, Jason, Henrick, Tony, Howard, & Fakhreddine, 2006; Forest, Alberto, Audisio, Marco, Sangiovanni, & Marco, 2008) along with a micro controller. Anti-lock Braking Systems (ABS) assembly, Airbag lock assembly control, dedicated communication network, Real time observer like various addition features were incorporated along with software and hardware. Due to various limitations in standard hardware design it forces the technology to think about reconfigurable based designs.

Soft microprocessor FPGA which can be programmable as per the need of the real time situation and promises to overcome all contemporary issues. Apart from the FPGA reconfigurable hardware, the usage of Internet of Things (IoT) is also used in the smart automotive systems. IoT based next generation vehicle (Ulrich, Helmut, Daniel, & Stefan, 2012) promises to give more comfortable self-driving vehicles like autopilot, analyzing traffic jam and moving into the appropriate lane through smart devices and finally targets for driverless vehicle. Present development in Artificial Intelligence (AI) technique also helps to develop autonomous vehicles, navigating complex traffic situations, smart detection of pedestrian, other vehicles, road work and other obstacles. Thus, future automotive system requirement will be satisfied by using the reconfigurable FPGA, IoT and AI based design.

Tradeoff Between Various Technologies

- **Microprocessor:** This technology is more applicable to general purpose applications. It helps to develop generic computer systems and its applications can be controlled by user programs.
- **Microcontroller:** This technology consists of a processing unit, peripherals, I/O and Memory (RAM and ROM) all on a single chip. It is most suitable for specific purpose applications. It supports interfacing of multifeatured devices and typically used in Embedded based design.
- **Digital Signal Processor (DSP) -** This technology supports faster in mathematical operations and various signal processing like transformation / quantization algorithms. Particularly, it is much faster in floating point

operations. It also supports Single Instruction Multiple Data (SIMD) to fasten multiple data information in the execution stage.

- **Application Specific Integrated Circuit (ASIC):** This technology gives more comfort to specific purpose and custom-made design. It contains analog, digital and mix of both components. Typical ASIC designs work in high performance and utilize low power consumption. On the other side, it is more expensive, time consuming and need more resource to develop.
- **Field Programmable Gate Array (FPGA):** This technology is also known as reconfigurable hardware. It means, possible to change the design and target to the same FPGA design. It consists of a set of an array along with programmable blocks which connected with programmable interconnect. It is possible to program and implement any digital combinational functions with parallel approach which results of quick and efficiency of data processing. It also contains soft and hard-core processing unit.

Table 1, shows the tradeoff between basic processor, ASIC and FPGA. It is evident that cost and flexibility of the design is more comfort with FPGA based technologies. Thus, FPGA based reconfigurable is best technology for IoT based design.

Table 1. Tradeoff between various technologies

Technology	Performance	Time to Change Code Function	Speed	Flexible	Cost
Basic Processor	Medium	Long	Medium	Medium	Medium
ASIC	High	Impossible	High	Low	High
FPGA	Moderate	Short	Moderate	High	Low

HISTORY OF SMART CAR

The following table 2, shows various evolution stages of smart car from the year of 1800 to present scenario.

- **Sensors and Actuator:** Smart vehicle contains hundreds of sensors (Leandro, Filippo, & Marco, 2011; Tzuu, Li, Shih, & Yi, 2003) and actuators to observe the real-time situation on the road and the health of the smart vehicle. Thus, the usage of sensors and actuators are very crucial in smart vehicles. Figure 1 shows various sensors and actuators which is monitoring several conditions of the smart vehicle.

Table 2. Evolution of smart car

Year	Development Function
1800	Machines communicating with one another
1830	Direct communications – Telegraph
1900	Wireless telegraphy
1950	Development of computers
1962	Internet, part of DARPA (Defense Advanced Research Projects Agency)
1969	ARPANET
1980	Commercial service and public use of ARPANET First IoT application in Coca Cola machine, Carnegie Melon University
1993	Global Positioning Satellites (GPS)
1996	General Motors - Emergency help in accident, Safety, GPS location
2000	RFID used in IoT
2001	Remote Diagnostics
2003	Vehicle health report
2007	Telematics
2013	IoT system using multiple technologies ranging from the Wireless communication, MEMS, Embedded systems and GPS.
2014	Audi and General motors use 4G – LTE Wi-fi Hotspot access
2015	Automated transmission, Fuel efficiency
2017	Predictive Intelligence for better vehicle manages
2018	Keyless entry, Hill-assist control
2019	Blind Spot Information System, Forward and Reverse Sensing Systems.
2020	Artificial Intelligence, Deep Learning and Machine Learning

Broad Classification of Vehicle Connectivity

- **Vehicle to Infrastructure (V2I)**: This connectivity helps to connect the information which is data generated by the vehicle along with the information of infrastructure. Thus, it helps the vehicle drive to understand the real-time issues. It is also used to communicate the information about environment-related conditions such as safety and mobility of the vehicle.
- **Vehicle to Vehicle (V2V)**: It helps to communicates information between one vehicles to another vehicle. It provides various information about the position and speed of the surrounding vehicles through a wireless information. It is basically used to avoid accidents and make traffic free environment.

Figure 1. Sensors and actuators in smart vehicle
(Source: CISCO)

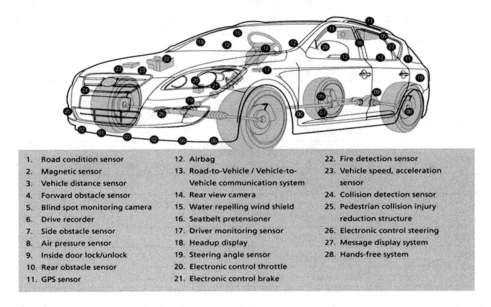

1. Road condition sensor	12. Airbag	22. Fire detection sensor
2. Magnetic sensor	13. Road-to-Vehicle / Vehicle-to-	23. Vehicle speed, acceleration
3. Vehicle distance sensor	Vehicle communication system	sensor
4. Forward obstacle sensor	14. Rear view camera	24. Collision detection sensor
5. Blind spot monitoring camera	15. Water repelling wind shield	25. Pedestrian collision injury
6. Drive recorder	16. Seatbelt pretensioner	reduction structure
7. Side obstacle sensor	17. Driver monitoring sensor	26. Electronic control steering
8. Air pressure sensor	18. Headup display	27. Message display system
9. Inside door lock/unlock	19. Steering angle sensor	28. Hands-free system
10. Rear obstacle sensor	20. Electronic control throttle	
11. GPS sensor	21. Electronic control brake	

- **Vehicle to Cloud (V2C)**: This technology helps to exchanges information about the vehicles with a cloud-based data storage. It is used to allow the vehicle to get the cloud-based information like smart home, insurance business, energy and transportations.
- **Vehicle to Pedestrian (V2P)**: This technology helps to sense the information about the real-time environment of the pedestrian with on-road vehicles. It is used to improve safety and mobility of the pedestrian.
- **Vehicle to Everything (V2X)**: This communication interconnects all types of vehicles and all type of infrastructure systems. Thus, it is named as everything can be connected with vehicle which includes highway centers, base control rooms, other vehicles, ships, trains and airplanes.

FPGA FOR SMART AUTOMOTIVE SYSTEMS

- **Basic of FPGA:** This device (Francisco, & Mariano, 2012; Jonas, 1983; Jurgen, Adam, & Michael, 2007; Michael, Valentina, & Dietmar, 2001) consist of matrix based reconfigurable gate array. FPGA can be configured or programmed, the internal hardware circuitry for any desired applications. Unlike any other general-purpose processors, it uses dedicated internal hardware to process the necessary logic. This computing process is not depended on any kind of operating system. Thus, a single FPGA can replace several electronics component by integrating millions of logic gates in a single integrated circuit (IC). Basic block of FPGA consists of collections of matrix-based configurable logic blocks (CLBs). It is surrounded by a various I/O pins for external periphery usage. Programmable interconnect wire and switches uses to route the required signals which is generated by programs. Figure 2, shows the basic structure of FPGA.

Figure 2. Basic structure of FPGA

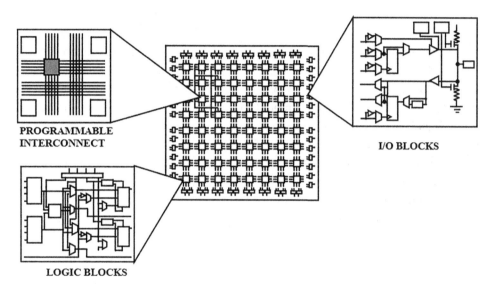

Since FPGAs reconfigurable (Naoya, 2002; Oliver, et. al 2001; Oliver, Michael, Jurgen, & Matthias, 2008; Ratan, Tatikonda, & Vinayak, Kulkarni, 2016; Shreejith, Fahmy, Lukasiewycz, 2013; Ubaid, Henry, Owen, & Joseph, 1993) contains huge programmable gates and possible to process the given program in parallel method. Due the advantage of parallel process in FPGA, it can compute different programs in the same FPAG. It also supports automatic map technique to give processing solutions directly to the FPGA programmable hardware.

FPAG permits to the user to create various task-specific cores that all run parallelly inside one FPGA chip. Thus, FPGA configurable execution provides efficient performance and determinism when compared with other processor-based software solutions. It also helps to increase the range of throughput of the data. VHDL and Verilog languages are used for programming the FPGA design. Once application code gets compiled it is possible to target any desired FPGA (Jurgen, Adam, & Michael, 2007) as per the need of applications.

Advantages

- Quick time-to-market
- More flexible to change the design
- Less cost in Bill of Material (BoM) and inventory management
- Reduce the complexity of PCB and cost
- Best alternative to software designs

Reasons for FPGA Technologies in Automobile Industries

- **Determination:** FPGA uses dedicated resources as programmable logic hardware. The latency of the computation is also highly deterministic.
- **Performance**: FPGA also enables best fit for performance optimization.
- **IO Flexibility**: With programmable logic it is possible to create any interface which is necessary as per the application.
- **Rapid Standard Adoption**: In future the communication standards will change rapidly from one standard to another standard like 4G to 5G. Thus, FPGA can help to migrate from any standard and easily adopt as per the future requirement.
- **Security**: FPGA contains inbuild high grade of encrypted secure algorithms. It gives more secure for vehicle network.
- **Execution Speed**: Concurrent based process support by FPGA rather than sequential operations.
- **Flexible in Complex Functions**: FPAG provide separate hardware and confined space for complex functions.
- **Intellectual Property (IP) Core**: Various interfaces and communication protocol are available in the form of IP core. It also supports soft and hard IP core for time to market requirement.
- **High Reliability:** FPGA systems promises to perform for several years without environmental effects like single event upsets (SEU). Thus, it provides zero Failure In Time (FIT) rate and also supports redundancy requirement for critical situations.

COMMUNICATION PROTOCOLS

In the last two decades, the utilization of electronic components was huge in automobiles. Various automobiles manufacturers integrated the number of electronics devices, which causes immense wire connection and result with more expensive. To address this issue, a specialized vehicle communication protocol (Gabriel, Donal, & Alan, 1999; ISO, 1994) was introduced in modern automobiles. This protocol made more compact in-vehicle network and reduces the cost of wiring, complexity, and weight. At present, there are numerous types of vehicle protocol used in smart automobiles and developed by various manufacturers.

Popular Vehicle Protocols

- FlexRay Network
- Vehicle Area Network (VAN)
- Controller Area Network (CAN)
- Local Interconnect Network (LIN)

In-vehicle communication protocols are classified into three major class. They are Class A networks, Class B networks and Class C networks. In Class A network, low Speed (<10K bits/second) data transfer is considered. It is convenient for entertainment, audio and computer activation. In Class B networks, medium speed (10K b/s to 125K b/s) data transfer is considered. It supports general information transfer like cluster of instruments, speed of the vehicle and data diagnostics. In Class C networks, it is used for high Speed (125K b/s to 1M b/s or greater) data rate information. It helps for real-time critical control, powertrain control, braking and dynamic control of the vehicles.

FLEXRAY PROTOCOL

The FlexRay protocol (Flexray, 2016) was developed by companies including BMW, Bosch, General Motors, DaimlerChrysler, Philips, Volkswagen and Freescale. FlexRay is one of the popular automotive communications networks. It consists of various advantages like high-speed, efficient fault tolerant, better performance, enrich in comfortable, secure communication and better deterministic function. It is possible to transfer the information with 10Mbps. High-Performance is activated with powertrain mechanism. It also promises to support the requirement of next-generation automobiles.

FlexRay's is more reliable and 30 time faster than CAN protocol. It has 3 CRC checks than CAN protocol. It is also a deterministic system, which provides efficient reliability in communications. It can be easily adopted by any kind of network configuration. It provides scalable fault-tolerance. It gives fast error detection and signaling. It is more expensive, so it is considered in the last smart vehicles which require efficient reliability such as high-performance power train, drive-by-wire, active suspension, and adaptive cruise control systems.

Xilinx: FlexRay IP

Spartan-3 from Xilinx contains FlexRay IP for automobiles communications. This FPGA has Logicore FlexRay controller IP. It is used as a single-channel controller for the automotive data bus system. FlexRay supports time-triggered approach and also provides tenfold increase in bandwidth over CAN protocol. Thus, it helps to strengthen automotive applications including gateway, driver assistance, security and other real-time observation in automobiles. This Xilinx IP offers streamlined process with the FlexRay protocol as middleware and drivers from Informatik vector.

Features

- Process data rate can support up to 10 Mbps
- Provides single communication channel
- It supports automotive Industrial and Extended Temperature
- Scalable data transmission - asynchronous and synchronous
- Configurable payload range up to a maximum of 256 bytes
- Configurable Tx, Rx buffers to store up to 128 messages

VEHICLE AREA NETWORK(VAN) PROTOCOL

Vehicle Area Network (VAN) is one of the popular networks with broadband connected Wi-Fi network. It is used to exchange secure information's like data, image, and video between various mobile users to headquarters. This technology will be best fit with any base agencies that can deploys many personnel to one location, especially if more than one person is occupied in each vehicle. It operates over mobile broadband router which connects cellular network or any other internet connections.

CONTROLLED AREA NETWORK (CAN) PROTOCOL

Controlled Area Network (Gianluca, & Adriano, 1999; Robert (1991) is a very popular in-vehicle network with the international standard of ISO 11898. It was developed by Bosch Company and has been adopted for the automotive industry. This in-vehicle network also called as multi-master which supports multiple CAN device communicate with one another without the host control. All nodes are connected with each other through nominal twisted pair bus via CAN H and CAN L wires.

A CAN is a serial communication protocol with multi-master support. It supports multicast protocol with any nodes. It offers to use the communication bus with any node and possible to send a message and receive message from any nodes. Thus, it is known as multi-task support. Transmitter node initiates the message and receiver node will receive that particular message. Messages are assigned to static priorities in the communication network. It means, transmitting node will remain a transmitter until the bus becomes idle. A CAN arbitration helps to superseded by a node with a higher priority message through a process. Basic CAN message may contain up to 8 bytes of data. Bit rates in short network ($\leq$ 40 m) support up to 1 Mbit/s and longer network distance reduces the bit rate up to 125 kbit/s. For example, High speed CAN will support bit rate up to 500 kbit/s.

XilinxL CAN Core

The Xilinx CAN IP core is ideally suited for automotive test equipment, vehicle body control units, automotive gateways, sensor controls and instrument clusters. This Xilinx CAN core supports ultimate flexibility in the process of multiple Electronic Control Unit (ECU) based applications. This CAN core can be used as stand-alone mode and also possible to connected with Xilinx MicroBlaze or PowerPC processors. This Xilinx core provides the solutions to meet the requirement of Bosch licensing terms and condition. Thus, it help to provide a complete flexible IP core to fulfil the user requirement.

Features

- Designed with the standard of ISO 11898-1.
- Various specification support - CAN2.0A and CAN2.0B
- Bit rates ranges up to 1Mbps as per CAN2.0B specification
- Rx and Tx message FIFOs with a user-configurable 64 messages
- Parameterized Acceptance Filtering support
- Supports sleep mode with automatic wakeup
- Transmit prioritization - one High Priority Transmit buffer

- Maskable error and status interrupts
- Supports for Processor Local Bus (PLB) and On-chip Peripheral Bus (OPB)
- Optional support for generic microcontroller interfaces

LOCAL INTERCONNECT NETWORK - LIN PROTOCOL

LIN protocol does not support equal access to the bus due to the arrangements of Master-Slave architecture. LIN master supports delegate's communication, which is known as delegated token principle. Based on the message addressing the required message will be distributed. It supports 64 message addresses for identifiers. This protocol is slower when compared with CAN protocol. But, it is very simple in design and more cost effective than any other in-vehicle protocol.

Xilinx: LIN Core

Local Interconnect Network (LIN) protocol performs serial communication and especially used for automobile-based applications. Xilinx provides the soft core of LIN. It can be operated like single master and multi-slave on LIN network 1.3, 2.0, 2.1 or 2.2. The message transfer can be controlled by a microprocessor interface. It also supports transmission speed between 1 and 20kb/s in the communication network. DLIN is defined by RTL level, and this softcore contains programmable timer and error messages. The LIN soft IP core is microcode-free design and very compatible to target and reuse in any FPGA implementations.

Features

- 8-bit host controller interface (native).
- Automatic bit rate detection (for slave) and time-out detection.
- Master – Slave Configurable can be supported.
- Programmable data rate range between 1 Kbit/s and 20 Kbit/s.
- Verified robustly and proven IP core.
- Slave can be implemented with or without clock synchronization.
- Support of LIN specification 2.0, 2.1, and 2.2A.

Altera: LIN Core

Altera FPGA's LIN core is very popular for vehicle protocols. It helps to interface one vehicle to other vehicle with more efficient. This FPGA contains various family types such as Arria and Cyclone.

Features

- OpenCore evaluation method
- Interface Protocols for communications
- Intel Arria 10, Arria V, Cyclone IV, Cyclone V, Cyclone V SoC are popular LIN IP

Protocol comparison is shown in table 3, between four popular communication networks. It is observed that, depends upon the communication speed FlexRay protocol is the best among other protocols. But it also contains huge cost. CAN protocol is moderate in cost and it can help of transmit the data at the rate of 1 Mbits/s. Depends upon the need of the application the protocol is utilized.

Table 3. Communication protocol comparison

Bus	FlexRay	CAN	LIN	VAN
Communication Speed	10 Mbit/s	1 Mbits/s	40 kbit/s	125 kbit/s
Cost	More	Moderate	Less	Moderate
Communication Wires	2 or 4	2	1	2
Application	Safety, Drive-by-wire Powertrain, High Performance, Adaptive cruise control	Powertrain Engine, Transmission	Body Electronics, Power Seats, Accessories	Secure Information, data, Image, Video

The comparison of in-vehicle communication protocol in terms of cost and speed. From this figure 3, it is evident that the need of high speed or low cost can be decided from the proper need of the applications.

Secure communication (Kizheppatt, Shanker, Suhaib, Fahmy, & Arvind, 2014; Liu, Zhu, Bian, & Xue, 2001; Marko, & Timo, 2012; Shanker, Bezborah, Suhaib, & Fahmy, 2016; Tim, et.al 2003) is one of the major parameters need to be addressed in in-vehicle communication. Due to huge data transfer it is necessary to have trusted communication. Thus, hackers will find more difficult to break the network information in the smart vehicles.

Figure 3. Cost and Speed comparison of in-vehicle communication protocol

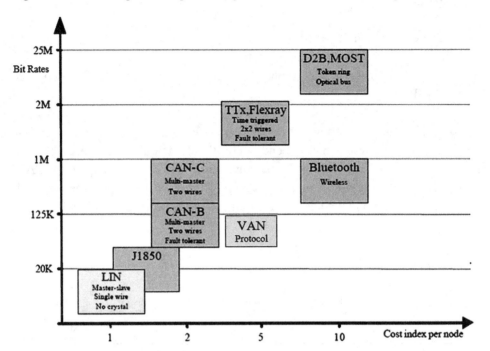

ADVANCED DRIVER ASSISTANCE SYSTEMS (ADAS)

A system which helps for driving process and provides more comfort in driving is known an Advanced Driver Assistance Systems (ADAS). It is basically a human machine interaction for increasing safety in vehicles and road users. It is also developed to enhance vehicle for better driving, automation and adaption. More safety features are designed to avoid accidents and collisions by providing smart technologies that helps the driver to take overall control of the vehicle. Human error is the major cause for road accidents. Thus, usage of ADAS promises to reduce road fatalities, potentially observing the road usage problems and provides over all control of the vehicle.

It was initiated by US Department of Transportation's National Highway Traffic Safety Administration (NHTSA) to have ADAS in all the modern vehicles. General Motors (GM) offers vibrating seat warning in 2013. Alcohol ignition interlock devices was introduced in 2014. In September 2016, the NHTSA published a policy related to Highly Automated Vehicles (HAV) which forces all the vehicles need to have ADAS. Basic function of ADAS is given in figure 4.

Figure 4. Basic function of ADAS
(Source: www.eenewseurope.com)

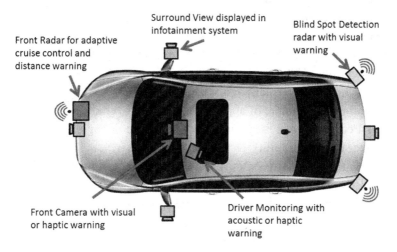

FPGA in ADAS

For smart vehicles, it is mandatory to support the requirement of dynamic market. So, ADAS need more flexibility of computational process as per future demand of smart vehicles. FPGA promises for the demand of future ADAS by providing improved computational benefits with multi-function process. Single FPGA can be used for more than 10 functions in parallel approach.

Basic ADAS consists of two main functions named as vision and sensor fusion. For vision functionality cameras are used in a smart car, which provide the information about vehicle detection and its tracking method. In sensor fusion functionality, it helps to combine different sensor type and its signal information to observe the real-time environment. Thus, FPGA based ADAS provide better results and safer decisions to the driver.

Reasons for Considering FPGA Design in ADAS

- **Reconfigurable**: Due to FPGA reprogrammable facility, it provides more flexible to accommodate late-stage design changes in ADAS.
- **High-Performance Computing**: ADAS systems will rely on sensor input to compute the next step, and fast processing power is needed to pick up on sudden environmental changes.
- **Parallel Processing**: FPGA supports simultaneous processing or parallel processing. For example, when ADAS system is engaged with Land Departure

Warning (LDW), it also supports parallel Pedestrian Detection (PD). Thus, FPGA can process two different algorithms simultaneously.

- **Low Power Consumption**: One of the major advantages of FPGA is the utilization of less power when it is in process. Thus, FPGA based ADAS will be more comfort for huge integrating more sensors and actuator signals.
- **High Reliable**: FPGA are highly reliable to withstand industrial based standard. For example, temperatures between -40°C ~ 100°C, making them suitable for a wide range of applications in smart vehicles.
- **Rapid Prototyping**: FPGA supports for simple debugging, and lower-risk parameter in undesirability.
- **Security:** FPGA provides security in terms of programmable anti-tampering and it also prevents reserve engineering attempts. This security mechanism is very important in ADAS particularly to secure the sensors signal information form hackers.
- **XILINX – ADAS CORE:** This FPGA supports next generation vehicles with SDSOC development environments and heterogeneous processing of Zynq 7000 SoC and Zynq Ultra-scale FPGAs. It provides more flexible and reliable platform for next-generation safety systems in vehicles. Xilinx based IP operates in parallel processing and multi-threading capability to improve the computational process. It supports Collision Avoidance, Eye and head tracking. Gesture recognition and Semi-Autonomous operation. It also supports Lane Departure Warning (LDW) and Pedestrian Detection (PD) with efficient algorithms.
- **ALTERA – ADAS CORE:** It supports unique features for better performance and efficiency in ADAS. Intel Cyclone V SoC family supports ADAS and qualified for ISO 26262 standard which the policy of Automotive Functional Safety Data Pack (AFSDP). It supports Anti-Lock braking systems (ABS), Electronic Stability Programs (ESP), Line Keep Assist (LKA), LDW and TSR. These ADAS core provides more comfort to present existing technology and the future standard. Altera FPAG also gives tremendous advantage over Commercial-of-the-shelf (COTS) products. It gives promises in increasing the diagnostic coverage of the smart vehicles by providing custom monitoring and custom watchdog timers for ADAS based applications. It also helps in better video streaming process, low power consumption and increased performance. Many COTS products have not been designed with functional safety and using a dynamic platform, better real-time environment and efficient in overall vehicle safety.
- **MICROSEMI – ADAS CORE:** This FPGA's SmartFusion2 SOC and IGLOO2 FPGA's are very popular for ADAS applications. This FPGA cores promises to supports next-generation ADAS design, which helps for audio

processing for early hazard identification, secure platform, Human machine interface and better video processing. It also supports hard and soft core of data acquisition, processing and display functions. Microsemi FPGA core's also offers best-in-class security for vehicle-to-vehicle (V2V) and vehicle-to-infrastructure (V2I) communication. It provides greater security services with help of SRAM based physically unclonable function (PUF). It also helps for dedicated hardware processing and reliable key authentication in ADAS based application.

Various Application Related to ADAS

- Detection of Blind-spot
- Warning of Lane departure
- Control of Electronic stability
- Advanced Emergency braking system
- Monitoring of Tire pressure
- Electrical power steering
- Intelligent in speed adaptation
- Automatic parking
- Adaptive headlights and cruise
- Smart vision features like
- Adaptive Cruise Control (ACC)
- Driver Monitoring System
- Glare-free high beam and pixel light
- Forward Collision Warning
- Emergency driver assistant

IoT for Smart Automotive System

Internet of Things (IoT) can be defined with various parameters. In general, it is defined as the Sensors and Actuators integrated with any physical components and connected through wired and wireless networks, often using Internet with the same Internet Protocol (IP). IoT technology uses in many applications. This chapter focuses only on IoT based smart vehicles. Due to its various advantages like efficient resource utilization and reduce human resources forces to adopt in future smart vehicles.

Basic development of IoT starts from the year of 2000 for the application of RFID tag routing. It helps for supply chain helpers. In the year of 2010, IoT started to support vetical market applications like surveiliance, security, healthcare, transport, food safety and document management. In the year of 2020, IoT is predicted for Ubiquitous positiong to locate people and everyday objects. In near future IoT technology will support for physical word web like teleoperation, monitoing and controlling distant objects. Thus, the roadmap of IoT promises to over the entire world in the single window. Figure 5, shows IoT technology roadmap.

Figure 5. IoT technology roadmap
(Source: SRI Consulting Business Intelligence)

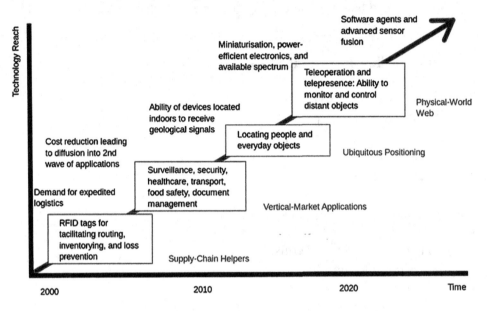

IoT integrated view as shown in figure 6, contains security, social network, mobility and device chain-based solutions as base layer. Hacking is possible in IoT based design (Andry, 2014; Gabriel, & Donal, 2002; Hermann, 1999). Thus, Providing better security in the base layer is very essential. From this paradigm the last layer consists of Cloud based apps and its services, which helps for virtualization and optimization hosting. The last before layer consist of Data management, which is used for analytical and standardization. It also supports artificial intelligence and machine learning methods. In the second top layer consist of applications and services of various standards. In the initial top layer consist of sensor and actuator-based device and its signals. Thus, this diagram shows the necessary layers of IoT based design.

Figure 6. IoT integrated view

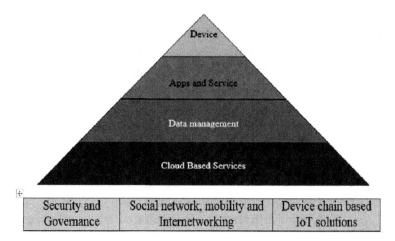

Advantages of IoT

- **Efficient Resource Utilization**: IoT can be effectively use the available resources. It is more adoptable with each device and monitor all real-time natural resources.
- **Minimize Human Effort:** As the devices of IoT interact and communicate with each other and do lot of task as per the requirement. Thus, it reduces human effort involving for the same effort.
- **Save Time:** Though it reduces the human effort certainly it is possible to save the time of the work. It promises time saving thorough out the IoT design platform.
- **Improve Security:** IoT also moves very close of security issues. Various preventions are made in IoT technology from network hackers.
- **Cost**: IoT helps to reduce the financial cost by replacing human efforts who are in charge of monitoring and maintaining the control of the application.

Disadvantages of IoT

- **Privacy:** IoT system provides maximum personal data or real-time data, which is not necessary for all the situations. Thus, the privacy is very less when IoT technology is involved.
- **Complexity:** Due to the designing, developing, and maintaining and enabling the large technology to IoT system is quite complicated. It is also necessary to address several possibilities of failure from sensor signals.

AI for Smart Automotive System

Artificial Intelligence (AI) technique supports smart vehicles to perform as a virtual human. This technique consist of deep learning with neural network concepts and mimic as the behavior of human brain. An AI integrates real time environmental conditions, building positions, road approach and pedestrian movements. It helps to reduce traffic accidents and congestions, minimized searching time for vehicle parking, and indicates the level of SO_2, CO and NO_x vehicle gas. With the support of this AI development, it address all the above issues and proves solution.

Basic structure of AI is classified into four important aspects. i) Artificial Neural Network (ANN), is the base network which consist of neural computational with other heavily connected neural. ii) Deep learning gives deep neural network for extracting and transforming different levels of neurons. iii) Support of vector neural machine is used to classify the neuron information. iv) Simulated annealing method is used to schedule neurons and also help to control the neural network.

Various comparative study (table 4) has been identified between automotive manufacturing companies along with present AI development.

FUTURE DIRECTION OF SMART VEHICLES

In the future, the exponential growth of internet usage is unavoidable. It is not only the integration of smart devices like computers, laptops, personal assistance, tablet and smart phones. It is also used by multitude of devices with high speed internet connection. It also connects with smart homes, wearable devices, smart cities and cloud storage. Various future directions of IoT based smart vehicles (Umar, Abdul, Hairi, & Dilip, 2018), are listed below

- **IoT Dominated Vehicles** – Several smart IoT devices connected to the high-speed internet and provides more comfort and safety in future vehicles.
- **Cyber Threat**: Distributed Denial of Service (DDoS) attack and various malfunctions will be very common due to overwhelm internet traffic in websites.
- **Impact of Smart Cities**: IoT based smart vehicles will adopt smart technologies which is used in smart cities and companies like automation, remote manage, video camera surveillance and hiring vehicles etc.,
- **Influence of Artificial Intelligence**: Deep machine learning promises to observe human habits and unique pattern recognition. IoT based smart vehicles also adopt this AI technology for better and smart connectivity of human need.

Table 4. Comparative between various automotive manufacturing company along with the development of AI features

Automobile Manufacturing Company	Reference	Year	Latest Feature Development
TATA Motors	(www.tatamotors.com, 2017)	2017	Collaborated with Microsoft for AI, ML and IoT on Azure cloud. It also supports automobile industry protocol such as Firmware over the air (FOTA) and Software over the air (SOTA)
Mahindra & Tech Mahindra Ltd	(www.techmahindra.com, 2019)	2019	GAiA open source AI based platform (powered by Acumos AI) used to reshape automobile industry
Maruti Suzuki	(https://cio.economictimes.indiatimes.com, 2018)	2018	Collaborated with Google with an AI voice enable assistant in automobiles
Hero Motor Corp Ltd	(www.heromotocorp.com, 2018)	2018	Adopted Robotic Process Automation, AI, IoT, Block Chain and ML for sophisticated automobiles
Bajaj Auto Limited	(www.analyticsinsight.net, 2019)	2019	Universal Robots helps Bajaj automobiles in assembly lines by providing compactness, lightweight, accuracy and cost effectiveness
Toyota Motor Corporation	(https://toyota-ai.ventures, 2018)	2018	Toyoto Research Institute (TRI) adopts AI, Robotics, Data centre and Cloud Platform
General Motors	(www.autodesk.com, 2018)	2018	Collaborated with Autodesk for optimized seat bracket. AI and cloud platform also used in adaptive manufacturing with 3D printing
Mitsubishi Motors Corporation	(www.mitsubishi-motors.com, 2017)	2017	AI based personal assistant system, voice operation, context recognition and connective with diverse device & content
Honda Motor Co Ltd. Company	(www.theverge.com, 2017)	2017	Adopted AI system with supervised machine learning for self-driving car autonomous level
Ford Motor Company	(www.forbes.com, 2019)	2019	AI (CarStory platform) adopted for automate quality assurance, detects wrinkles in the driver seats and improves fuel efficiency
Audi Car Automotive	(www.manufacturingtodayindia.com, 2020)	2020	Two innovations: Special vision and on-demand offer

Table 5. Comparative between various automotive component design companies along with the present features development

Automobile Components Design Company	Reference	Year	Latest Feature Development
Qualcomm	(www.just-auto.com, 2020)	2020	Dual MAC Wi-Fi, Connect up to 32 clients with improved WPA3 Protocols
LG Electronics	(www.lgcorp.com, 2019)	2019	Linux based in-vehicle infotainment (IVI), AI and Gesture recognition using Human Machine Interface WebOS auto platform with voice commands
Wipro Digital	(https://wiprodigital.com, 2018)	2018	Dedicated Short Range Communication (DSRC) and Long Term Evolution (LTE) Suitable for V2X and supports for 5G network
BlackBerry	(www.fleetowner.com, 2019)	2019	AI, ML and QNX platform used for cybersecurity and safety on vehicles
Bosch	(https://www.dealerscope.com, 2020)	2020	Transparent LCD display with 3D approach which connects interior monitoring camera detects the position of driver's eye movements.

- **Growth of 5G Networks**: In future 5G and its next generation wireless communication is expected. Thus 5th generation cellular service provides very high-speed internet connections and it is mandatory to improve the performance of IoT based smart device in vehicles. It also promises for driverless cars and smart connected cars which is already on the road.
- **New Protocols for IoT**: Due to 5G based IoT smart devices, it is necessary to develop smart Wi-Fi router with great security. Thus, this new IoT protocol will give more secure to smart vehicles.
- **Cloud based Storage** – Future smart vehicles uses IoT for most of the comfort and secure purpose. Thus, the usage of cloud-based storage will also use more to store all trusted data and information. Increasing of data usage need next level of technology in cloud storage for better security and smart accessing of data information.
- **Smart IoT Platforms** – Future IoT based smart vehicle expected to consider various different platforms into single integrated platform. Need to develop smart platform for low level devices and applications such as communication, security update data acquisition and device monitoring operations. Due to huge data transfer, Distributed Stream Computing Platforms (DSCP) technology need to be utilized for parallel architectures to analyze real-time process.

CONCLUSION

This chapter contributes various technology supports to full fill the need of future smart automotive systems. Three important technology promises to address the above need in terms reconfigurable FPGA design, Internet of Things (IoT) and Artificial Intelligence (AI) techniques. A Soft processor like reconfigurable FPGA can be the best fit for next generation automotive systems in terms of Intellectual Property (IP) in Communication protocols. It also supports efficient Advanced Driver Assistance Systems (ADAS) to full fill the need of smart automotive systems. This chapter also provides the importance of IoT technique along with its advantages and disadvantages. This chapter promotes the significance of IoT technique in terms of its network backbone support for future smart vehicles. Finally, the overall present development in Artificial Intelligent (AI) were compared with various automobile manufacturing companies and also with automotive component design. These two major comparative studies will help the audience to understand the present scenario of AI development in smart automotive systems. Thus, this chapter promises the reader to understand the need for reconfigurable FPGA, IoT and AI to explore their knowledge towards future smart automotive systems.

REFERENCES

Abelein, U., Lochner, H., Hahn, D., & Straube, S. (2012). Complexity, quality and robustness– the challenges of tomorrow's automotive electronics. *Proceedings of the International Conference on Design, Automation Test in Europe Conference Exhibition (DATE)*, 870–871. 10.1109/DATE.2012.6176573

Becker, J., Donlin, A., & Hu¨bner, M. (2007). New Tool Support and Architectures in Adaptive Reconfigurable Computing. *Proceedings of IFIP International Conference on Very Large-Scale Integration (VLSI–SoC)*. 10.1109/VLSISOC.2007.4402486

Bereisa, J. (1983). Applications of Microcomputers in Automotive Electronics. *Transactions on Industrial Electronics*, *30*(2), 87–96. doi:10.1109/TIE.1983.356715

Cena, G., & Valenzano, A. (1999). Overclocking of Controller Area Networks. *Electronics Letters*, *35*(22), 1923–1925. doi:10.1049/el:19991289

Chujo. (2002). Fail-safe ECU System Using Dynamic Reconfiguration of FPGA. *R & D Review of Toyota CRDL*, *37*, 54–60.

Dorazio, L., Visintainer, F., & Darin, M. (2011). Sensor Networks on the Car: State of the Art and Future Challenges. *Proceedings of the Design Automation and Test in Europe (DATE) Conference.*

Eberli, F. (2010). Automotive embedded driver assistance: A real-time low-power FPGA stereo engine using semi-global matching. *Proceedings of the International Conference on Computer Design (ICCD).* 10.1109/ICCD.2010.5647552

FlexRay Automotive Communication Bus Overview. (2016). www.ni.com/white-paper/3352/en/

Fons & Fons. (2012). FPGA-based Automotive ECU Design Addresses AUTOSAR and ISO 26262 Standards. *Xcell Journal, 78,* 20–31.

Forest, Ferrari, Audisio, Sabatini, Vincentelli, & Natale. (2008). Physical Architectures of Automotive Systems. *Proceedings of the Design Automation and Test in Europe (DATE) Conference,* 391–395.

Gschwind, M., Salapura, V., & Maurer, D. (2001). FPGA proto typing of a RISC processor core for embedded applications. *IEEE Transactions on VLSI Systems, 9*(2), 241–250. doi:10.1109/92.924027

International Organisation for Standardisation (ISO). (1994). *Road Vehicles— Interchange of Digital Information— Controller Area Network for High-Speed Communication.* Author.

Khan, & Owen, & Hughes. (1993). FPGA architectures for ASIC hardware emulators. *Proceedings of the ASIC Conference and Exhibit,* 336- 340. 10.1109/ASIC.1993.410733

Kopetz, H. (1999). Automotive electronics. *Proceedings of the 11th Euromicro Conference on Real-Time Systems,* 132–140. 10.1109/EMRTS.1999.777459

Leen, G., & Heffernan, D. (2002). Expanding automotive electronic systems. *Computer, 35*(1), 88–93. doi:10.1109/2.976923

Leen, G., Heffernan, D., & Dunne, A. (1999). Digital networks in the automotive vehicle. *Computing & Control Engineering Journal, 10*(6), 257–266. doi:10.1049/cce:19990604

Leinmuller, T., Buttyan, L., Hubaux, J.-P., Kargl, F., Kroh, R., Papadimitratos, P., ... Schoch, E. SEVECOM – Secure Vehicle Communication. *Proceedings of the IST Mobile and Wireless Communication Summit.*

Li, T.-H. S., Chang, S.-J., & Chen, Y.-X. (2003). Implementation of Human-like Driving Skills by Autonomous Fuzzy Behavior Control on an FPGA-Based Car-Like Mobile Robot. *IEEE Transactions on Industrial Electronics, 50*(5), 867–880. doi:10.1109/TIE.2003.817490

Liu, J., Ming, Z., Bian, J., & Xue, H. (2001). A debug sub-system for embedded-system co-verification. *Proceedings of the Conference on ASIC*, 777–780.

Rakotonirainy, A. (2014), Car hacking - Car hacking: The security threat facing our vehicles. *Popular Science*. https://www.sciencedaily.com/releases/2014/09/140917120705.htm

Robert Bosch GmbH. (1991). *CAN Specification, Version 2.0*. Author.

Sander, Becker, Hubner, Dreschmann, Luka, Traub, & Weber. (2001). *Modular system concept for a FPGA-based Automotive Gateway*. Academic Press.

Sander, O., Hubner, M., Becker, J., & Traub, M. (2008). Reducing latency times by accelerated routing mechanisms for an FPGA gateway in the automotive domain. *Proceedings of the International Conference on ICECE Technology (FPT)*, 97–104. 10.1109/FPT.2008.4762371

Shreejith, Anshuman, A., & Fahmy. (2016). Accelerated Artificial Neural Networks on FPGA for fault detection in automotive systems. *Design, Automation & Test in Europe Conference & Exhibition (DATE)*.

Shreejith, S., Fahmy, A., & Lukasiewycz, M. (2013). Accelerating Validation of Time Triggered Automotive Systems on FPGAs, *Proceedings of the International Conference on Field Programmable Technology (FPT)*, 4. 10.1109/FPT.2013.6718322

Song, I., Gowan, K., Nery, J., Han, H., Sheng, T., Li, H., & Karray, F. (2006). Intelligent Parking System Design Using FPGA. *Proceedings of the International Conference on Field Programmable Logic and Applications*, 1-6.

Tatikonda, R. R., & Kulkarni, V. B. (2016). FPGA based exhaust gas analysis for automotive vehicles. *International Conference on Internet of Things and Applications (IOTA)*. 10.1109/IOTA.2016.7562721

Vipin, K., Shreejith, S., Fahmy, S. A., & Easwaran, A. (2014). Mapping Time-Critical Safety-Critical Cyber Physical Systems to Hybrid FPGAs. *Proceedings of the International Conference on Cyber Physical Systems, Networks, and Applications (CPSNA)*, 31–36. 10.1109/CPSNA.2014.14

Wolf, M., & Gendrullis, T. (2012). Design, Implementation, and Evaluation of a Vehicular Hardware Security Module. *Proceedings of the International Conference on Information Security and Cryptology (ICISC)*, 302–318. 10.1007/978-3-642-31912-9_20

Xilinx Inc. (2013). *UG909: Vivado Design Suite User Guide: Partial Reconfiguration.* www.xilinx.com

Hamid, Zamzuri, & Limbu. (2018). Internet of Vehicle (IoV) Applications in Expediting the Implementation of Smart Highway of Autonomous Vehicle: A Survey. *Performability in Internet of Things,* 137-157.

Chapter 7
High-Performance Computing Using FPGAs for Improving the DTC Performances of Induction Motors

Saber Krim
University of Monastir, Tunisia

Mohamed Faouzi Mimouni
National Engineering School of Monastir, Tunisia

ABSTRACT

The conventional direct torque control (DTC) of induction motors has become the most used control strategy. This control method is known by its simplicity, fast torque response, and its lack of dependence on machine parameters. Despite the cited advantages, the conventional DTC suffers from several limitations, like the torque ripples. This chapter aims to improve the conventional DTC performances by keeping its advantages. These ripples depend on the hysteresis bandwidth of the torque and the sampling frequency. The conventional DTC limitations can be prevented by increasing the sampling frequency. Nevertheless, the operation with higher sampling frequency is not possible with the software solutions, like the digital signal processor (DSP), due to the serial processing of the implemented algorithm. To overcome the DSP limitations, the field programmable gate array (FPGA) can be chosen as an alternative solution to implement the DTC algorithm with shorter execution time. In this chapter, the FPGA is chosen thanks to its parallel processing.

DOI: 10.4018/978-1-5225-9806-0.ch007

INTRODUCTION

Recently, the Direct Torque Control (DTC) method can be considered as the most used control technique for electrical motors (Lin et al, 2006). This type of torque and flux control was firstly proposed as direct self control by Depenbrock (1988) and direct torque control by Takahashi (1986). This control strategy presents an outstanding dynamic performance as well as good robustness under variations in the motor parameters. It seems well suited to applications in traction or electric vehicle. However, this control strategy presents many disadvantages, such as the ripples in the torque and flux, and the distortion in the stator current waves; due to the presence of the hysteresis comparators used to control the torque and the stator flux (Luis et al, 2003; Deng et al, n.d). In fact, the basic structure of the conventional DTC was developed by Takahashi in 1986 and integrates two hysteresis controllers in order to control the torque and the flux in an independent way. The ripples of the torque and flux are limited by the bands of the hysteresis controllers in order to satisfy the torque and flux demand. Yet, in practice, it is difficult to guarantee this operation conditions due to the time delay between the sampling instant of the torque which follows a discrete computation approach and the located time to calculate the inverter switching states (Jidin et al, 2010). In this case, the torque ripples surpass the hysteresis bands, which leads to select a voltage vector causing a rapid increase or decrease of the torque (Idris et al, 2004). This consequently increases the torque ripples, the stator current distortions and degrades the conventional DTC performances. To overcome these problems, novel DTC structures have been developed, like the combination between the DTC and the Space Vector Modulation (SVM), this novel structure is known by DTC-SVM (Kyo-Beum et al, 2008). The DTC-SVM reduces considerably the ripples and guarantees an operation with fixed switching frequency. Generally, the DTC-SVM uses Proportional-Integral (PI) controllers to control the torque and the rotor speed. The gains of the PI controllers are estimated with the parameters of the motor model which cannot work well in practice and affect the robustness of the control strategy. Other researchers have replaced the PI controllers by Sliding Mode Controllers (SMCs) to improve the robustness of the control strategy. Hence, the combination of the DTC-SVM with SMCs increases the algorithm complexity (Saber et al, 2017). Alternatively, other DTC structure based on predictive controller has been developed by (Zhu et al, 2012; Preind et al, 2013), deadbeat direct torque control (Xu et al, 2014), duty ration control (Xia et al, 2014) and root mean square criteria (Shyu et al, 2010). The cited control techniques reduce the torque ripples and improve the DTC performances, but the algorithm uses more parameters of the motor and it is more complex. In paper (Singh et al, 2013), the authors propose a DTC with a modified switching table. Thus, this method cannot be considered as a definitive solution to prevent the flux ripples caused by sector exchange. In paper

(Zhang et al, 2012; Geyer et al, 2012), the authors have used multilevel inverters with more levels of the hysteresis controllers and more sectors number in order to select an appropriate voltage vector in each sampling time. This method reduces the torque ripples, but the multilevel inverter increases the control system cost and the commutation losses. Another method is based on the intelligent technique like the neural networks and the fuzzy logic, but in this method the switching frequency remains variable and does not provide a good performance in terms of torque and flux ripples (Uddin et al, 2012; Abbou et al, 2009) Moreover, the conventional DTC offers good performances in terms of ripples reduction if the sampling frequency is higher which require processors with high processing speed.

Traditionally, the DTC algorithm has been implemented utilized the software solutions like the digital signal processor (DSP) (Lianberg et al, 2002) which can be programmed using C language or graphical programming tool in order to reduce the prototyping time. It is known that these solution execute the control algorithm sequentially which increases the sampling time if the algorithm is complex. Normally, for DSP (DSPACE 1104) the sampling frequency can reach 20 kHz for the conventional DTC algorithm. However, this sampling frequency is insufficient for the operation of the discrete torque hysteresis controller, so that the torque ripples can be limited between the hysteresis bands, nay at very low speeds operations that cause high torque slope. To solve this problem, the Field Programmable Gate Array (FPGA) can be considered as the better solution to grantee an operation with a higher sampling frequency, thanks to its parallel processing of the implemented algorithm. The FPGA is recently utilized by some researchers in order to improve the electrical systems performances by reducing the sampling time (Krim et al, 20145).

The main contribution of this work is to implement the conventional DTC on an FPGA, in order to achieve a sampling frequency of 200 kHz. In fact, if the sampling frequency is higher the torque ripples will be limited within the hysteresis bands and then minimize the ripple by reducing the band size. Moreover, the hardware implementation method is based on Xilinx System Generator, which is a toolbox developed by Xilinx added to Matlab/Simulink and used for the implementation of control algorithms on FPGA (Xilinx et al, n.d.). The XSG is proposed to reduce the prototyping time and then the time-to-market. In addition, the XSG tool is a simple way for the hardware implementation on FPGAs. In fact, from the architecture of the DTC with XSG it's possible to test the functionality of the control system by digital simulation and then generate the (VHSIC Hardware Description Language) VHDL code and the bitstream file (Saidani et al, 2010).

CONVENTIONAL DTC SCHEME

In the Concordia reference (α, β), the mathematical model of the induction motor is given by the Equation (1):

$$\begin{cases} \dfrac{d\varphi_{s\alpha}}{dt} = \nu_{s\alpha} - R_s i_{s\alpha} \\[2mm] \dfrac{d\varphi_{s\beta}}{dt} = \nu_{s\beta} - R_s i_{s\beta} \\[2mm] \dfrac{d\varphi_{r\alpha}}{dt} = -R_r i_{r\alpha} - \omega\varphi_{r\beta} \\[2mm] \dfrac{d\varphi_{r\beta}}{dt} = -R_r i_{r\beta} - \omega\varphi_{r\alpha} \end{cases} \tag{1}$$

with

- $\left(\nu_{s\alpha},\nu_{s\beta}\right), \left(\varphi_{s\alpha},\varphi_{s\beta}\right), \left(\varphi_{r\alpha},\varphi_{r\beta}\right) \text{ and } \left(i_{s\alpha}, i_{s\beta}\right)$: are the components of the voltage, the stator flux, the rotor flux and stator current respectively, in the Concordia reference (α, β).
- $R_s, R_r \text{ and } \omega$: The stator and the rotor resistances and the electric rotor speed.
  The relation between current and flux is presented by Equation (2):

$$\begin{cases} \varphi_{s\alpha} = L_s i_{s\alpha} + M i_{r\alpha} \\[2mm] \varphi_{s\beta} = L_s i_{s\beta} + M i_{r\beta} \\[2mm] \varphi_{r\alpha} = L_r i_{r\alpha} + M i_{s\alpha} \\[2mm] \varphi_{r\alpha} = L_r i_{r\beta} + M i_{s\beta} \end{cases} \tag{2}$$

where $L_s, L_r \text{ and } M$: the induction motor inductances.

From a mechanical point of view, the behavior of the induction motor can be described by Equation (3):

$$\begin{cases} J\dfrac{d\Omega}{dt} = T_e - T_l - f\Omega \\[2mm] T_{em} = \dfrac{3}{2} N_p \left(\varphi_{s\alpha} i_{s\beta} - \varphi_{s\beta} i_{s\alpha}\right) \end{cases} \tag{3}$$

where T_l and T_{em} are the load and the electromagnetic torques, respectively. *Np, J and f* the number of the pair poles, the viscous friction coefficient and rotor inertia, respectively.

The basic DTC diagram is given in Figure 1.

Figure 1. Conventional DTC diagram

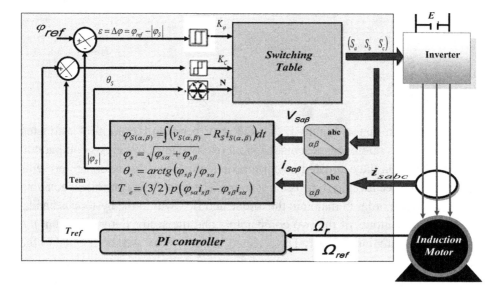

The (α, β) current signals can be estimated from the real stator current as:

$$\begin{cases} i_{s\alpha} = \sqrt{\dfrac{3}{2}} i_{s\alpha} \\ i_{s\beta} = \dfrac{1}{\sqrt{2}} \left(i_{sb} - i_{sc} \right) \end{cases} \tag{4}$$

The norm of the stator flux can be calculated by Equation (5):

$$\left| \varphi_s \right| = \sqrt{\varphi_{s\alpha}^2 + \varphi_{s\beta}^2} \tag{5}$$

The (α, β) flux signals can be estimated by Equation (6):

$$\begin{cases} \varphi_{s\alpha} = \int \left(v_{s\alpha} - R_s i_{s\alpha} \right) dt \\ \varphi_{s\beta} = \int \left(v_{s\beta} - R_s i_{s\beta} \right) dt \end{cases} \tag{6}$$

The (α, β) voltage signals can be estimated from the inverter switching states (S_a, S_b, S_c) as:

$$\begin{cases} v_{s\alpha} = \frac{2}{3} E \left(S_a - \frac{S_b - S_c}{2} \right) \\ v_{s\beta} = \frac{2}{3} E \frac{S_b - S_c}{\sqrt{3}} \end{cases} \tag{7}$$

It can be seen that in Figure 1, that the error between the norm of estimated stator flux and its reference presents the input of a two level hysteresis comparator. The error between the estimated electromagnetic torque and its reference presents the input of a three level hysteresis comparator. The hysteresis controllers generate logical signals in order to maintain the torque and flux within the hysteresis bands.

Finally, the outputs of the two comparators and the sector number present the inputs of the switching Table 1. The selected voltage vector will be applied to the induction motor in each sampling period. Figure 2-3 illustrate the used hysteresis controllers.

Figure 2. Two-level hysteresis controller of stator flux

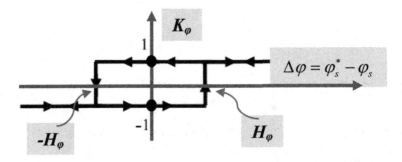

The choice of voltage vector Vs depends on desired variation of the stator flux and the desired evolution of the electromagnetic torque. When the stator flux is in zone i:

Figure 3. Three-level hysteresis controller of torque

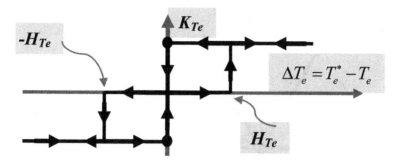

- If V_{i+1} is selected, then the stator flux amplitude increases and the electromagnetic torque increases.
- If V_{i+2} is selected, then the stator flux amplitude decreases and the electromagnetic torque increases.
- If V_{i-1} is selected, then the stators flux amplitude increases and the electromagnetic torque decreases.
- If V_{i-2} is selected, then the stators flux amplitude decreases and the electromagnetic torque decreases.
- If V_0 or V_7 are selected, then the stator flux vector stops and the electromagnetic torque kept constant.

The stator flux position in the reference (α, β) can be calculated by the Equation (8):

$$\theta_s = arctg\left(\frac{\varphi_{s\beta}}{\varphi_{s\alpha}}\right) \tag{8}$$

The basic DTC consists in subdividing the Concordia (α, β) reference in six sectors (sector 1 to sector 6); each sector is defined by an angle of 60° as given by Figure 4 (Takahsi et al, 1986). The different sectors and voltage-vector positions are illustrated in Figure 4.

As presented in Figure 1, the voltage vector is selected using the hysteresis controller's decisions (K_φ, K_T) and the position of the stator flux vector (N). According to the effect of the voltage vector on the couple and the stator flux magnitude, a switching table is used, as given by Table 1.

Figure 4. Sectors and voltage vectors

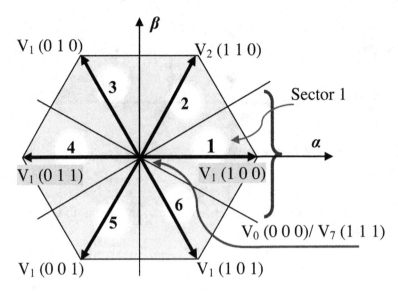

Table 1. Switching table

K_φ	K_C	S1	S2	S3	S4	S5	S6
	1	V2	V3	V4	V5	V6	V1
1	0	V7	V0	V7	V0	V7	V0
	-1	V6	V1	V2	V3	V4	V5
	1	V3	V4	V5	V6	V1	V2
0	0	V0	V7	V0	V7	V0	V7
	-1	V5	V6	V1	V2	V3	V4

Based on the selected voltage vector, the switching states of the inverter can be determinate using the following relationship, presented by Equation (9).

$$V_S = \sqrt{\frac{2}{3}} U_{dc} \left(S_A + S_B e^{j\frac{2\pi}{3}} + S_C e^{j\frac{4\pi}{3}} \right) \tag{9}$$

with S_A, S_B and S_C being the inverter switching states, and U_{dc} being the DC, bus voltage.

Major Problem in Hysteresis-Based DTC

Despite its simplicity, the conventional DTC uses two hysteresis controllers which cause some drawbacks like the variation of the switching frequency, important torque ripples and a higher sampling period required for the digital implementation (Idris et al, 2004; Tripathi et al, 2005). In this chapter the sampling frequency is increased to reach 200 kHz in order to reduce the torque ripples, thanks to the parallel processing of the FPGA.

Requirement of High Processing Speed

Decreasing the width of the hysteresis controller band is useless if the sampling frequency of the digital processor is limited. In fact, with a processing delay caused by the processor, the torque ripples cannot be limited exactly by the hysteresis band. If the too small hysteresis band, the torque variation can exceed this band which causes the selection of a reverse active voltage vector instead of a zero voltage vector. The selection of a reverse voltage vector leads to a rapid decrease of the torque and as a result an increase of the torque ripples (Jidin et al, 2011). However, the torque ripples can be prevented with higher sampling frequency of the digital processor.

DESIGN OF THE CONVENTIONAL DTC IN THE XSG

The XSG is actually a toolbox developed by Xilinx that can be integrated within Simulink and is composed of several block sets that are used for the system design and for testing the hardware system's functionality by simulation. When the design is achieved, giving the desired results of simulation the XSG offer the possibility of automatically generating the VHDL code. The generated VHDL code can be then synthesized and implemented on the FPGA. Figure 5 presents the design flow using the XSG.

The direct torque control algorithm is composed of several blocks, as Concordia transformation of the stator current, Concordia transformation of the voltage, the electromagnetic torque estimator, the stator flux module, calculation of angle Θ_s, determination of the sector N, the two hysteresis comparators and the switching table. The full architecture of the conventional DTC from the XSG is given by Figure 6.

The internal architectures of some DTC blocks are given by Figs.7 and 8:

Figure 5. XSG Design Flow

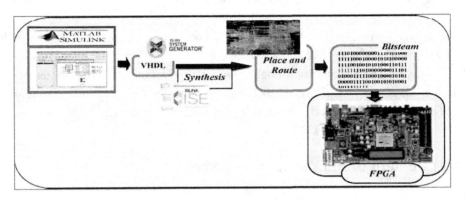

Figure 6. Full architecture of the conventional DTC from the XSG

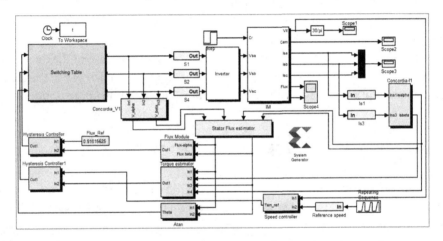

Figure 7. XSG internal architecture of the: (a) Concordia transformation of the Voltage, (b) stator flux estimator

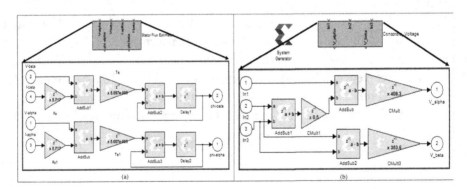

Figure 8. XSG internal architecture of the: (a) Module of the estimator flux, (b) Torque estimator

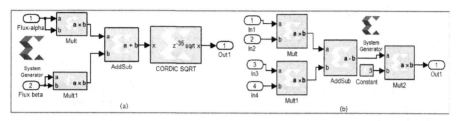

(a)   (b)

DIGITAL SIMULATION

This section presents the digital simulation of the conventional DTC architecture with two sampling frequency. The reference flux $\left|\phi_s^*\right| = 0.91Wb$, the reference of the rotor speed is applied at t=0.1sec, which is equal to 150 rad/sec. The rated load is applied at t=0.5 Nm. The hysteresis bands the torque and flux are given as:

$$\begin{cases} \Delta H_{Tem} = \left(5\%\right)T_{em-n} \\ \Delta H_\phi = \left(5\%\right)\left|\phi_s^*\right| \end{cases} \tag{10}$$

With T_{em_n} is the rate torque. The induction motor parameters are given by Table 2:
Figure 9 (a and b) presents the developed electromagnetic torque when the motor is controlled by the conventional DTC under two sampling frequency. In general, torque has fast response and reached quickly its reference value. However, it can be seen that the torque ripples are considerably reduced if the sampling frequency increased, as demonstrated by Figure 9 a). Referring to Figure 10, the stator flux reached quickly its reference value which is equal to 0.91Wb. It can be noticed that the flux ripples are reduced for higher sampling frequency.

Table 2. Induction motor parameters

P_u	Nominal Power	1.5 KW	R_s	Stator resistance
V	Nominal Voltage	230/400 v	R_s	Rotor resistance
I_n	Nominal current	3.2 /5.5 A	Ls	Stator inductance
N_n	Nominal Speed	1435 rpm	L_r	Rotor inductance
F	Frequency	50 Hz	M	Mutual inductance
P	Pair pole number	2	J	Moment of inertia
			f	Viscous friction coefficient

Figure 9. Torque response for the conventional DTC with two sampling frequency: (a) 200 kHz, (b) 20 kHz

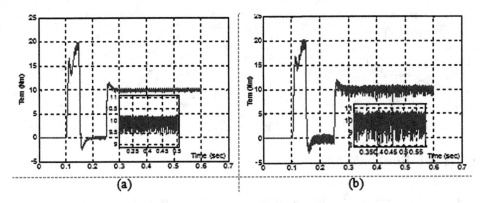

(a)   (b)

Figure 10. Norm of the stator flux for the conventional DTC with two sampling frequency: (a) 20 kHz, (b) 200 kHz

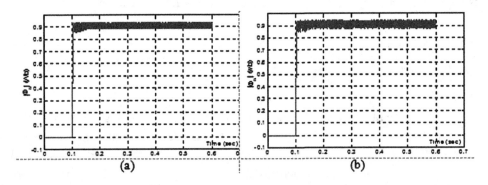

(a)   (b)

Figure 11. Speed response for the conventional DTC with two sampling frequency: (a) 20 kHz, (b) 200 kHz

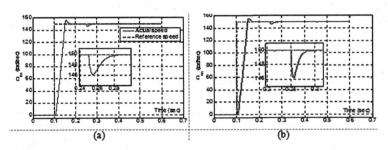

(a)   (b)

Figure 12. Speed response for the conventional DTC with two sampling frequency: (a) 200 kHz, (b) 20 kHz

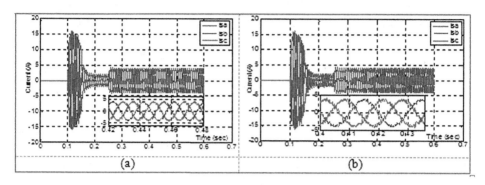

(a)   (b)

The rotor speed evolution is presented in Figure 11, it can be seen that the actual speed reached quickly its reference value, thanks to the high dynamic offered by the DTC. The raise of the sampling frequency reduce the speed ripples, as demonstrated by Figure 11(a). As shown in Figure 12, the stator current harmonic waves are reduced for higher sampling frequency. The performance of the implementation method in terms of ripple reduction is given in Table 3.

Table 3. Ripples analysis

	Conventional DTC at 20 kHz	Conventional DTC at 200 kHz
	Max-Min	Max-Min
Torque ripple (Nm)	2.25	0.7
Flux ripple (Wb)	0.06	0.045
Stator current ripple (A)	0.5	0.15

Synthesis Results and Hardware Co-Simulation

The conventional DTC algorithm is verified by digital simulation with the XSG tool and under Matlab/Simulink environment. The VHDL code is generated using the Xilinx ISE 12.4 tool. The Implementation results using the Xilinx FPGA Virtex 5 ML507 are given as follows. The area resources and the execution time are presented in Table 4.

Table 4. Area resources / time

	Used Resources	Ready Resources
Number of bonded IOBs	68	640
Number of Slices	1601	44800
Number of Slice LUTs	4	32
Number of MULT18X18s	749	44800
Execution Time (µs)		
Concordia transformation	0,12	
Torque and flux Estimators	0,16	
Sector and hysteresis controllers	0,16	
PI speed	0,16	
Execution Time (µs):	0, 6	
Total Execution Time (µs):	0,6 +t$_{ADC}$	

t$_{ADC}$: Analogue to digital conversion time

The estimated processing time is 0.6 +t_{ADC} µs using a Xilinx Virtex-5 FPGA ML507 with an xc5vfx70t-3ff1136 package. In paper (Shyu et al, 2010) the total execution time is not less than the 100µs, due to the serial treatment of the software solutions. However, the execution time using the FPGA does not exceed 5µs with a sampling frequency equal to 200 kHz.

The hardware co-simulation can be considered as an experimental implementation using the FPGA board. This step aimed to verify the performances of the algorithm executed by the FPGA. The co-simulation consists firstly, to generate the JTAG block and the bitstream file. Secondly, The DTC design in Simulink must be replaced by the generated JTAG block, then connect the FPGA to PC computer through JTAG cable and click start simulation, in this step the FPGA board executes the algorithm. In fact, the FPGA receive the stator current, the real speed and the reference speed, and then send the inverter switching states through JTAG cable. The Hardware co-simulation environment based on the personal computer, Xilinx FPGA Virtex V ML507 is represented in Figure 13.

The Hardware Co-simulation results are given by Figure 14. In this study, the stator flux reference and the load torque are equal to 0.91 Wb and 10 Nm, respectively. The load torque is applied at t=0.25 sec. The reference speed is variable, at start up the reference speed is equal 100 rad/sec. At t=0.5 sec, the reference speed is reduced with a rump form to reach 50 rad/sec at t=1 sec. It can be seen that the obtained results are similar to those obtained by digital simulation. The torque ripples and the current distortions are reduced. Figure 14 (b, c) has demonstrated that the torque and flux ripples are restricted between the hysteresis bands, thanks to the high processing

Figure 13. Hardware Co-simulation environment

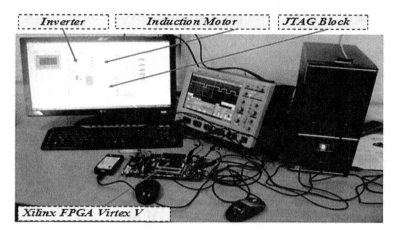

Figure 14. Hardware Co-simulation results: (a) Rotor speed, (b) Torque, (c) Norm of the stator flux, (d) Stator current

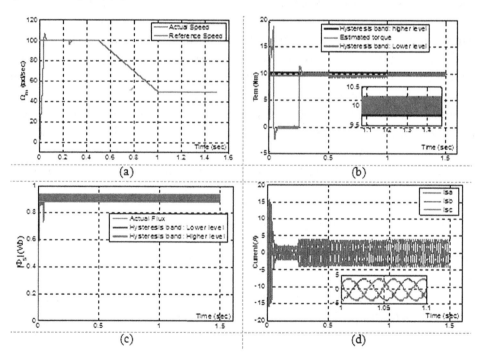

speed offered by the FPGA. In this study, the sampling frequency reached 200 kHz (the sampling period is equal to 5μs). The actual speed follows its reference value with good accuracy. The fast speed response and the high dynamic of the DTC are also demonstrated by these results. Finally, the FPGA implementation of the conventional DTC reduces the torque/flux ripples and the current distortions which consequently reduces the mechanical vibrations, the faults in the stator windings and increases the motor service life.

CONCLUSION

In this chapter a reduction of the sampling time (the raise of the sampling frequency) has been achieved utilizing an FPGA Virtex 5 ML507. In fact, the torque ripples are considerably reduced by the decrease of the hysteresis bands and the increase of the sampling frequency, thanks to the parallel processing and the high computation power of the FPGA. Nevertheless, an effective way about the design, the simulation and the hardware implementation are presented in this paper. The VHDL code is generated using the DTC algorithm architecture designed from the XSG tool, which can be considered as an interesting implementation method. The using of this method is very practical since the VHDL knowledge is unnecessary and so the implementation time is reduced. To obtain satisfactory calculation accuracy, we propose 16 bits fixed point format. The digital simulation of the DTC under Matlab/ Simulink is presented. The obtained results are compared with variations in the hysteresis band width and the sampling time. Thus, the torque ripples is reduced if the sampling frequency increased and the hysteresis band width reduced. In fact, comparatively with the DSPs, the execution time offered by the FPGA is very short. In addition, the DTC algorithm has been verified by hardware co-simulation using an FPGA Virtex 5 ML507.

REFERENCES

Abbou, A., & Mahmoudi, H. (2009). Performance of a sensorless speed control for induction motor using DTFC strategy and intelligent techniques. *J. Electr. Syst.*, *5*, 64–81.

Saber, Soufien, & Abdellatif. (2018). Control with high performances based DTC strategy: FPGA implementation and experimental validation. *EPE Journal*, 1–17.

Cruz, S. M. A., Toliyat, H. A., & Cardoso, A. J. M. (2005). DSP implementation of the multiple reference frames theory for the diagnosis of stator faults in a DTC induction motor drive. *IEEE Transactions on Energy Conversion, 20*(2), 329–335. doi:10.1109/TEC.2005.845531

Deng, J., & Tu, L. (n.d.). *Improvement of Direct Torque Control Low-speed Performance by Using Fuzzy Logic Technique.* International Conference on Mechatronics and Automation, Luoyang, China.

Depenbrock, M. (1988, October). Direct Self Control of Inverter-Fed Induction Machines. *IEEE Trans. On Power Electr., PE-3*(4), 420–429. doi:10.1109/63.17963

Gadoue, S. M., Giaouris, D., & Finch, J. W. (2009). Arti̅cial intelligence-based speed control of DTC induction motor drives: A comparative study. *Electric Power Systems Research, 79*(1), 210–219. doi:10.1016/j.epsr.2008.05.024

Geyer, T., & Mastellone, S. (2012). Model predictive direct torque control of a five-level ANPC converter drive system. *IEEE Transactions on Industry Applications, 48*(5), 1565–1575. doi:10.1109/TIA.2012.2210174

Idris, N. R. N., & Yatim, A. H. M. (2004, August). Direct torque control of induction machines with constant switching frequency and reduced torque ripple. *IEEE Transactions on Industrial Electronics, 51*(4), 758–767. doi:10.1109/TIE.2004.831718

Idris, N. R. N., & Yatim, A. H. M. (2004, August). Direct torque control of induction machines with constant switching frequency and reduced torque ripple. *IEEE Transactions on Industrial Electronics, 51*(4), 758–767. doi:10.1109/TIE.2004.831718

Inoue, Y., Morimoto, S., & Sanada, M. (2010). Examination and linearization of torque control system for direct torque controlled IPMSM. *IEEE Transactions on Industry Applications, 46*(1), 159–166. doi:10.1109/TIA.2009.2036540

Jidin, A. (2010). Torque ripple minimization in DTC induction motor drive using constant frequency torque controller. *Proc. Int. Conf. Electr. Machines Syst.*, 919–924.

Jidin, A., Idris, N. R. N., Yatim, A. H. M., & Sutikno, T. (2011). An optimized switching strategy for quick dynamic torque control in DTC-hysteresis-based induction machines. IEEE Trans. Ind. Electron., 58(8), 3391–3400.

Kang, J. W., & Sul, S. K. (2001, June). Analysis and prediction of inverter switching frequency in direct torque control of induction machine based on hysteresis bands and machine parameters. *IEEE Transactions on Industrial Electronics, 48*(3), 545–553. doi:10.1109/41.925581

Krim. (2014). Real Time Implementation of High Performance's Direct Torque Control of Induction Motor on FPGA. *International Review of Electrical Engineering, 9*(5), 919–629.

Krim, S., Gdaim, S., Mtibaa, A., & Mimouni, M. F. (2015). Design and implementation of direct torque control based on an intelligent technique of induction motor on FPGA. *Journal of Electrical Engineering & Technology, 10*(4), 1527–1539. doi:10.5370/JEET.2015.10.4.1527

Kyo-Beum, L., & Blaabjerg, F. (2008). Sensorless DTC-SVM for Induction Motor Driven by a Matrix Converter Using a Parameter Estimation Strategy. *IEEE Transactions on Industrial Electronics, 55*(2), 512–521. doi:10.1109/TIE.2007.911940

Lascu, C., Boldea, I., & Blaabjerg, F. (2000, January–February). Amodified direct torque control for induction motor sensorless drive. *IEEE Transactions on Industry Applications, 36*(1), 122–130. doi:10.1109/28.821806

Lianbing, L. (2002). A high-performance direct torque control based on DSP in permanent magnet synchronous motor drive. *Proc. 4th World Congress Intell. Control Automat., 2,* 1622–1625. 10.1109/WCICA.2002.1020862

Lin, L., Songhua, S., Shengping, L., Qiang, L., & Wei, L. (2006). Stator Resistance Identification of Induction Motor in DTC System Based on Wavelet Network. *Intelligent Control and Automation, 2006. WCICA 2006. 2006 IEEE.*

Luis, R., Antoni, A., Emiliano, A., & Marcel, G. (2003, June). Novel Direct Torque Control (DTC) Sheme With Fuzzy Adaptive Torque- Ripple Reduction. *IEEE Transactions on Industrial Electronics, 50*(3).

Monmasson, E., & Cirstea, M. (2007). FPGA design methodology for industrial control systems— A review. *IEEE Transactions on Industrial Electronics, 54*(4), 1824–1842. doi:10.1109/TIE.2007.898281

Monmasson, E., Idkhajine, L., Cirstea, M. N., Bahri, I., Tisan, A., & Naouar, M. W. (2011). FPGAs in industrial control applications. *IEEE Transactions on Industrial Informatics, 7*(2), 224–243. doi:10.1109/TII.2011.2123908

Monmasson, E., Idkhajine, L., Cirstea, M. N., Bahri, I., Tisan, A., Naouar, M. W., & Charaabi, L. (2011). FPGAs in industrial control applications. *IEEE Transactions on Industrial Informatics*, *7*(2), 224–243. doi:10.1109/TII.2011.2123908

Noguchi, Yamamoto, Kondo, & Takahashi. (1999). Enlarging switching frequency in direct torque-controlled inverter by means of dithering. *IEEE Trans. Ind. Appl.*, *35*(6), 1358–1366.

Noguchi, T., Yamamoto, M., Kondo, S., & Takahashi, I. (1999, November – December). Enlarging switching frequency in direct torque-controlled inverter by means of dithering. *IEEE Transactions on Industry Applications*, *35*(6), 1358–1366. doi:10.1109/28.806050

Preindl, M., & Bolognani, S. (2013). Model predictive direct torque control with finite control set for PMSM drive systems, part: Maximum torque perampere operation. *IEEE Transactions on Industrial Informatics*, *9*(4), 1912–1921. doi:10.1109/TII.2012.2227265

Rodriguez-Andina, J. J., Moure, M. J., & Valdes, M. D. (2007). Features, design tools, and application domains of FPGAs. *IEEE Transactions on Industrial Electronics*, *54*(4), 1810–1823. doi:10.1109/TIE.2007.898279

Saber, K. R. I. M. (2017). Implementation on the FPGA of DTC-SVM Based Proportional Integral and Sliding Mode Controllers of an Induction Motor: A Comparative Study. *Journal of Circuits, Systems, and Computers*, *26*(3).

Saber, K. R. I. M., Soufien, G. D. A. I. M., & Abdellatif, M. T. I. B. A. A. (2017). Modeling and Hardware Implementation on the FPGA of a Variable Structure Control Associated with a DTC-SVM of an Induction Motor. *Electric Power Components and Systems*, *45*(16), 1806–1821. doi:10.1080/15325008.2017.1351010

Saber, Soufien, & Abdellatif. (2015a). FPGA implementation of the direct torque control with constant switching frequency of induction motor. In Systems, Signals & Devices (SSD), 2015 12th International Multi-Conference on. IEEE.

Saber, Soufien, & Abdellatif. (2015b). Hardware Implementation of a Predictive DTC-SVM with a Sliding Mode Observer of an Induction Motor on the FPGA. *WSEAS Transactions on Systems and Control, 10*, 249-269.

Saidani, T., Atri, M., Dia, D., & Tourki, R. (2010). Using Xilinx System Generator for Real Time Hardware Co-simulation of Video Processing System. *Electronic Engineering and Computing Technology*, *60*, 227–236. doi:10.1007/978-90-481-8776-8_20

Shyu, K. K., Lin, J. K., Pham, V. T., & Yang, M. J. (2010). Global minimum torque ripple design for direct torque control of induction motor drives. *IEEE Transactions on Industrial Electronics*, *57*(9), 3148–3156. doi:10.1109/TIE.2009.2038401

Singh, B., Jain, S., & Dwivedi, S. (2013). Torque ripple reduction technique with improved flux response for a direct torque control induction motor drive. *IET Power Electronics*, *6*(2), 326–342. doi:10.1049/iet-pel.2012.0121

Takahashi, I., & Noguchi, T. (1986). A new quick-response and high efficiency control strategy of an induction motor. IEEE Trans., 22(5). doi:10.1109/TIA.1986.4504799

Toh, C., Idris, N., Yatim, A., Muhamad, N., & Elbuluk, M. (2005). Implementation of a New Torque and Flux Controllers for Direct Torque Control (DTC) of Induction Machine Utilizing Digital Signal Processor (DSP) and Field Programmable Gate Arrays (FPGA). *Power Electronics Specialists Conference, 2005. IEEE 36th*. 10.1109/PESC.2005.1581843

Tripathi, A., Khambadkone, A. M., & Panda, S. K. (2005, March). Torque ripple analysis and dynamic performance of a space vector modulation based control method for AC-drives. *IEEE Transactions on Power Electronics*, *20*(2), 485–492. doi:10.1109/TPEL.2004.842956

Uddin, N., & Hafeez, M. (2012). FLC-based DTC scheme to improve the dynamic performance of an IM drive. *IEEE Transactions on Industry Applications*, *48*(2), 823–831. doi:10.1109/TIA.2011.2181287

Wang, Y., Li, H., & Shi, X. (n.d.). Direct Torque Control with Space Vector Modulation for Induction Motors Fed by Cascaded Multilevel Inverters. *32nd IEEE Annual Conference on Industrial Electronics IECON*, 1575-9. 10.1109/IECON.2006.347240

Xia, C., Zhao, J., Yan, Y., & Shi, T. (2014). A novel direct torque control of matrix converter-fed PMSM drives using duty cycle control for torque ripple reduction. *IEEE Transactions on Industrial Electronics*, *61*(6), 2700–2713. doi:10.1109/TIE.2013.2276039

Xilinx System Generator v2.1 for Simulink User's Guide Online. (n.d.). www.mathworks.com/applications/dsp_comm/xilinx_ref_guide.pdf

Xu, W., & Lorenz, R. D. (2014). Dynamic loss minimization using improved deadbeat-direct torque and flux control for interior permanent-magnet synchronous machines. *IEEE Transactions on Industry Applications*, *50*(2), 1053–1065. doi:10.1109/TIA.2013.2272052

Zhang, Y., Zhu, J., Zhao, Z., & Xu, W. (2012). An improved direct torque control for three-level inverter fed induction motor sensorless drive. *IEEE Transactions on Power Electronics*, *27*(3), 1502–1513. doi:10.1109/TPEL.2010.2043543

Zhang, Z., Tang, R., Bai, B., & Xie, D. (2010). Novel direct torque control based on space vector modulation with adaptive stator flux observer for induction motors. *IEEE Transactions on Magnetics*, *46*(8), 3133–3134. doi:10.1109/TMAG.2010.2051142

Zhu, H., Xiao, X., & Li, Y. (2012). Torque ripple reduction of the torque predictive control scheme for permanent-magnet synchronous motors. *IEEE Transactions on Industrial Electronics*, *59*(2), 871–877. doi:10.1109/TIE.2011.2157278

Chapter 8
Wireless Sensor Networking in Biomedical Engineering

Chandrasekaran R.
Vels Institute of Science, Technology and Advanced Studies, India

Hemalatha R. J.
Vels Institute of Science, Technology and Advanced Studies, India

Josephin Arockia Dhivya A.
Vels Institute of Science Technology and Advanced Studies, India

Thamizhvani T. R.
Vels Institute of Science Technology and Advanced Studies, India

ABSTRACT

Wireless sensor networking plays an important role in sensor signal communication and data transfer. The WSN is one of the trending fields in medical data mining. WSN provides the connecting link between the real physical world and virtual environment. In this study, the various WSN network algorithm, topologies, architectures, and their applications to medical technology are discussed. This study will be useful for the readers to know about various communicative technologies and standards followed in biomedical technology.

DOI: 10.4018/978-1-5225-9806-0.ch008

INTRODUCTION

The Wireless Sensor Network is defined as small sensor nodes connected together using radio signals for the purpose of real-time sensing of the physical environment. The WSN provides a bridge between the physical and virtual world. The WSN has various applications in various fields. The WSN networks are used in the stream of Biomedical Engineering in recent days for the monitoring and diagnosing the various physiological parameters of the subject wirelessly. The WSN plays major role in the Telemedicine and Tele Ambulatory services. In this study the various wireless sensor networking in Biomedical Engineering is surveyed. The increase in technology in communication and increase in Micro and Nano communication spectrum leads to the development of healthcare monitoring system. The wearable devices create new milestone in disease diagnosis and healthcare management systems (Lymberis et al, 2005). The Basic Structure of the WSN consists of Sensors, Sensor Nodes, Base Station, Server, Host Computer. The Sensor system consists of various sensors connected to the node called Sensor Node. The data collected from the different sensors are transmitted to the sensor node. The sensor system consists of three sub systems – Sub sensor system, Controller system, Communication system. The sub sensor system converts the Analogue data of the sensor to digital format. The Digitized data values are sent to the controller system. The Controller system detects the data and sends the data to the base station. The Base station is connected to the controller system wirelessly. The Controller system controls the sensors, sensor nodes and base station. The controller system should consist of wide range of memory for storing and data transmission. The larger the memory capacity faster the data transmission. The data transmission speed is based on the memory capacity of the controller system. The Controller is connected to the base station wirelessly. Base station is the place where the data is transmitted to the host computer wirelessly, it is the gateway for the WSN.

Figure 1. Block diagram of WSN

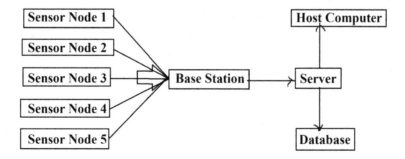

NETWORK TOPOLOGY

- **Bus Topology**: In Bus Topology the data sent from one to another node in single path (one-way communication). The data send through the network, where all nodes can see the data but only the recipient can access the data and receive the data. Bus Topology has more traffic of data due to single path communication. It is very easy to configure, install and access. If more nodes are attached to the Bus Topology the performance of the system gets affected and gets slow down.

- **Tree Topology**: In Tree Topology the network has one central root hub, where all the sensor nodes are connected to the root hub. The main disadvantage of the Tree topology is the complexity of the architecture of the nodes, the traffic of data from node to hub and hub to host computer, the link damage to the single node or single hub damages the communication link of whole networks.

- **Star Topology**: Here Nodes cannot communicate directly to each other and Networks are connected to the central Hub. Each node is a client and central Hub is called as the server or sink.

- **Ring Topology**: It has 2 neighbours and every message pass through the same direction (ring like direction – Either Clockwise / Anti-clock wise). Failure in any network takes down the whole network.

- **Mesh Topology**: Each node is connected to one another node called full mesh. The data transmitted here has high integrity and secured. The complexity can be increased or reduced based on the number of nodes present. The number of nodes can be increased based on the data circulated. There is also partial mesh network which connects indirectly with the other nodes.

- **Circular Topology**: In this Topology, the main sink is placed at the centre, the other nodes are connected in circular shape. It is easy to establish communication between the nodes. It is secured way of transmission of data and reliable also. The nodes are randomly deployed with node uniform density all around the sink.

- **Grid Topology**: The Network is divided in number of grids. Each grid are works as the node. The data transmitted here is fast with less complexity. The grids can be added additionally based on incrementation of the sensor nodes. The Routing is performed grid by grid manner. This algorithm is useful in low level node energy consumption.

Figure 2. Applications of WSN

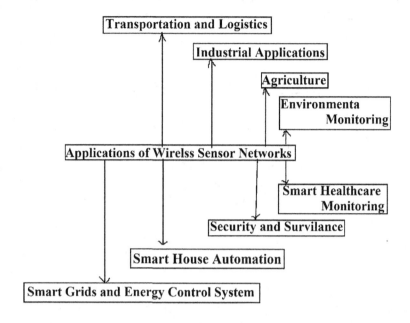

BIOMEDICAL APPLICATIONS OF WIRELESS SENSOR NETWORKS

The sensors are used in Biomedical Technology for monitoring, diagnosing the physiological parameters of the patients. The various physiological parameters that can be measured using the sensors are Heart rate, Pulse rate, Respiration rate, Body Temperature, Non-Invasive Blood Pressure measuring etc. The most common mode for wireless communication used in Biomedical Technology is RF (Radio Frequency), Bluetooth, Zigbee, recently IoT (Internet of Things). The IoT is preferred in recent times because of its connectivity and easy data retrieval and reliable. The Moving range of wireless signal / sensor acquisition to Body Area Network (BAN) and Personal Area Network (PAN) for carrying important healthcare monitoring information are next level of healthcare monitoring through WSN.

COMMON REQUIREMENTS FOR WSN

The Three main requirements of the WSN are 1. Reliability and synchronization of measurements 2. Reliable delivery of synchronization of measurements 3. Minimization of human Intervention on network. The other requirements of the WSN network are Global Synchronization, 2-way data communication, Data retrieval, Encryption, Identification, Authentication, Power Consumption, Error Detection/Correction, On board or on Chip A/D conversion, On board or on chip Micro-controller.

OPEN SYSTEM INTERCONNECT LAYERED ARCHITECTURE

The ISO standard for networking is OSI architecture is shown in figure 7. The main concept of OSI is that the process of communication between two endpoints in a network can be divided into seven distinct groups of related functions, or layers. Each communicating user or program is on a device that can provide those seven layers of function. In this architecture, each layer serves the layer above it and, in turn, is served by the layer below it. So, in a given message between users, there will be a flow of data down through the layers in the source computer, across the network, and then up through the layers in the receiving computer.

OVERVIEW OF THE IEEE 802.15.4 – 2003 STANDARDS

It uses the wide band technology and Direct Sequence Spread Spectrum. It functions on 3 operating frequencies, it ranges from

1. **2.4 GHZ:** Worldwide ISM band, that supports 16channel of data rate 25 kb/s and modulated using Offset Quadrature Phase Shift Keying.
2. **868 MHZ:** The European Band, that supports 1 Channel of data rate 20 kb/s and modulated using Binary Phase Shift Keying.
3. **915 MHZ:** The American Band, that supports 10 channels of data rate 40 kb/s and also modulated using Binary Phase Shift Keying.

IEEE 1451 STANDARD

The IEEE 1451.0 standards are the set of protocols or command for IEEE 1451.0 wired and wireless networking of Transducer Electronic Data Sheets and Network Capable Application Processor.

IEEE 1451.5 STANDARD

The IEEE 1451.5 standards are the set of protocols or command for WTIM (Wireless Transducer Interface Module and Network Capable Application Processor. It comprises of 802.11 Bluetooth, ZigBee as its wireless communication protocol.

IMPLEMENTATION OF BIOMEDIAL SENSORS IN WSN

The Biomedical Sensors are of different types. The sensors like Pulse rate, ECG, EMG etc are traditional Biosensors whereas there are some other categories of sensors are used, like Bio Chemical Sensors, Gas Sensors, Bio MEMS etc (Neuman et al, 1988). The Wireless sensor Networking works on two nodes, they are **i. NCAP Node ii. WTIM Node.** The Sensors are primarily connected to the Wireless Transmission Internet Module Via Serial Port. The Next Step is NCAP Communication is established with WTIM wirelessly using IEEE 1451.0 and 1451.5 Protocols using the client server and publisher - subscriber communication model. The client server and publisher – subscriber communication is established using Transmission Control Protocol / Internet Protocol and Transmission Control Protocol / User Datagram Protocol.

BLUETOOTH BASED BIOMEDICAL HEALTHCARE MONITORING

The Wireless technologies are very rapid in development of remote health monitoring services. The Recent Telecommunication services consists of the easily accessible cloud or online data storage for saving the patient records and retrieval of patient data (Sandeep et al, 2001). The Smart Home Health care monitoring systems uses X10 Technology which are implemented and used in European countries. The Electrical Lines are used for message transmission in X10 Technology. It consumes low power and it has reduced noise and power distortion (Alam et al, 2012). The patients in the critical care units or Intensive care units should be monitored continuously. The various physiological parameters of the patients should be monitored to estimate the recovery rate and normality of the patients. If sudden changes in any physiological parameter leads to pathological conditions. The cable less, wireless devices are in need of monitoring patients at critical care units. The Bluetooth is one of the best ideas for short range of communication. For example, in an Intensive Care Unit- if the patient is put under a patient monitoring system, which monitors and records his/her physiological parameters like heart rate, pulse rate, ECG, NIBP, Body

Temperature, etc. The sensed data of the patient in patient monitor can also be monitored by the physician from his personal computer or mobile using Bluetooth. Here the Bluetooth acts as the connectivity protocol. Using Bluetooth, the data can be shared at short range and secured.

ZIGBEE BASED BIOMEDICAL APPLICATIONS

ZigBee is the first Industrial standard Wireless Personal Area Network, that provides more secure connection, low power consumption, and supports multi-hopping network. The recent advancement is the secured wireless transmission of health care monitoring. It works on the standards of IEEE 802.15.4. Wireless Communication Protocol (Zahurul et al, 2010). More Number of Zigbee nodes can be connected together to form a Zigbee network. If two or more Zigbee networks connected together then power consumption is the biggest problem to overcome. The power consumption will be more if there are too many Zigbee network connected together (Jhang et al, 2010). The Phase shift keying modulation techniques consumes low power due to increased sleeping time of the node and increased EEMAC MAC layer Algorithm (Chen et al, 2012). The Energy Efficiency is improved using the European En Ocean Technology and the introduction of very short message service for acknowledgement to overcome the message collision probability. The En Ocean Technology uses the Direct Media Access on MAC control and implementation (Ploennigs et al, 2010). The Advanced Technologies like Wavenis has various license free ISM bands of frequency ranges 868 MHZ, 915 MHZ, 433 MHZ. It has automated 2 way communication with ultra low power and energy consumption (Kuo et al, 2010).

NODE SENSOR WIRELESS NETWORKS

IoT Private Area Networoring

A private network is more of a usage designation rather than a proper network type or topology. There is not much of a technical difference between a private and a public network in terms of hardware technology and infrastructure, except for the way that access rights and security measures are set up. The terms "private" and "public" simply denote who can and cannot use the network. However, it is more complicated to set up a private network due to all the security measures and access restrictions that need to be put in place; sometimes even extra hardware not that's not required on public networks is used. Private networks are most preferred in businesses and private organizations because they provide high security for vital information. There are some factors that need to be addressed in order to have a secured connection, making private networks more complicated to set up. First is the number of users or devices that can connect. Next, Web servers need to be protected, since exposure to the Internet makes these networks susceptible to malicious attacks. Lastly, high-security hardware and applications like firewalls need to be installed, as they can greatly help in making the network private and secure. There is no doubt that a private network, with all of its bells and whistles, is more expensive to set up compared to public networks, which only needs to have some access points and a proper connection to the Internet to function.

IoT BASED BIOMEDICAL APPLICATIONS

Wifi is one of the trending and ever popular wireless technology based on the IEEE standard 802.11 standards that has enormous speed of data transmission ranges from 11 to 300 Mbps. For security reasons the wifi can be used as WPA -2- 802.11i standard Protocol. It consumes more power and 802.11 g (Zahurul et al, 2010) protocol for 35m in doors and 802.11 b protocol for 100 m out doors connectivity. The Internet of Things is a physical system of inter- related computing devices. Using IoT the computing devices is connected always via Internet. The IoT has wide range of Biomedical and Industrial Applications. The low power consuming Biosensors are applied in the wireless technology for the transfer of data wirelessly. The Biosensor implemented in IoT should have more space for storage of data and less traffic on data communication (Ren et al, 2005). The Introduction of Nano Technology in development of miniature IC & Sensors leads to the invention of Bio-MEMS technology. The Bio-MEMS are often used in IoT applications (Blount et al, 2007).

BIOMEDICAL DEVICE MANAGEMENT

The smart wireless sensing technology for surgical tools and computer assisted surgery uses the wireless sensing protocols. The wearable sensing devices are in trend for all kind of non-invasive diagnosis of diseases (Mohd et al, 2012). Using the IoT & RFID – The Biomedical Devices and Equipment's can be managed and serviced easily. The RFID is used to track the Medical Devices and its details. The Medical Device Management plays primarily role in the field of Biomedical Engineering and Technology. The Medical Devices should be maintained properly in such way that it should be ready to use at any instant of time. The Medical Devices and its service information should be maintained carefully and accurately. The RFID and

IoT plays main role in maintaining the information regarding Biomedical Device Management.

REAL TIME MONITORING

The Real Time Monitoring refers to the real time patient physiological data monitoring. The various physiological parameters can be monitored using various bio sensors. The sensed data can be transmitted through the IoT via Internet to any mobiles, Clouds, Host Computers etc. The main key feature for IoT based Health care monitoring is its real time, secured data transmission, easy connectivity and low data management system.

MEDICAL INFORMATION MANAGEMENT

The Medical Information System refers to maintenance of patient data, patient history, medical records, manuals, files, procedures etc. In recent days the maintenance of patient data plays major role. The patient data must be transmitted in a secured way. The IoT plays major role is maintaining patient records in online storages. The online storage of data is easy to access and easy to retrieve. The Cloud based patient storage has become very easy and efficient in data storage. The cloud storage has huge memory capacity and can be accessed anytime using the smart phones. The data can be retrieved easily (Ghosh et al, 2016). The Wireless Wearable systems are used in recent times for easy and fast recording and monitoring of patient data. The vital parameters like ECG, Respiration rate, Non-Invasive Blood Pressure, Pulse rate are easily sensed and monitored using the sensors. The Sensors like Glucose sensing sensors, Airflow sensors, LM 35 Temperature Analogue sensors, Accelerometer are used as wearable sensors to monitor the physiological parameters of the body (Hameed et al, 2016). The Real time wireless health monitoring using the mobile application is trending in healthcare and software industries. The main advantage of the mobile application-based healthcare monitoring is the patient can be monitored at instant of time and the patient is connected online via internet (WLAN, LAN) etc (Abdullah et al, 2015). The Smart Fitness management applications are increased in recent times. The Fitness monitoring is very attractive in recent days. The healthcare – fitness mobile applications designed in recent days are very easy to use and track the fitness of the peoples. The fitness applications can track the daily work out, daily calories intake, heart rate, etc (Bui et al, 2011).

The SENTINAL IoT is specialized IoT for more secured and authenticated communication. This IoT Gateway is used for office, Industrial, Defence purposes.

It is not mostly preferred for Home IoT and Security purposes (Miettinen et al, 2017). The Sentinal IoT is trending in healthcare Networking. The Main Purpose of Implementing of the Sentianl IoT in Healthcare is secured sharing of Patient Data. It is mandatory for hospitals to secure the patient data. The Hospitals follows the Ethics of securing the patient data. Now a days the patient data are available in analogue and digital formats. The securing the patient data in digital formats needs more care and work. The fraudsters and hackers can easily access the data. Hence a secured and authenticated portal- gateway is much needed for the protection of patient data in hospitals. The Sentinal IoT provides more secure and authenticated Portal for protection of patient data by cloud computing, communication via secured gateway, secured connectivity of the devices, sensors to the hub and servers. The IoT can be implemented for transport and logistics purposes also. IoT can implemented for 3D based visualization and LiFi based networking (Sun et al, 2010).

RECENT INNOVATIONS IN BIOMEDICAL ENGINEERING USING WIRELESS SENSOR NETWORKING

The Biomedical Technology is improving day by day. The wireless sensor networking is the fast-growing technology in various fields. The usage of Internet is now become mandatory for the effective functioning of all other fields of science, Engineering & Technology. The recent advancements include development of the Biomedical Signal acquisition, Signal Processing, Biomedical Data Analytics, Imaging & Imaging solutions. The recently implemented wireless sensors are the IoT controlled Drones that consists of the various sensors for health care monitoring. Sensor like hear rate monitoring sensor (Non-contact IR type), Temperature sensors, GPS tracking device etc are placed in the sensor for monitoring the patient healthcare at emergency periods. These drones are designed for assisting Alzheimer's patients. This assistive aid is very much useful in monitoring the Alzheimer's patient health conditions. The Drones are also used in Biomedical Technology for transferring the blood required for the patients from one place to another (Kuo et al, 2010).

CONCLUSION

The Conclusion can be made that the Internet of Things are trending in recent days in all sectors. The Medical and Health care Industries are using the Internet of Things for developing smart health care systems and protocols. However, the IoT in Medical and Healthcare Technology is still challenging and required effective algorithms and secured gateway. A Computer Aided tool is required for smart decision making in IoT.

The Self Learning tools and Self Improvement tools can be included or upgraded for reducing the complexity of IoT. Genetic Algorithm, Ant Colony Algorithm can be upgraded for improving the data mining and classification. Second biggest problem that each IoT devices faces is battery – power issues and memory management. The power sources used for different devices has different specifications. The Battery used in the IoT devices should be long life and should not be drained easily and frequent changing of battery should be avoided. The Memory capacity of the devices should be more and it has to be extended when additional memory required. The data management of the IoT systems requires more memory. Hence the memory management of the IoT devices should be improved. Security issues are the most common problem faced by the IoT. The IoT used in private as well as public areas requires secured gateway for establishing the communication. The Transfer of data from and to communication link can be easily damaged by intruders or hackers, if the communication link is not secured and authenticated. The secured and authenticated gateway protocol is required for secured IoT communications.

REFERENCES

Abdullah, Ismael, Rashid, Nour, & Tarique. (2015). Real time wireless health monitoring application using mobile devices. *IJCNC, 7*(3).

Alam, Reaz, & Ali. (2012). A review of smart homes- past, present, and future. *IEEE Trans. on Systems, Man, and Cybernetics-part C. Applications and Reviews*, *42*(6), 1190–1203.

Anliker, U., Ward, J. A., Lukowicz, P., Troster, G., Dolveck, F., Baer, M., ... Vuskovic, M. (2004, December). AMON: A wearable multiparameter medical monitoring and alert system. *IEEE Transactions on Information Technology in Biomedicine, 8*(4), 415–427. doi:10.1109/TITB.2004.837888 PMID:15615032

Blount, M., Batra, V. M., Capella, A. N., Ebling, M. R., Jerome, W. F., Martin, S. M., ... Wright, S. P. (2007). Remote health-care monitoring using Personal Care Connect. *IBM Systems Journal, 46*(1), 95–113. doi:10.1147j.461.0095

Bui & Zorzi. (2011). *Health care applications: a solution based on the internet of things*. Academic Press.

Chen, Ma, Song, Lai, & Hu. (2016). *Smart Clothing: Connecting Human with Clouds and Big Data for Sustainable Health Monitoring*. Academic Press.

Chen, S., Yao, J., & Wu, Y. (2012). Analysis of the power consumption for wireless sensor network node based on Zigbee. *International Workshop on Information and Electronics Engineering*, 29, 1994-1998. 10.1016/j.proeng.2012.01.250

Coyle, S., Lau, K.-T., Moyna, N., O'Gorman, D., Diamond, D., Di Francesco, F., ... Bini, C. (2010, March). BIO- TEX—Biosensing Textiles for Personalised Healthcare Management. *IEEE Transactions on Information Technology in Biomedicine, 14*(2), 364–370. doi:10.1109/TITB.2009.2038484 PMID:20064761

Curone, D., Secco, E. L., Tognetti, A., Loriga, G., Dudnik, G., Risatti, M., ... Magenes, G. (2010, May). Smart Garments for Emergency Operators: The ProeTEX Project. *IEEE Transactions on Information Technology in Biomedicine, 14*(3), 694–701. doi:10.1109/TITB.2010.2045003 PMID:20371413

Ghosh, A. M., Halder, D., & Hossain, S. K. A. (2016). *Remote Health Monitoring System through IoT (5th ed.)*. ICIEV.

Gonzalez, J., Blanco, J. L., Galindo, C., Ortiz-de-Galisteo, A., Fernandez-Madrigal, J. A., Moreno, F. A., & Martinez, J. L. (2007). Combination of UWB and GPS for indoor-outdoor vehicle localization. *Proceedings of the 2007 IEEE International Symposium on Intelligent Signal Processing*, 1–6. 10.1109/WISP.2007.4447550

Gopalsamy, C., Park, S., Rajamanickam, R., & Jayaraman, S. (1999, September). The Wearable Motherboard™: The first generation of adaptive and responsive textile structures (ARTS) for medical applications. *Virtual Reality (Waltham Cross), 4*(3), 152–168. doi:10.1007/BF01418152

Hameed, Abdulwahabe, & Găpuú. (2016). Health Monitoring System Based on Wearable Sensors and Cloud Platform. *20th ICSTCC*.

Huq & Islam. (2010). Home area network technology assessment for demand response in smart grid environment. *Universities Power Engineering Conference*, 1-6.

Jhang, Sun, & Cui. (2010). Application and analysis of ZigBee technology for smart grid. *International conference on Computer and Information Application*, 171-174.

Kuo, W. H., Chen, Y. S., Jen, G. T., & Lu, T. W. (2010). An intelligent positioning approach: RSSI-based indoor and outdoor localization scheme in Zigbee networks. *Proceedings of the 2010 International Conference on Machine Learning and Cybernetics*, 2754–2759. 10.1109/ICMLC.2010.5580783

Lee & Lee. (2015). *The Internet of Things (iot): Applications, investments, and challenges for enterprises*. Academic Press.

Lymberis. (2005). Progress in R&D on Wearable and Implantable Biomedical Sensors for Better Healthcare and Medicine. *Proceeding of the 3rd Annual International IEEE EMBS Special Topic Conference on Microtechnologies in Medicine and Biology.*

Mahfouz, To, & Khun. (2012). Smart instruments: wireless technology invades the operating room. *IEEE Topical conference on Biomedical Wireless Technologies, Networks and Sensing Systems*, 33-36.

Michael, R. (1988, September). Biomedical Sensors in Interventional Systems: Present Problems and Future Strategies. *Proceedings of the IEEE, 76*(9).

Miettinen, M., Marchal, S., Hafeez, I., Asokan, N., Sadeghi, A.-R., & Tarkoma, S. (2017). IoT SENTINEL: Automated Device-Type Identification for Security Enforcement in IoT. *2017 IEEE 37th International Conference on Distributed Computing Systems (ICDCS).* doi:10.1109/icdcs.2017.283

Millner, H., Ebelt, R., Hoffmann, G., & Vossiek, M. (2009). Wireless 3D localization of animals for trait and behaviour analysis in indoor and outdoor areas. *Proceedings of the IEEE MTT-S International Microwave Workshop on Wireless Sensing, Local Positioning, and RFID*, 1–4.

Mohammed, Lung, Ocneanu, Thakral, Jones, & Adler. (2014). *Internet of Things: Remote Patient Monitoring Using Internet Services and Cloud Computing.* Academic Press.

Ploennigs, J., Ryssel, U., & Kabitzsch, K. (2010). Performance analysis of the EnOcean wireless sensor network protocol. *IEEE Conf. on Emerging Technologies and Factory Automation*, 1-9. 10.1109/ETFA.2010.5641313

Ren, H., Meng, M. Q.-H., & Chen, X. (2005). Physiological Information Acquisition through Wireless Biomedical Sensor Networks. *Proceedings of the 2005 IEEE International Conference on Information Acquisition.*

Schwiebert, L. (2001). Research Challenges in Wireless Networks of Biomedical Sensor. Academic Press.

Sun, L., Zhang, D., Li, B., Guo, B., & Li, S. (2010). Activity recognition on an accelerometer embedded mobile phone with varying positions and orientations. In *Ubiquitous Intelligence and Computing* (pp. 548–562). Berlin, Germany: Springer. doi:10.1007/978-3-642-16355-5_42

Tada, Y., Amano, Y., Sato, T., Saito, S., & Inoue, M. (2015, November). A smart shirt made with conductive ink and conductive foam for the measurement of electrocardiogram signals with unipolar precordial leads. *Fibers (Basel, Switzerland)*, *3*(4), 463–477. doi:10.3390/fib3040463

Wavenis Technology Homepage. (n.d.). http://www.coronis.com/ en/wavenis_technology.html

Zhang, H. (2013). Environmental Effect Removal Based Structural Health Monitoring in the Internet of Things. Academic Press.

Chapter 9
Multi–Processor Job Scheduling in High–Performance Computing (HPC) Systems

Annu Priya

https://orcid.org/0000-0001-6772-6509
Birla Institute of Technology, Mesra, India

Sudip Kumar Sahana

https://orcid.org/0000-0002-2493-3695
Birla Institute of Technology, Mesra, India

ABSTRACT

Processor scheduling is one of the thrust areas in the field of computer science. The future technologies use a huge amount of processors for execution of their tasks like huge games, programming software, and in the field of quantum computing. In hard real-time, many complex problems are solved by GPU programming. The primary concern of scheduling is to reduce the time complexity and manpower. There are several traditional techniques for processor scheduling. The performance of traditional techniques is reduced when it comes under huge processing of tasks. Most scheduling problems are NP-hard in nature. Many of the complex problems are recently solved by the GPU programming. GPU scheduling is another complex issue as it runs thousands of threads in parallel and needs to be scheduled efficiently. For such large-scale scheduling problem, the performance of state-of-the-art algorithms is very poor. It is observed that evolutionary and genetic-based algorithms exhibit better performance for large-scale combinatorial problems.

DOI: 10.4018/978-1-5225-9806-0.ch009

INTRODUCTION

The science of scheduling is not new; the first citation of scheduling was seen 3000 years ago by Egyptians. After that, 2500 years ago, Sun Tzu wrote a scheduling strategy for military perspective. In the 1980s scheduling was only used for very expensive assets that required significant training and skill for lengthy manual scheduling calculations. Changing and development continuously increase in the field of the industry by the arrival of scheduling tools with GUI. The scheduling is required in every field such as the business sector, cooperate, etc. In a computing environment, the scheduling algorithm is used to organize the data correctly. It also helps to create plans and structure the complex tasks in an efficient and reliable manner. Task scheduling is one of the tedious operations in computer science for that the scheduler requires a highly precise algorithm to reduce the time frame of the task in the waiting queue for execution. There are various stochastic process is present for processor scheduling. Processor scheduling is the way to determine which process will get the computer power to run while another process is on hold condition. The process that assigns by CPU has various states. CPU decisions may take place by considering the following four circumstances which is shown below in Figure 1 (Cera et al, 2007).

Figure 1. Process state of CPU various states

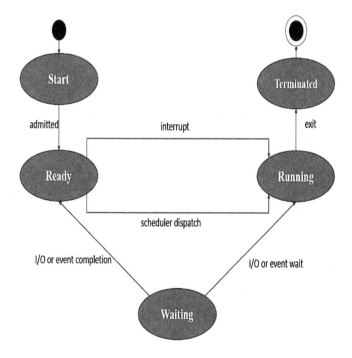

The Data Flow Diagram (DFD) represents various states of the process in CPU. The start state shows the process has been created and wait for the ready queue. In the ready state, the initialize process is waiting for the queue and assign to the processor. Running state is used some instruction set to assign the process to the processor. The process is waiting for some event to occur (such as an I/O completion or reception of a signal) in the waiting state. Finally, in the termination state, the process is executed. There are various criteria for CPU scheduling such as:

CPU Utilization: The amount of work is handled by CPU at a certain period of time. It is also used for estimating the performance of the system. The CPU utilization is varied according to the type of task because some tasks require heavy CPU time while others require less CPU time. The other name of CPU time is process time, where the amount of time is used by CPU to process the instruction of an operating system. The unit of CPU time is clock ticks or seconds. CPU utilization represents the burden on the processor in terms of percentage. It means that if there are any changes to be made in the system or otherwise it may get exhausted by capacity. Let us define CPU utilization as **U** = 100% - (Percentage of time that is spent in the idle task) then, Percentage of time in idle task calculation is given below in Eq. (1)

$$\% \, time \, in \, idle \, task = \frac{\left(Take \, the \, average \, time \, period \, of \, background \, task \, without \, load\right) * 100\%}{Avg. \, period \, of \, background \, task \, including \, some \, load}$$

$$(1)$$

Throughput: It is measured that the amount of data is transferred from one place to another or processed in a specified amount of time. Data transfer rates for disk drives and networks are measured in terms of throughput. Typically, throughputs are measured in kbps, Mbps and Gbps.

Turnaround Time (TAT): It is the time taken by the task for the submission to the completion of the process. Turnaround time is an important metric for the evaluation of the scheduling algorithm. Which is given below in Eq. (2)

$$Turnaround\_Time \, (TAT) = Compeltion\_Time \, (CT) - Arrival\_Time \, (AT) \qquad (2)$$

Waiting Time: The task has to wait after placing a request for action and before the action/service actually occurs. Waiting time is calculated based on Eq. (3)

$$Waiting\_Time \, (wt) = Turnaround\_Time \, (TAT) - Burst\_time \, (BT) \qquad (3)$$

Response time: It is the elapsed time between the request and the response of the request. It is mainly used for performance measurement. Low response times may be critical to successful computing.

CPU scheduling is dealing with the problem of the waiting queue, where it decided which process is allocated to the processor for the execution. CPU scheduling is basically two types (i) Scheduling in which a running process cannot be interrupted by any other process is called non-preemptive scheduling, (ii) Scheduling in which running process can be interrupted if a high priority process enters the queue and is allocated to the CPU is called preemptive scheduling. If scheduling an algorithm applies to the single operating system then it is called single processor scheduling. The problem with sequential processing is waiting for a job in queue and deadlock. It is very hard to schedule using a single processor. In multiprocessor scheduling there are multiple processors are available for execution of the task. The efficient processing of jobs is very complex because there are multiple numbers of CPUs are present as compared to a single processor (Kato et al, 2011). Today's CPU becomes very complex and heterogeneous with various microarchitecture. Now it is commonly design system with multicore CPU's, and graphics processing unit (GPU). Parallel computing is required to solve the hardcore complex problem. Another way of solving the multiprocessor problem is by using FPGA+CPU. Field Programmable Gate Arrays (FPGAs) extensively configure to solve multiprocessors. FPGA has different microarchitecture as compare to CPUs, GPUs, and others. CPU and GPU design are used to schedule the big tasks such as intensive game and video editing tasks associated with GPU. The key challenge of scheduling is the massive irregular process that required multiple threads for sorting.

Purpose of the Work

Scheduling is a natural phenomenon that is adopted by every human being in day to day life. In computer science, most of the effort is given for efficient task allocation. Scheduling is used in various fields such as sensor networks, irrigation, commercial and small-scale farms, automated planning of spacecraft application, scheduling of deep space network communications, class schedule, etc. Scheduling has a very long history of research and development but in the recent era, the cutting-edge techniques addressed various technical challenges inefficient allocation of the task. History of computing is very diverse in terms of the vacuum tube, to registers, to semiconductor devices. Nowadays, huge computing of task is carried out by CPU's. The proper utilization of the processor is required for computing those huge tasks. Traditional algorithms provide good results for small sets of the job but for large sets computation evolutionary-based scheduling techniques are required for better performance.

BACKGROUND

Scheduling Algorithms for a Single Processor (CPU)

CPU Scheduling is very significant for a multi-programmed operating system (OS). For CPU scheduling, the selection of an appropriate CPU distribution is required. CPU scheduling is done by short-term schedulers that decide which of process allocate to processors. CPU scheduling is considered as preemptive and non-preemptive CPU scheduling. In preemptive scheduling, the process allocated to the CPU is in waiting for the state until it terminates. But in the case of non-preemptive scheduling, the allocated process is required to release control on the occurrence of another interrupt. The main known traditional non-preemptive scheduling techniques are First to Come First Serve (FCFS), Priority and Shortest Job First (SJF) techniques. The traditional preemptive scheduling techniques are Shortest Remaining Time First (SRTF), Round Robin (RR), and Priority (preemptive).

Traditional Non-Preemptive CPU Scheduling

1. **First Come First Serve (FCFS)** is a principle derives from the concept of real-life customer service. It is an efficient, simple, and error-free process that saves valuable CPU resources. In this scheduling technique process with less burst time have to wait till the firstly arrived big process with high burst time complete their execution. This is easy to implement and understand. The disadvantage of the FCFS scheduling algorithm is it doesn't provide optimal average waiting time in parallel resource utilization. It is also not possible to obey the Convoy Effect (i.e. many processes who need a resource for a very short time period are blocked by a single process that holds resources for the very long-time period) which causes the resource utilization in a very poor manner.
2. **SJF (Shortest Job First)** scheduling algorithm is based on their arrival time which has the lowest burst time among the ready queue of processes. The priority queue is based on the smallest processor time requirement. When a job exceeds the resource is considered as aborted. The implementation of these techniques is very difficult as it provides maximum throughput and minimum average waiting and turnaround time. The disadvantage of this technique is starvation. Because of non-preemptive like FCFS, SJF is not in the time-sharing environment. When the same CPU bursts time for all processes consider it works as FCFS scheduling.

3. **Priority Scheduling** chooses the tasks based on their priority that is assigned to every process. The higher priority processes are carried out first if every process has equal priority then it works as FCFS scheduling. It can be either dynamic or static in nature. The priority of processes decision based on memory required, memory requirements, and time requirements. Following types of priority scheduling are:

    a. **Preemptive Scheduling:** It preempts the CPU when the arrived process has greater priority than the existing one.

    b. **Non- Preemptive Scheduling:** This type of scheduling add the new process on the top of the given ready queue.

Problem with priority scheduling indefinite blocking (or starvation) in the case of low priority process sometimes never execute.

Traditional Preemptive CPU Scheduling

1. **Shortest Remaining Time First (SRTF):** This technique is a preemptive version of the shortest job next schedule. It is very useful in a time-sharing environment system. In this scheduling technique, the process which has the smallest amount of time remaining until completion is selected for execution. SRTF provides optimally minimum average waiting time for the given burst time of the processes. SRTF keeps records of time elapsed by service of the running process and also handle them.

2. **Round Robin (RR)** is similar to FCFS, with the help of switching in between processes it allows preemption and allows fixed time to each process (i.e. quantum time) for execution. All the process execution requires quantum time to leave the CPU. Operating System used RR and its application to serve multiple client's requests to use the system resources. These requests handle by circular First-In-First-Out (FIFO). The order of execution is considered as a cyclic executive. These scheduling algorithm works well with single CPU scheduling to achieve their goals.

Scheduling Algorithms for Multiprocessor

Today's modern society working with smart massive parallel-connected CPUs. They work together to get the optimal solution for scheduling. Load sharing is possible in multiprocessor scheduling to handle the processors.

Evolutionary Technique

In multiprocessor scheduling processes are working independently. Multiprocessor scheduling difficult as compare to single processor scheduling. Multi-processor (CPU) evolutionary techniques are used for parallel computations for a multiprocessor. To reach the high performance of the system, parallel execution of the task is required to schedule the execution time of the task and maximize the CPU utilization. To solve multiprocessor scheduling problems evolutionary techniques provide good results. The evolutionary technique is an optimization approach to solve the high complex scheduling problems. Due to its robust and flexible nature, it becomes very popular. These techniques are able to solve optimistic tasks by using the limitation of some aspects of natural evolution. This algorithm contains basically four steps:

1. Initialization
2. Selection.
3. Crossover and Mutation
4. Termination.

These steps are shown in Figure 2.

Figure 2. Genetic Algorithm basic working steps

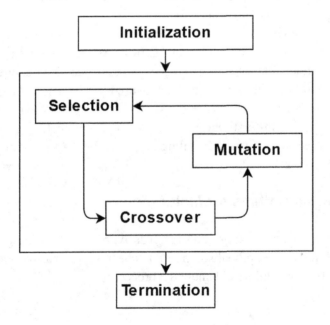

- **Initialization**: At the beginning of the algorithm initial population of the solutions is created in the initialization process. It creates random solution sets which contain a possible number of a solution to the given problem that needs to be solved.
- **Selection**: After the creation of the population the fitness function is applied for the evaluation. The fitness function is defined as a mathematical function that takes the candidate problem. It also decides to fit the solution with respect to given problem consideration. Maximization and minimization of the objective function are required to achieve the optimal solution. Complex problems required multiple objectives with their constraints.
- **Crossover and Mutation**: After selecting the top members (typically top 2, but this number can vary), these members are now used to create the next generation. Using the characteristics of the selected parents, new children are created that are a mixture of the parents' qualities. Doing this can often be difficult depending on the type of data, but typically in combinatorial problems, it is possible to mix combinations and output valid combinations from these inputs. Now, we must introduce new genetic material into the generation. If we do not do this crucial step, we will become stuck in local extrema very quickly, and will not obtain optimal results. This next step is Mutation where we do, quite simply by changing a small portion of the children such that they no longer perfectly mirror subsets of the parents' genes. Mutation typically occurs probabilistically, in that the chance of a child receiving a mutation as well as the severity of the mutation are governed by a probability distribution.
- **Termination**: Eventually the algorithm must end. There are two cases in which this usually occurs: either the algorithm has reached some maximum runtime, or the algorithm has extended to some threshold of performance. At this point, a final solution is selected and returned.

Ant Colony

Scheduling is the key approach to ensure tasks to meet their timing constraints. Traditionally, real-time systems (RTSs) are designed to perform a given set of computational tasks where each task is bounded by time constraints. Multiprocessor provides an effective computing platform for hard RTSs, the problem of scheduling RTSs tasks in a multiprocessor environment continued to be a challenging research topic. Scheduling RTSs tasks in a multiprocessor environment is to determine effective Task-to-Processor Allocation (TPA) sequence. In multiprocessor, the scheduling algorithm needs to efficiently handle TPA. Multiprocessor Tasks can be scheduled either *dynamically* or *statically*. The production scheduling problems of NP-hard, as a focus on combinatorial optimization, also become the main objects of ACO research. Ant Colony Optimization (ACO) is a highly innovative combinatorial meta-heuristics approach proposed by Italian scholars Dorigo, Maniezzo & Colorni (1990). It is inspired by ants' foraging behavior which is based on pheromone indirect communication mechanism. They proposed the first ACO algorithm-Ant System (AS) and tested it by solving the Traveling Salesman Problem (TSP). ACO is a constructive, population-based meta-heuristics algorithm. It has advantages as robustness, which demonstrates its excellent performance and great potential while applied to solve many complex optimization problems. Figure 3. Shows that the basic flowchart of ant colony optimization.

Figure 3. Basic flowchart of ant colony optimization

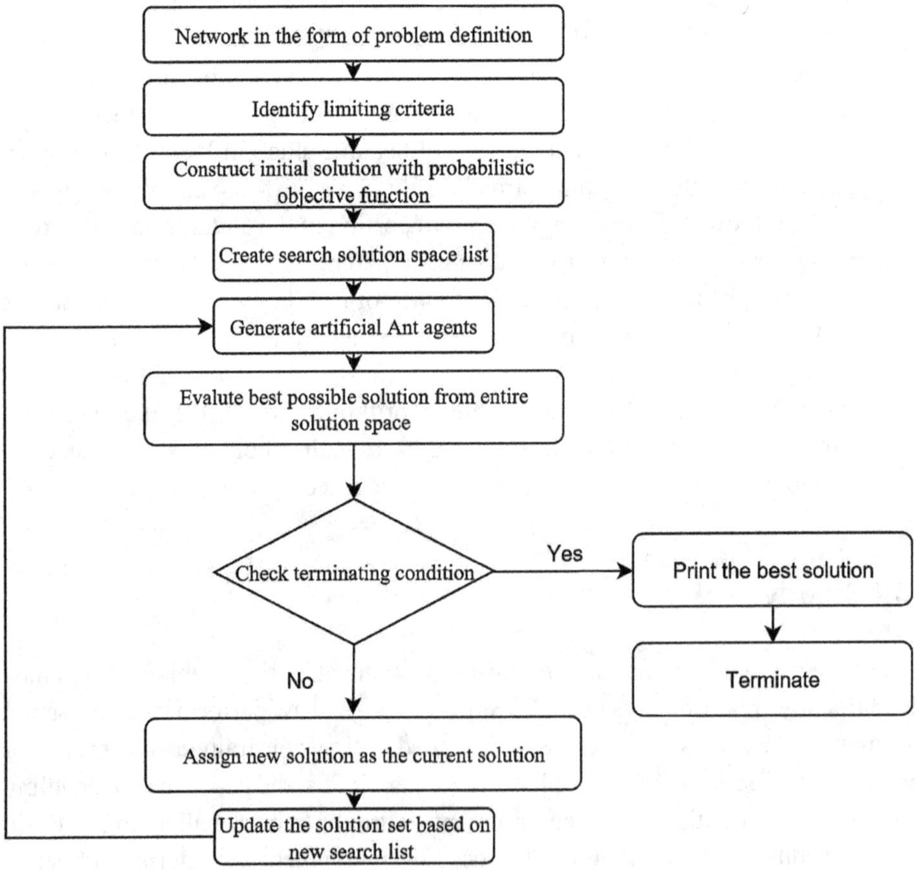

The production scheduling problems are NP-hard in nature, its focus on combinatorial optimization. This algorithm contains basically five steps:

- **Initial Population**: The population of ants is uniformly distributed across the nodes of the graph. The distribution of ants across the node is very important because all nodes to have an equal chance as the starting point. The starting node is considered as an optimal starting node.
- **Ant Movement:** The ant movement is based on the probability equation. Eq. 4 given below used to identify the next edge taken by the ant to complete a tour.

$$P = \frac{\tau(r,u)^{\alpha} * \eta(r,u)^{\beta}}{\sum_{k}(r,u)^{\alpha} * \eta(r,u)^{\beta}}
\qquad (4)$$

Where,

$\tau(r,u)$ – Intensity of the pheromone

(r,u) – The edge between the nodes r and u.

$\eta(r,u)$ – the desirability of state transition r, u.

α – weight for the pheromone

β – Weight for the heuristic

- **Pheromone Calculation:** The pheromone trail is calculated as follows in Eq. 5. At any particular time instance ant can visit the node and once the ant tour is completed length of the entire tour is computed. It is some of all distances traveled by the ant the equation given below the amount of pheromone left on each edge of the tour for ant 'k'.

$$\Delta\tau_{ij}^{k}(t) = \frac{Q}{L^{k}(t)}
\qquad (5)$$

Where,

Q – Constant.

$L^{k}(t)$ – Tour length of the ant.

The pheromone increase along with edge tour is calculated by the Eq. 6 given below

$$\tau_{ij}\left(t\right) = t_{ij}\left(t\right) + \left(\tau_{ij}^{k}\left(t\right) * \rho\right)$$ (6)

Where, ρ is the constant value lies between $[0, 1]$.

- **Pheromone Evaporation** takes place through all the edge of the nodes. Initially, each edge probability is taken as same. We can calculate evaporation by using Eq. 7 given below.

$$\tau_{ij}\left(t\right) = \tau_{ij}\left(t\right) * \left(1 - \rho\right)$$ (7)

ρ is constant.

Particle Swarm Optimization (PSO)

Particle Swarm Optimization (PSO) was introduced by Russell Eberhart and James Kennedy in 1995. It is inspired by the flocking of birds and fish. It works well on the number of iterations, and the group of variables has its values adjusted closer to the target at any given moment. This algorithm keeps track of three global variables:

- Target value or condition
- Global best (gBest) value indicating which particle's data is currently closest to the target
- Stopping value indicates the algorithm should stop if the target isn't found

Each particle consists of:

- Data representing a possible solution
- A velocity value indicating how much the data can be changed
- A personal best (pBest) value indicating the closest the particle's data has ever come to the target.

Figure 4 shows Basic Flow Chart of particle swarm optimization. The particles' data could be considered anything. These would be coordinates of each bird. The gBest of bird coordinates is nearer to food and each bird would try to move closer. The individual coordinates of each bird would try to move closer to the coordinates of the bird which is closer to the food's coordinates (gBest). The data would be manipulated until the pattern matches the target pattern. Based on how far an individual's data from the target velocity value is calculated.

Figure 4. Basic flow chart of particle swarm optimization

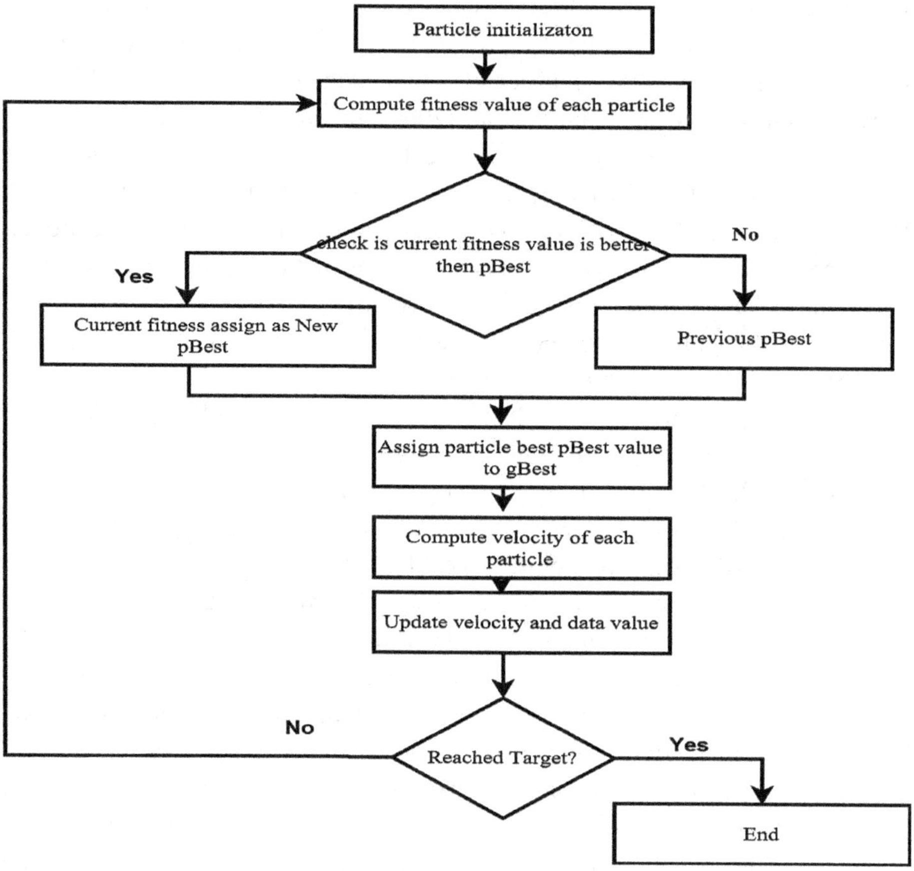

LITERATURE REVIEW

Many researchers have proposed several techniques in the field of scheduling. According to Z. Zhou et al, (2016), a scheduling technique is used to simulate annealing of resource on a high-performance computing environment. Queue based FCFS with backfilling technique simulate workload on the high-performance computing environment. These techniques reduced the waiting time of process on the system by 40% and also reduced response time by 30% of the process. It has the ability to solve the difficult scheduling problem online. B. S. Yoo & C. R. Das (2001) proposed a novel fast efficient processor allocation technique that works for messy interconnected multicomputer which is based on stack allocation to locate free sub mesh for the process using simple coordination and spatial subtraction to prevent deadlock and also reduce response time by minimizing the queue delay for the process. Hsiu-Jay Ho, & Wei-Ming Lin. (2004) addressed scheduling technique by self-adjustment between two orders in real-time according to the size and variance among the process in the process queue. The advantage of this method is to preserve significantly diminishing the chance of blocking and starvation situation. Ding Shun-li et al, (2004), demonstrate a model and agent structure-based processor management that follows the adoption scheme of the local processor. FCFS scheduling technique achieves the task scheduling goals. W. Leinberger et al, (1999), developed a heuristic-based technique using process selection for resource balancing that supports the construction of the global K-resource scheduling technique. This technique achieves high average response time up to 50% over existing scheduling techniques such as FCFS with the First-Fit backfill. P. K. Saraswat, & P. Gupta, (2006), designed and implemented a scheduling technique to enhance the performance of MMOs (Multimedia Operating System) in a batch process. M. C. Cera, et. al. (2007), was developed a scheduler that is implemented by using MPI-2. That support for parallel programming it established during the execution of tasks, on a processor that a process runs with priority. Chang Wen-Chih et. al. (2008) designed a web-based card game through which the learner can access the game by using the network to manage the process of different events and resources. Network help to break limits of time and space constraints. M. Vestias, & H. Neto (2014), compare the trends of FPGA, General Purpose Graphics Unit (GPGU) architecture for high-performance computing and also did a survey on these platforms in the field of the different scientific application domain. F. Chi et. al. (2014) proposed a cloud gaming design technique i.e. fine-grained scheduling in the cloud (FGCG) with fine-grained scheduling that improves resource utilization as on heterogeneous CPU-GPU cluster as compared to the existing cloud gaming system. S. Kato (2011) represents the Graphics processing unit (GPU) commonly used for parallel computing to speed up the execution of the time graph for real-time GPU scheduler to protect GPU workload from the performance interface. This graph also adopts an event-driven based model that helps to synchronize the GPU and CPU. This graph supports priority-based scheduling policies to address the tradeoff between throughput and response time. They used OpenGL graphics to demonstrate a time graph. Okamoto, S. et.al (1994) describe a new parallel algorithm which is basically parallelization of the usual branch-and-bound method for flow-shop problems. It takes advantage of all search methods to keep the high efficiency of parallel processing. This algorithm is implemented on nCUBE2 and LUNA88k2 processors. The author Allahverdi et al, (2008) reviewed the scheduling problem with setup times and also provide literature models which cover more than 300 papers which classify scheduling problem based on batching and non-batching. After that, it further categorized according to shop environments. The author Fernandez-Viagas et.al (2014) present a new tie-breaking mechanism. It is based on the estimation of the idle times of the different subsequences and computational results showed that the proposed mechanism outperforms the existing ones. S.-W. Lin et al, (2013) developed a hybrid artificial bee colony (HABC) algorithm to minimize makespan for flow shop problems with multi-processor tasks. The author LIU, C. L et.al (2002) studied problems of single processor scheduling with multiprogramming. They showed high processor utilization can be achieved by assigning dynamic priorities based on their current deadlines. R. Ruiz, & C Maroto, (2005), is reviewed the comparative evaluation of heuristics and metaheuristics for permutation flow shop problem with the makespan criterion and also proposed a comparison of 25 methods including classical Johnson's algorithm or dispatching rules to the most recent metaheuristics, tabu search, simulated annealing, genetic algorithms, iterated local search and hybrid techniques. They used the Taillard benchmark for testing. Tan, K.-C. (2000) Considered a single machine scheduling problem to minimize total tardiness in sequence-dependent setup environment and also deal with the class of difficult scheduling problems which are considered by the researcher as well as practitioners. They suggested that simulated annealing and random-start pairwise interchange are viable solution techniques for tardiness objective with sequence-dependent setup times. Ying, K.-C., & Lin, S.-W. (2018). Tried to solve the distributed hybrid flowshop scheduling problem with multiprocessor tasks on the distributed system by using self-tuning iterated greed (SIG) technique and also present an adaptive cocktail decoding mechanism to minimize the makespan. X. Yuming, L.Kenli (2012) *et.al* examine the task scheduling problems for distributed systems as well as parallel heterogeneous computing systems and also suggested multiple priorities queuing genetic scheduling. They used the HEFT technique to search an optimal solution for mapping tasks on to the processor. lotfii, H . (2010) *et.al* used a new coarse-grain genetic technique to schedule the tasks by reducing the solution search space to prevent the speedy convergence between the subpopulation and also this technique helped to reduce the makespan. M Akbari et al, (2017) developed a genetic-based scheduling technique i.e. a meta-heuristic method that works for static task scheduling in heterogeneous computing environment processors. This technique minimizes processor execution time to achieve their objectives. The advantage of this method is to minimize processor execution time to achieve their objectives. The author J.-J Hwang et al, (1988) tested scheduling technique speedup issues in multiprocessors and also compute the network for fast execution of model the analyzed the system based on three important factors: communication overhead of the processor, scheduling, and the application method. This model provides a brief idea about the integrated effects of these factors. A Majd et al, (2017) proposed a technique that is inspired by the biological behavior method to find the near-optimal solution for scheduling. Which guarantees performance for multiple applications on a multiprocessor system. Ahmad, I., & Dhodhi, (1996) Used a technique based on the problem space genetic algorithm that reduced response-time on to homogeneous multiprocessor system. The main advantage of this technique is the combination of a genetic algorithm with a list scheduling heuristic approach to find the efficient large solution for the best possible solution in processor time. It provides an average 3.6% improvement in response time as compared to CP/MISF Methods.

CASE STUDY 1: GAME SCHEDULING

Game Scheduling on CPU

Games are the software designed by using the concept of operating systems. The online games will run through the network by using different events and resources to manage the process. According to W. Zhang (2018), games provide entertainment and interaction interface to the users. There are lots of research works have been done in the field of game scheduling. The game can be in the form of anything such as multimedia, animation, physical cards, and many others. For online games, CPU scheduling is done on the basis of the operating system scheduler. Let us assume that, if we want to play the game online what are the steps we have to follow.

Steps for a web-based card game:

1. Process lifecycle drew with five status i.e. read, ready, etc.
2. First shuffling all process cards.
3. Event cards, priority cards, and resource cards shuffle together.
4. Decide the sequence of playing.

There is a number of rounds to play the game and each round is separated by the following steps:

1. Cards drawn by the first player each player has five cards in each round of the game.
2. The player has to decide to move forward to the next stage on the map.
3. Playing cards depends on the stage.
4. Discard out of work card.
5. The player has five cards of discarded cards in one round will not consider.

There are four kinds of cards in this game:

1. Process card.
2. Resource card.

3. Event card.
4. Priority card.

Process card is consists of two types (i) I/O bound process card and (ii) CPU bound process card. Process cards help us to record the CPU time, I/O time and also schedule priority. Resource card includes the I/O resource and memory resource. Event card includes the event situation such as starvation, deadlock and convoy situation. Priority card is selected by different types of CPU scheduling techniques. Such as Round-Robin, Shortest job first, Priority scheduling FCFS. Here the priority used in CPU scheduling player uses priority card and after that enter next status. Flowchart of the operating card game based on the web learning environment is given below in Figure 5.

Figure 5. Game scheduling process steps

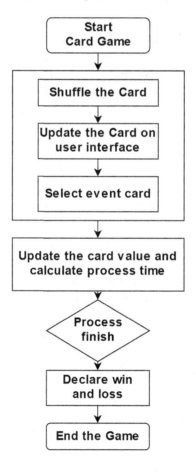

The game scheduling steps:

1. **Game Start:** Initial stage of the game to play.
2. **Build Cards:** The operating system will generate the score and build learner's cards.
3. **Update User Interface:** For random card distribution of game operating system update user interface.
4. **Card Selection and Play by the Learner**: Learner play cards with rules.
5. Dynamically update information about process time and status.
6. Checking process status that is finished or not.
7. Find out defeat or victory.
8. The game ended if it is the last one.

This technique established an operation on the operating system to process games and also assist practical experience. Another form of game scheduling problem is the N-Queen problem. Where it schedule the chess moves. In chess, the queen has to move as far as she pleases in both horizontally, vertically, and diagonally. A chessboard considers being an 8×8 matrix board. In standard 8×8 Queen's problem, it is used to place queens on an ordinary chessboard so that none of them can hit any other in one move. Besides being an entertaining puzzle this is very interesting for the kids. It also considers as a teaching tool for the higher level student to create a strategy and defeat the enemy. It is also great for the programmer to solve the exercises. In chess, it turns out that there are 12 essentially distinct solutions. (Two solutions are not essentially distinct if you can obtain one from another by rotating your chessboard, or placing it in front of a mirror, or combining these two operations). Even though the solution shown here looks pretty natural and straightforward, it is not that simple to find any others, or even this one if I hadn't displayed it here. An obvious modification of the 8 by 8 problem is to consider an N by N "chessboard" and ask if one can place N-queens on such board. It's pretty easy to see that this is impossible if 'N' is 2 or 3, and it's reasonably straightforward to find solutions when N is 4, 5, 6, or 7. The problem begins to become difficult for manual solution precisely when N is 8, in fact, this number coincidentally equals the dimensions of an ordinary chessboard that has contributed to the popularity of the problem.

Game Scheduling on CPU+GPU

The Graphics Processing Unit (GPU) is widely used for parallel computing of data and graphics. GPU provides a multi-tasking environment for the application. GPU provides a livelier interface to the user it provides 3-Dimensionals windows, high-quality graphics, and smooth transition these are very difficult to implement in CPU.

To provide high-quality gaming service to mobile device cloud gaming is widely used. To maximize the resource utilization on heterogeneous CPU-GPU clusters on cloud gaming. Cloud gaming provides the power of a GPU gaming CPU to any other device these are very user-friendly, less hassle and simple to use. In this cluster, the game workload decomposes into a small independent task that is dispatch to different machines. To provide good quality of game resource scheduling at the cloud becomes critical because of the cloud gaming system either streaming or graphics streaming. To design a scheduling algorithm on cloud gaming consider two types of resources i.e. CPU and GPU. Suppose, there is a '*j*' tasks require resource machine '*i*' at a given time '*t*' slot for every resource. Then resource allocation is given by Eq. 8,

$$Resource = x_{ij}^r(t) \tag{8}$$

Whereas, i.e. r $\in$ {CPU, GPU}
And the resource volume on the system is given by Eq. 9.

$$Resource\_Volume = v_i^r(t) \tag{9}$$

The total capacity of resources is given by the Eq. 10.

$$Resource\_Capacity = c_j^r \tag{10}$$

The maximum utility is achieved when the resources are fully utilized. The utility function is used to achieve the maximum value given below in Eq. 11.

$$Max = \frac{\sum_{i=0}^{n} \sum_r \left\{ \left[\left(\frac{u_i^r(t)}{c_i^r} \right) \right]^{k_r} \right\}}{n} \tag{11}$$

Where,

n = total number of server

K_r = positive integer for resource preference

According to W. Zhang et al, (2018), fine-grained scheduling techniques are used to increase resource utilization and decomposes workload to other physical machines that have ideal resources. This technique follows the client-server paradigm of the cloud. For cloud gaming, there are mainly three-component at the server side (i) Master, (ii) Worker, and (iii) Manager. Master usually deployed along with their game application in virtual machines and worker-run on the physical server side. Game operation sends by the client to master that generate tasks and also assign them to a worker with the help of a worker it generates video stream for a client connected through the cloud. The master always assigns with the worker to manage and collect server status and it also monitors the cluster. The dispatch management commands are triggered when the scheduling strategy is activated on the server.

CASE STUDY 2: SCHEDULING ALGORITHM USING CUDA

Here, in this section, we have discussed a processor scheduling technique using CPU and GPU. We already saw that the operating system technique is to work on a single thread. Now the above single thread scheduling technique in GPU environment using Compute Unified Device Architecture (CUDA). It is basically a general-purpose computing on graphics processing units (GPU) architecture which is developed by NVIDIA. It supports the extension of C, C++, FORTRAN, and Python and C#. In recent years parallel programming becomes increasingly important to speed up the processor. The CPU scheduling algorithm FCFS, SJF, RR, PBS implemented in a single thread CPU environment. The basic code implementation process of scheduling algorithm is given below:

1.   Memory allocation on CPU.
2.   Allocate memory on GPU the same as CPU using the function "CudaMalloc".
3.   Insert data as input in memory allocated in CPU.
4.   CPU data will copy to GPU memory using function CudaMemCpy.
5.   By using kernel calls processing performed in GPU. It supports parallelism.
6.   Final data copy to the GPU to the CPU.
7.   Release GPU memory.

When running the FCFS, SJF, and RR parallel in the GPU environment it is found that the execution time is lesser for FCFS, SJF, and RR single thread scheduling technique in CPU. In Table. 1, it shows that there are 3 processes taken to scheduling and burst time taken accordingly. So the total waiting time is calculated using Eq. 12. Here arrival times of the processes are zero so total waiting time (T) is equal to total burst time (BT).

Total Waiting time (T) = Total Burst time (BT)   (12)

Table 1. FCFS Scheduling technique in CUDA

Process No.	Burst Time(Sec)	Arrival Time(Sec)
1	4	0
2	3	0
3	6	0

Total waiting time = 13.0 sec
Execution time taken by processor = 0.0000972 sec

Table 2, represents the FCFS Execution time taken by the processor using a single thread CPU scheduling technique environment taken more time (sec) than then FCFS GPU scheduling technique.

Table 2. FCFS Scheduling technique in CPU

Process No	Burst Time (Sec)	Arrival Time(Sec)
1	4	0
2	3	0
3	6	0

Total waiting time (T) = 13.0 sec
Execution time taken by processor = 6.666667 sec

SJF Scheduling Technique in GPU

In Table 3, represents the Shortest job first scheduling initially taken burst time p1=3, p2=4, p3= 5, p4=3. So the shortest job is to assign to the processor in descending orders.

Table 3. SJF Scheduling technique in CUDA

Process No.	Burst Time(Sec)	Waiting Time (Sec)	Turnaround(Sec)
p1	3	0	3
p4	3	3	6
p2	4	6	10
p3	5	10	15

Average waiting time (T) = 4.75sec
Turnaround Time = 8.50sec
Execution time taken by processor = 0.0000783sec

SJF Scheduling Technique in CPU

In Table 4, represents the SJF Execution time is taken by the processor using a single thread CPU scheduling technique environment taken more time (sec) then SJF GPU scheduling technique.

Table 4. SJF Scheduling technique in CPU

Process No.	Burst Time (Sec)	Waiting Time (Sec)	Turnaround (Sec)
p1	3	0	3
p4	3	3	6
p2	4	6	10
p3	5	10	15

Average waiting time (T) = 4.75sec
Turnaround Time = 8.50sec
Execution time taken by processor =0.001sec

RR Scheduling Technique in GPU

Table 5, represents the RR Execution time (sec) taken by the processor using a single thread GPU scheduling technique using CUDA.

Table 5. RR Scheduling technique in CUDA

Process No.	Burst Time (Sec)	Waiting Time (Sec)
P1	3	0
P2	4	11
P3	5	12
P4	2	9
P5	6	14

Total waiting time = 46sec
The total average waiting time= 9.2sec
Execution time is taken by processor =0.0001498sec

RR Scheduling Technique in CPU

Table 6, represents the RR Execution time (sec) taken by the processor using a single thread CPU scheduling technique is less average waiting time than the RR GPU scheduling technique. From the above results, it is found that the GPU scheduling technique provides a better result than single thread CPU scheduling.

Table 6. RR Scheduling technique in CPU

Process No.	Burst Time (Sec)	Waiting Time (Sec)
P1	2	0
P2	4	10
P3	5	11
P4	2	8
P5	6	13

Total waiting time = 42sec
Total average waiting time= 8.4sec
Execution time taken by processor =0.002000sec

Figure 6. Abstraction layer of MPI Architecture

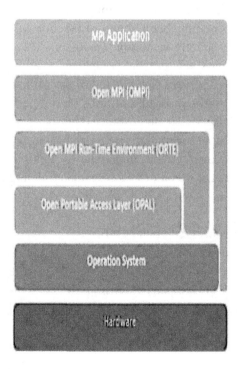

CASE STUDY 3: MULTIPROCESSOR SCHEDULING

Like CPU-GPU, Intel provides the CPU and Field Programmable Gate Array (FPGA) chips onto one package. GPU and FPGA can be used in two ways offload and inline. First coming data goes through CPU before moved to FPGA processing that is called offload. Inline means coming data goes directly 'in' and 'out' for FPGA processing and CPU has to stay out. FPGA perform is better than GPU. CPU and FPGA processors provide very high processing capacity. These computing architecture come up with High-Performance Computing (HPC). In the field of computational science engineering and natural science and many others, they required very high computer simulation to obtain scientific results and they are too difficult to solve. HPC also called a supercomputer with high processing capacity, speed calculation. Early days (around 1970) super-computer use only a few CPUs. In the year 1990s machines with thousands of CPUs appear. By the end of the 20th century massively parallel supercomputer has been created. To work on that system we need a study about the parallel programming language which is important in the field of computer science development. In the real world, parallelization is very important especially, when we have an asynchronous event. Parallelism is an important abstraction for software designing and computation. Parallel processing includes ideas from theoretical computer science, computer architecture, programming languages, algorithms and application areas such as computer graphics (GUI) and artificial intelligence (AI). Processor scheduling techniques are implemented with the Message passing interface (MPI). MPI is nothing but a library of function calls that coordinate with programs and run independently on multiple processors. These programs run parallel on multiple nodes of massively parallel computers. It allows flexible division of work among processes. The very first version of the MPI standard, MPI-1.0, was published in 1994. MPI-2.0, a set of additions on top of MPI-1, was completed in 1996. OpenMPI provides an open-source high-performance implementation of MPI. It works on Single Instruction stream and Multiple Data Stream (SIMD) class that includes one instructional unit issue to multiple processing elements (PEs). It also represents the union of four research/academic for open source MPI implementations such as:

1. LAM (Local Area Multicomputer)/MPI,
2. LA (Los Alamos)/MPI,
3. FT-MPI (Fault-Tolerant MPI) and
4. PACX-MPI (Parallel Computer extension MPI).

It has mainly three project layers of abstraction given in Figure 6. That shows the architecture view of Open MPI which has mainly three layers: OPAL, ORTE, and OMPI.

- **Open Portable Access Layer (OPAL):** Open MPI's core portability between different operating systems and basic utilities.
- **Open MPI Run-Time Environment (ORTE):** Launch, monitor individual processes, and group individual processes in to "jobs"
- **Open MPI (OMPI):** Public MPI API and only one exposed to applications.

When there are multiple numbers of processors available for scheduling and it is very difficult to schedule by using the traditional algorithm. But for this type of case evolutionary scheduling techniques required that are inspired by different families of biology. Such as a Genetic algorithm (GA), Ant Colony Optimization (ACO), and Particle Swarm Optimization (PSO), etc. Evolutionary techniques required huge execution time to schedule multi-processors problems. This issue parallel programming support to minimize the execution time on the High-performance Computing environment. Let's our study is about how the process allocation is done in HPC environment. Here, we have implemented a matrix multiplication algorithm using MPI in the HPC environment and also FCFS using MPI on a parallel platform of the HPC environment. In terms of mathematics, a matrix product is basically a binary operator that produces a matrix from two matrices having a number of rows and columns. Here we are taking two matrices for multiplication is shown in Eq. 13 and Eq. 14.

$$A = A [i, k] \tag{13}$$

Whereas,
    i= number of a row of matrix A and
    k= number of column of matrix A

$$B = B [k, j] \tag{14}$$

Whereas,
    j = number of column of matrix B and
    k= number of a row of matrix B

To do multiplication the condition is to be satisfied: a number of columns of matrix A are equal to the number of rows of matrix B.

Algorithm for Matrix Multiplication

Step 1: To multiply two matrixes sufficient and necessary condition is a number of columns in matrix A = number of rows in matrix B.
Step 2: Apply Loop condition for each row in matrix A.
Step 3: Apply Loop for each column in matrix B and initialize output matrix C to 0.
Step 4: This loop will run for each row of matrix A.
Step 5: this Loop will run for each column in matrix A.
Step 6: Multiply A [i, k] to B [k, j] and add this value to C [i, j].
Step 7: Return output matrix C.

MATRIX MULTIPLICATION ON SINGLE PROCESSOR

Here in Eq. 15 and Eq. 16, we see the basic steps for Matrix multiplication that is performed on two matrices A, B of dimension ranged from [100×100]. Sequential multiplication runs on the single operating system. It used a ready queue of the processes for scheduling. After the multiplication value stored in C which has 'm' number of rows and 'p' number of columns. The complexity of this algorithm is $O(n^2)$.

$$A_{m \times n} = \begin{vmatrix} a_{11} & a_{12} & . & . & a_{1n} \\ a_{21} & a_{22} & . & . & a_{2n} \\ . & . & . & . & . \\ . & . & . & . & . \\ a_{m1} & a_{m2} & . & . & a_{mn} \end{vmatrix} \tag{15}$$

$$B_{n \times p} = \begin{vmatrix} b_{11} & b_{12} & . & . & b_{1p} \\ b_{21} & b_{22} & . & . & b_{2p} \\ . & . & . & . & . \\ . & . & . & . & . \\ b_{n1} & b_{n2} & & & b_{np} \end{vmatrix} \tag{16}$$

C = A*B. C will have m rows and p columns.

Sequential brute force algorithm takes O (m*n*p) time

Test Parameters for Single Processor

- Sequential matrix multiplication runs on a single processor/core.
- A number of rows and columns were equal. Both matrices had the same dimensions
- Matrix dimensions ranged from 100 to 100.
- The running time is for the computation part only. It does not include the time for distributing data to and gathering data from the nodes that do the computation.
- I used the 8-core nodes with 64 GB of RAM. Only 1 MPI process was used.

Matrix Multiplication on Multiprocessor (HPC)

In recent years the high-performance computing system relies heavily on parallel processing. The principles of parallelism are to increase the performance of the system and also incorporate it into the programming language. Such type of language is known as parallel programming. Parallel programming language explicitly in the feature. In the modern world, we need to go beyond the availability of sequential programming languages. Matrix multiplication is a highly structure problem which is needed to be run for the parallel processor environment. Scheduling of matrix multiplication uses the concept of master and slave model. It is found that the master and slave model is a very important application. In this paradigm, it involves two sets of processors one is acting as a master which is responsible for pre and post-processing of work orders and another one is acting as a salve which is the responsible actual execution of the orders. Figure 7, represent the one processor as master node which has processing of work order for matrix multiplication of A and B. It would partition the matrix multiplication problem into Q (Q = Number of slave processor) each of slave node involving submatrix of A and B. After that these sub-matrix pairs together with multiplication code that would be transmitted to the 'p' slaves and the salves would execute the code once they received data for multiplication and code. It would transmit the product of the submatrix back to the master node. Master node store the received sub-matrix into 'c'.

The Eq. 17 and Eq. 18, is used on each node to multiply the portion of A with the matrix B. The master node (MPI process with rank 0) generates random matrix data allocates m/Q rows from matrix A to each node. Each node also gets the entire matrix B. The master node also participates in the computation.

Figure 7. Matrix multiplication execution process on HPC using MPI

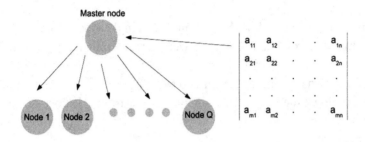

$$A_{\frac{m}{Q} \times n} = \begin{vmatrix} a_{11} & a_{12} & . & . & a_{1n} \\ a_{21} & a_{22} & . & . & a_{2n} \\ . & . & . & . & . \\ . & . & . & . & . \\ a_{\frac{m}{Q},1} & a_{\frac{m}{Q},2} & . & . & a_{\frac{m}{Q},n} \end{vmatrix} \tag{17}$$

$$B_{n \times p} = \begin{vmatrix} b_{11} & b_{12} & . & . & b_{1p} \\ b_{21} & b_{22} & . & . & b_{2p} \\ . & . & . & . & . \\ . & . & . & . & . \\ b_{n1} & b_{n2} & & & b_{np} \end{vmatrix} \tag{18}$$

Each node 'i' calculates the rows from $(i-1)*(m/Q) + 1$ to $i*(m/Q)$ of the matrix C. Basically, different portions of the matrix are calculated in parallel. The calculated results are sent back to the master node which can store the final result in a file. The complexity of this algorithm is O(n).

Test Parameters for Parallel Programming Using MPI

- Matrix dimensions ranged from 100 to 100.
- A number of rows and columns were equal. Both matrices had the same dimensions
- No. of processor used were 5, 10, 15, 25.
- The 8-core nodes used with 64 GB of RAM.

Figure 8. Average Execution time for parallel processing on a different number of processors

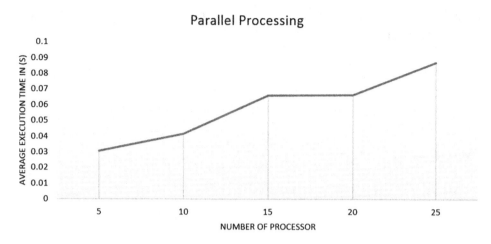

Figure 8, represents the running time of each matrix block. The computation part only including communication between nodes for computation. It does not include the time for distributing data or gathering of data from the nodes that do for computation.

FCFS Scheduling on Multiprocessor (HPC)

FCFS is a preemptive scheduling algorithm that runs on an HPC environment. The step by step procedure for processor scheduling using MPI on HPC is given as below. FCFS Algorithm using MPI is as follows:

Algorithm for FCFS on HPC

Step 1: Enter the number of processors.
Step 2: Enter the burst time (*bt*).
Step 3: Apply MPI
Step 4: Assign waiting time (*wt*) for all the processors.
Step 5: Waiting time for process '*1*' will be '*0*' i.e. *wt* [0] = 0.
Step 6: The manager sends tp p-1 number X_1, X_2... X_{p-1} to the workers.
Step 7: The worker receives the ith worker X_i in *f*. The manager copies X_0 to *f*: *f*=X_0.
   Eq. 19, represent every node process

$$f \rightarrow wt~[f] = bt~[f\text{-}1] + wt~[f\text{-}1] \tag{19}$$

Step 8: Every worker sends 'f' to the manager. The manager receives X_i from the ith worker, $i = 1, 2...$ p-1. Manager copies 'f' to X_0: $X_0=f$

Step 9: Print the result on every processor. The Eq. 20, represents the calculation of turnaround time for all processes.

$$Turnaround\_time = [wt + bt] \tag{20}$$

Step 10: The Eq. 21, shows the calculation of average waiting time.

$$Average\_waiting\_time = \frac{total\_waiting\_time}{no\_of\_processes} \tag{21}$$

Step 11: Similarly, Eq. 22 is used to find the average turnaround time.

$$Average\_turnaround\_time = \frac{total\_turn\_around\_time}{no\_of\_processes} \tag{22}$$

The result evidence that running FCFS on a single thread on CPU doesn't perform well as compare to FCFS running on the MPI scheduling technique on the HPC environment in the given Figure 9. FCFS using MPI taken less execution time for processor scheduling. It is performed for 5 different processors and the result is present in between execution time and a number of processors.

Figure 9. Execution Time(s) Comparison of FCFS scheduling technique on CPU and FCFS using MPI on CPU+FPGA

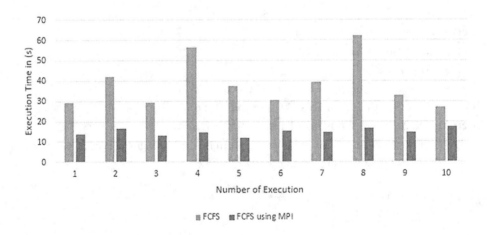

Genetic Algorithm on Multiprocessor (HPC)

We already discussed several ways of scheduling in a multi-processor system. But in the HPC environment, we apply evolution techniques to get a better result. As an example, we have taken the genetic algorithm technique for scheduling in an HPC environment. Here are some of the basic steps and fitness function which is used in the genetic algorithm.

Genetic Algorithm

According to A. Priya (2018) and K. Sinha et. al (2018) processor scheduling in an HPC environment is achieved by using the MPI package, which works as a master and salve model. The processor schedules working steps given in figure 10 using the evolutionary algorithm in the HPC environment using MPI is as follows: As a starting, we take an HPC system in ideal condition and all the jobs are coming at the Time (T=0 sec). To start the simulation and take a job in the input queue. The queue consists of Job (J) where (J=1, 2, ..., n) and execution time (Et). The next step is to apply the fitness function. It is an evaluation technique that is applied to the job, to evaluate the sequence of execution. As a result, we get a new sequence for evaluation. Here we have taken sphere function for the fitness evaluation. So, our next step is to check the stopping condition. If the stopping criteria are satisfied then stop the simulation and if not then go to the selection process.

Selection is the process where we remove the unwanted data and collect those data which is better for creating a new generation. After selection, we go for a crossover where two parents Job creates new child Job. The mutation is the other process which shows the one-bit change in the 1000 process. The mutation probability is taken in between randomize values from [0 to 1] i.e. {0.25, 0.5.0.75, 1}. The mutation operator is done by exchanging some genes in chromosomes. After that, it will for the fitness evaluation. This process is running in the loop up to stopping criteria is not achieved. Once it's complete the simulation it sends the jobs to the MPI queue. The working of MPI is to distribute the Job with the slave node (processors). Each processor executes the job parallels on their cores. Once the execution is complete then calculate the average waiting time and execution time for each processor. Stop the simulation process and generate the graph of execution time.

Figure 10. Flowchart of Genetic Algorithm on Multiprocessor (HPC)

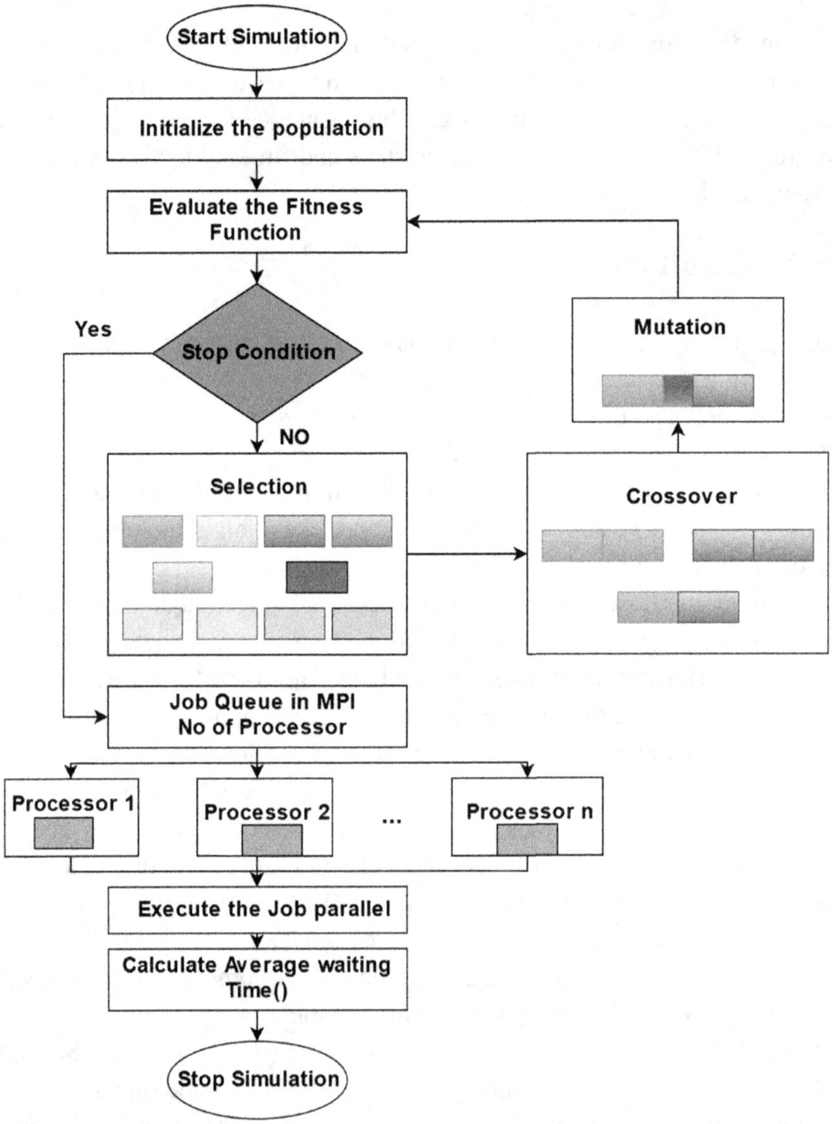

The advantages of the genetic algorithm are:

1. Supports Parallelism
2. GA provides wider Solution space.
3. Easley help to discover global optimum
4. The multi-objective function considers solving the problem.

5. Easily modified for different problems.
6. Good for multi-modal problems Returns a suite of solutions.
7. Very robust.
8. They perform very well for large-scale optimization problems.

The disadvantage of the genetic algorithm is:

1. The problem of identifying fitness function.
2. Definition of representation for the problem.
3. The problem with choosing the various parameters like the size of the population, mutation rate, crossover rate, the selection method, and its strength.
4. Cannot easily incorporate problem specific information.
5. No effective terminator.
6. Have trouble finding the exact fitness function evaluations.

Table 7, shows the computational time comparison of GA and proposed GA using MPI on an HPC environment for Taillard (Mohammad et al, 2009; Carlos et al, 2017) benchmark set. Which contains a large number of randomly generated problems of different size (group) of $\left(n \times p \right)$. Where 'n' is a number of jobs and 'p' is a number of processors which is used the execution of jobs. In the case of GA-MPI for 500 iteration simulation, it is shown that the minimum time about 1.64 sec for (20 jobs $\times$ 5 processor) and the maximum time 29.37 sec for (500 jobs $\times$ 20 processors). When we increase the iteration rate of 1000 and 2000. The minimum value is 2.64 and 5.12 sec respectively to the (20 jobs $\times$ 5 processor) set and the maximum value is 58.617 and 110.436 sec for (500 jobs $\times$ 20 processors) set. The computational complexity of the proposed technique is O (n^2p). Figure 11, shows that the execution time comparison of the algorithms. We found that GA_MPI takes less execution time as compared to the GA approach.

DISCUSSION AND CONCLUSION

The simulation is performed on the system consists of Master Node- 2, and Intel Xeon E5-2630 V3 processors. Which has the clock speed of 2.4GHz with 8 cores and 64 GB memory, 2*1 TB HDD, 500 GB Disk capacity for different data set of the benchmark on the different number of processors. There are different type's revolutionary techniques available such as GA, ACO, particle swarm optimization (PSO). The advantage and disadvantages of evolutionary techniques discussed properly. These techniques used to optimize the results when we have a large number

Table 7. Execution Time(s) comparison of GA scheduling technique on CPU and genetic based proposed approach on CPU+FPGA for different iteration

S. No	Dataset (n × p)	Genetic Algorithm (GA) in (sec)			Genetic Algorithm (GA_MPI) in (sec)		
		500	1000	2000	500	1000	2000
1	20 × 5	10.312	13.664	25.64	1.64	2.64	5.12
2	20 × 10	10.516	15.414	29.78	1.92	3.34	7.165
3	20 × 20	21.645	38.49	65.794	2.64	4.46	9.625
4	50 × 5	12.364	22.34	44.669	1.96	3.74	5.152
5	50 × 10	23.645	44.541	88.669	2.16	5.173	11.645
6	50 × 20	28.616	51.64	110.66	3.37	7.316	14.345
7	100 × 5	25.316	47.31	92.614	5.66	10.123	21.651
8	100 × 10	30.614	54.2166	116.34	7.22	15.345	24.644
9	100 × 20	37.614	65.4165	129.33	9.66	18.196	27.728
10	200 × 10	80.616	154.164	298.36	14.192	22.144	31.614
11	200 × 20	182.751	236.194	516.69	16.115	30.164	61.366
12	500 × 20	1255.357	2413.14	4361.36	29.37	58.617	110.436

Figure 11. Execution time comparison of GA and GA_MPI approach.

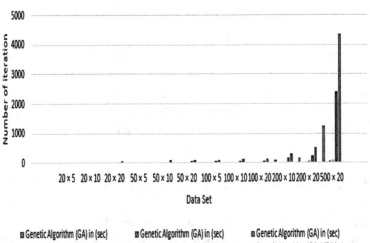

of processors available that need to norm for scheduling in a high-performance computing environment. There are various methods are available for processor scheduling to maximize the processor utilization and minimize throughput for fast execution. In this chapter, the author uses the processor scheduling technique with MPI in a high-performance computing system. The sequential dominating application required CPU scheduling to manage the workload for the game schedule. In case study 1, the author implemented game scheduling using single thread CPU power. Process control can't be easy by using the CPU scheduling technique. Game scheduling techniques are on uniform machines that have limitations for game scheduling they required high processor power for scheduling. These limitations are a cover-up by using CPU+GPU. GPU provides a parallel programming platform for the game scheduling.it has isolation priority capacity for huge game scheduling that required high power capacity. GPU scheduling policies are based on predictable response time (PRT). GPU supports a real-time multitasking environment. The logical problem with finite state machines and parallel computing that is sustainable performance and power efficiencies for the massively parallel process. In case study 2, the author demonstrates CPU scheduling techniques FCFS, SJF, and RR using CUDA. The results show that parallel programming platform gives better performance as compared to single thread CPU scheduling techniques. In case study 3, the author describes matrix multiplication and FCFS, an Evolutionary scheduling algorithm on HPC to provide high processing capacity. The author discusses the Openmpi architecture of parallel programming and evolutionary technique working principle in the parallel platform.

REFERENCES

A., & Sahana, S. K. (2018). A Survey on Multiprocessor Scheduling Using Evolutionary Technique. *Lecture Notes in Electrical Engineering*, 149–160. Doi:10.1007/978-981-13-0776-8_14

Carlos, C. R. A., & Albert, C. K. M. (2017). *Real-Time Multiprocessor Scheduling Algorithm Based on Information Theory Principles*. IEEE.

Cera, M. C., Pezzi, G. P., Pilla, M. L., Maillard, N., & Navaux, P. O. A. (2007). Scheduling Dynamically Spawned Processes in MPI-2. *Lecture Notes in Computer Science*, *4376*, 33–46. doi:10.1007/978-3-540-71035-6_2

Chang, W.-C., & Sung, C.-W. (2008). Process state integrated CPU scheduling game. *2008 First IEEE International Conference on Ubi-Media Computing.* 10.1109/ UMEDIA.2008.4570959

Chi, F., Wang, X., Cai, W., & Leung, V. C. M. (2014). Ad Hoc Cloudlet Based Cooperative Cloud Gaming. *2014 IEEE 6th International Conference on Cloud Computing Technology and Science.* DOI:10.1109/cloudcom.2014.112

Ding, S., Yuan, J., & Ju, J. (2004). An algorithm for agent-based task scheduling in grid environments. *Proceedings of 2004 International Conference on Machine Learning and Cybernetics* (IEEE Cat. No.04EX826). DOI:10.1109/icmlc.2004.1378510

Hsiu-Jay, Ho., & Lin, W.-M. (2004). A performance-optimizing scheduling technique for mesh-connected multicomputers based on real-time job size distribution. *Proceedings. Tenth International Conference on Parallel and Distributed Systems, 2004. ICPADS 2004.* DOI:10.1109/ICPADS.2004.1316150

Kato, S., Lakshmanan, K., Ishikawa, Y., & Rajkumar, R. (2011). Resource Sharing in GPU-Accelerated Windowing Systems. *2011 17th IEEE Real-Time and Embedded Technology and Applications Symposium.* DOI:10.1109/rtas.2011.26

Leinberger, W., Karypis, G., & Kumar, V. (1999). Job scheduling in the presence of multiple resource requirements. *Proceedings of the 1999 ACM/IEEE Conference on Supercomputing (CDROM) - Supercomputing '99.* 10.1145/331532.331579

Mohammad, M. R., & Mahmoud, N. (2009). Hard Real-Time Multiobjective Scheduling in Heterogeneous Systems Using Genetic Algorithms. *International CSI Computer Conference,* 437-445.

Sahana, S. K., Khowas, M., & Sinha, K. (2018). *Budget Optimization and Allocation: An Evolutionary Computing Based Model.* Doi:10.2174/97816810870781180101

Saraswat, P. K., & Gupta, P. (2006). Design and Implementation of a Process Scheduler Simulator and an Improved Process Scheduling Algorithm for Multimedia Operating Systems. *2006 International Conference on Advanced Computing and Communications.* 10.1109/ADCOM.2006.4289946

Vestias, M., & Neto, H. (2014). Trends of CPU, GPU, and FPGA for high-performance computing. *2014 24th International Conference on Field Programmable Logic and Applications (FPL).* DOI:10.1109/fpl.2014.6927483

Yoo, B. S., & Das, C. R. (2001). Efficient processor management schemes for mesh-connected multicomputers. *Parallel Computing*, *27*(8), 1057–1078. doi:10.1016/S0167-8191(01)00078-3

Zhang, W., Liao, X., Li, P., Jin, H., Lin, L., & Zhou, B. B. (2018). Fine-Grained Scheduling in Cloud Gaming on Heterogeneous CPU-GPU Clusters. *IEEE Network*, *32*(1), 172–178. doi:10.1109/MNET.2017.1700047

Zheng, X., Zhou, Z., Yang, X., Lan, Z., & Wang, J. (2016). Exploring Plan-Based Scheduling for Large-Scale Computing Systems. *2016 IEEE International Conference on Cluster Computing (CLUSTER)*. 10.1109/CLUSTER.2016.43

Compilation of References

A., & Sahana, S. K. (2018). A Survey on Multiprocessor Scheduling Using Evolutionary Technique. *Lecture Notes in Electrical Engineering*, 149–160. Doi:10.1007/978-981-13-0776-8_14

Abbas, Y. A., Jidin, R., Jamil, N., Z'aba, M. R., Rusli, M. E., & Tariq, B. (2014). Implementation of PRINCE Algorithm in FPGA. *International Conference on Information Technology and Multimedia (ICIMU)*. 10.1109/ICIMU.2014.7066593

Abbou, A., & Mahmoudi, H. (2009). Performance of a sensorless speed control for induction motor using DTFC strategy and intelligent techniques. *J. Electr. Syst.*, *5*, 64–81.

Abdullah, Ismael, Rashid, Nour, & Tarique. (2015). Real time wireless health monitoring application using mobile devices. *IJCNC, 7*(3).

Abelein, U., Lochner, H., Hahn, D., & Straube, S. (2012). Complexity, quality and robustness– the challenges of tomorrow's automotive electronics. *Proceedings of the International Conference on Design, Automation Test in Europe Conference Exhibition (DATE)*, 870–871. 10.1109/DATE.2012.6176573

Abrial, A., Bouvier, J., Renaudin, M., Senn, P., & Vivet, P. (2001). A new contactless smart card IC using an on-chip antenna and an asynchronous microcontroller. *IEEE Journal of Solid-State Circuits*, *36*(7), 1101–1107. doi:10.1109/4.933467

Alam, Reaz, & Ali. (2012). A review of smart homes– past, present, and future. *IEEE Trans. on Systems, Man, and Cybernetics-part C. Applications and Reviews*, *42*(6), 1190–1203.

Altera. (2014). *Altera SoC Embedded Design Suite User Guide*. Author.

Anliker, U., Ward, J. A., Lukowicz, P., Troster, G., Dolveck, F., Baer, M., ... Vuskovic, M. (2004, December). AMON: A wearable multiparameter medical monitoring and alert system. *IEEE Transactions on Information Technology in Biomedicine*, *8*(4), 415–427. doi:10.1109/TITB.2004.837888 PMID:15615032

Ashton, K. (2011). *In the real world, things matter more than ideas*. RFID Journal.

Autkar, Dhage, & Bholane. (2015). A Survey on Distributed Techniques for Detection of Node Clones in Wireless Sensor Networks. IEEE.

Bai, F., & Helmy, A. (2006). *Wireless Adhoc Networks*. Wireless Ad Hoc and Sensor Networks.

Banik, S. (2015). Selected Areas in Cryptography (SAC). *22nd International Conference.*

Bansod, G., Raval, N., & Pisharoty, N. (2015). *Implementation of a New Lightweight Encryption Design for Embedded Security. IEEE Transaction.* doi:10.1109/TIFS.2014.2365734

Baradaran & Diniz. (2008). A compiler approach to managing storage and memory bandwidth in configurable architectures. *ACM Trans. Des. Autom. Electron. Syst., 13*, 61:1–61:26.

Becher, A., Benenson, Z., & Dornseif, M. (2006). Tampering with Motes: Real-World Physical Attacks on Wireless Sensor Networks. In J. A. Clark, R. F. Paige, F. A. C. Polack, & P. J. Brooke (Eds.), *Security in pervasive computing* (pp. 104–118). Berlin: Springer Berlin Heidelberg. doi:10.1007/11734666_9

Becker, J., Donlin, A., & Hu¨bner, M. (2007). New Tool Support and Architectures in Adaptive Reconfigurable Computing. *Proceedings of IFIP International Conference on Very Large-Scale Integration (VLSI–SoC).* 10.1109/VLSISOC.2007.4402486

Bellas, N., Chai, S. M., Dwyer, M., & Linzmeier, D. (2006). FPGA implementation of a license plate recognition SoC using automatically generated streaming accelerators. *20th International Parallel and Distributed Processing Symposium, IPDPS 2006.* 10.1109/IPDPS.2006.1639437

Benabdellah, M., Regragui, F., & Bouyakhf, E. H. (2011). Hybrid Methods of Image Compression-Encryption. *J. of Commun. & Comput, 1*(1-2).

Bereisa, J. (1983). Applications of Microcomputers in Automotive Electronics. *Transactions on Industrial Electronics, 30*(2), 87–96. doi:10.1109/TIE.1983.356715

Bhushan, B., & Sahoo, G. (2019). Routing protocols in wireless sensor networks. Studies in Computational Intelligence. doi:10.1007/978-3-662-57277-1_10

Blount, M., Batra, V. M., Capella, A. N., Ebling, M. R., Jerome, W. F., Martin, S. M., ... Wright, S. P. (2007). Remote health-care monitoring using Personal Care Connect. *IBM Systems Journal, 46*(1), 95–113. doi:10.1147j.461.0095

Boeckl, K., Fagan, M., Fisher, W., Lefkovitz, N., Megas, K. N., Nadeau, E., . . . Scarfone, K. (2018). *Considerations for Managing Internet of Things (IoT) Cybersecurity and Privacy Risks.* National Institute of Standards and Technology. Retrieved from www.nist.gov

Bogdanov, A., Knezevic, M., Leander, G., Toz, D., Varici, K., & Verbauwhede, I. (2011). spongent: A Lightweight Hash Function. In B. Preneel & T. Takagi (Eds.), Cryptographic Hardware and Embedded Systems - CHES 2011 (pp. 312-325). Berlin: Springer Berlin Heidelberg.

Bogdanov, A., Knudsen, L. R., Leander, G., Paar, C., Poschmann, A., Robshaw, M. J. B., & Vikkelsoe, C. (2007). PRESENT: An Ultra-Lightweight Block Cipher. In P. Paillier & I. Verbauwhede (Eds.), *Cryptographic Hardware and Embedded Systems - CHES 2007* (pp. 450–466). Berlin: Springer Berlin Heidelberg. doi:10.1007/978-3-540-74735-2_31

Bradshaw, V. (2006). *The Building Environment: Active and Passive Control Systems*. River Street, NJ: John Wiley & Sons, Inc.

Bucci, M., Guglielmo, M., Luzzi, R., & Trifiletti, A. (2010). *A Power Consumption Randomization Countermeasure for DPA-Resistant Cryptographic Processors*. doi:10.1007/978-3-540-30205-6_50

Buchanan, W. J., Li, S., & Asif, R. (2017). Lightweight cryptography methods. *Journal of Cyber Security Technology*, *1*(3-4), 187–201. doi:10.1080/23742917.2017.1384917

Bui & Zorzi. (2011). *Health care applications: a solution based on the internet of things*. Academic Press.

Bui, D.-H., Puschini, D., Bacles-Min, S., & Tran, X.-T. (2017). *AES Datapath Optimization Strategies for Low-Power Low-Energy Multisecurity-Level Internet-of-Thing Applications. IEEE Transactions on Very Large Scale Integration (VLSI) Systems*.

Burger, A., & Schiele, G. (2018). Demo Abstract: Deep Learning on an Elastic Node for the Internet of Things. *2018 IEEE International Conference on Pervasive Computing and Communications Workshops, PerCom Workshops 2018*. 10.1109/PERCOMW.2018.8480160

Carlos, C. R. A., & Albert, C. K. M. (2017). *Real-Time Multiprocessor Scheduling Algorithm Based on Information Theory Principles*. IEEE.

Carvalho, P. F., Santos, B., Correia, M., Combo, Á. M., Rodrigues, A. P., Pereira, R. C., … Gonçalves, B. (2015). PCI express hotplug implementation for ATCA based instrumentation. Fusion Engineering and Design. doi:10.1016/j.fusengdes.2015.05.030

Cash, P., Krzewick, W., MacHado, P., Overstreet, K. R., Silveira, M., Stanczyk, M., … Zhang, X. (2018). Microsemi Chip Scale Atomic Clock (CSAC) technical status, applications, and future plans. *2018 European Frequency and Time Forum, EFTF 2018*. 10.1109/EFTF.2018.8408999

Catarinucci, L., De Donno, D., Mainetti, L., Palano, L., Patrono, L., Stefanizzi, M. L., & Tarricone, L. (2015). *An IoT-Aware Architecture for Smart Healthcare Systems*. IEEE Internet of Things Journal. doi:10.1109/JIOT.2015.2417684

Cena, G., & Valenzano, A. (1999). Overclocking of Controller Area Networks. *Electronics Letters*, *35*(22), 1923–1925. doi:10.1049/el:19991289

Cera, M. C., Pezzi, G. P., Pilla, M. L., Maillard, N., & Navaux, P. O. A. (2007). Scheduling Dynamically Spawned Processes in MPI-2. *Lecture Notes in Computer Science*, *4376*, 33–46. doi:10.1007/978-3-540-71035-6_2

Chakraborty, R. S., & Bhunia, S. (2011, December). Security Against Hardware Trojan Attacks Using Key-Based Design Obfuscation. *Journal of Electronic Testing*, *27*(6), 767–785. doi:10.100710836-011-5255-2

Chang', Y.-J., Zhung, W., & Chen, T. (2004). Biometrics-Based Cryptographic Key Generation *IEEE International Conference on Multimedia and Expo (ICME)*.

Chang, W.-C., & Sung, C.-W. (2008). Process state integrated CPU scheduling game. *2008 First IEEE International Conference on Ubi-Media Computing.* 10.1109/UMEDIA.2008.4570959

Chatterjee, S. R., Majumder, S., Pramanik, B., & Chakraborty, M. (2014). FPGA implementation of pipelined blowfish algorithm. *5th International Symposium.*

Chen, Ma, Song, Lai, & Hu. (2016). *Smart Clothing: Connecting Human with Clouds and Big Data for Sustainable Health Monitoring.* Academic Press.

Chen, S., Yao, J., & Wu, Y. (2012). Analysis of the power consumption for wireless sensor network node based on Zigbee. *International Workshop on Information and Electronics Engineering*, 29, 1994-1998. 10.1016/j.proeng.2012.01.250

Chen, W. (2017). Electrocardiogram. In *Seamless Healthcare Monitoring.* Advancements in Wearable, Attachable, and Invisible Devices; doi:10.1007/978-3-319-69362-0_1

Chi, F., Wang, X., Cai, W., & Leung, V. C. M. (2014). Ad Hoc Cloudlet Based Cooperative Cloud Gaming. *2014 IEEE 6th International Conference on Cloud Computing Technology and Science.* DOI:10.1109/cloudcom.2014.112

Chodowiec & Gaj. (2003). Very Compact FPGA Implementation of the AES Algorithm. *LNCS, 2779,* 319–333.

Chujo. (2002). Fail-safe ECU System Using Dynamic Reconfiguration of FPGA. *R & D Review of Toyota CRDL, 37,* 54–60.

Chung, E. S., Hoe, J. C., & Mai, K. (2011). Coram: An in-fabric memory architecture for fpga-based computing. In *Proceedings of the 19th ACM/SIGDA International Symposium on Field Programmable Gate Arrays* (pp. 97–106). ACM. 10.1145/1950413.1950435

Cilardo & Gallo. (2015). Improving multibank memory access parallelism with lattice-based partitioning. *ACM Trans. Archit. Code Optim., 11,* 45:1–45:25.

Cilardo, A., & Gallo, L. (2015). Interplay of loop unrolling and multidimensional memory partitioning in hls. 2015 Design, Automation Test in Europe Conference Exhibition (DATE), 163–168. doi:10.7873/DATE.2015.0798

Columbus, L. (2017). 2017 Roundup of Internet of Things Forecasts. *Forbes.* Retrieved from www.forbes.com

Cong, J., Wei, P., Yu, C. H., & Zhang, P. (2018). Automated accelerator generation and optimization with composable, parallel and pipeline architecture. *Proceedings of the 55th Annual Design Automation Conference,* 154:1–154:6.

Cong, J., Li, P., Xiao, B., & Zhang, P. (2016). An optimal microarchitecture for stencil computation acceleration based on nonuniform partitioning of data reuse buffers. *IEEE Transactions on Computer-Aided Design of Integrated Circuits and Systems, 35*(3), 407–418. doi:10.1109/TCAD.2015.2488491

Cong, J., Zhang, P., & Zou, Y. (2011). Combined loop transformation and hierarchy allocation for data reuse optimization. *2011 IEEE/ACM International Conference on Computer-Aided Design (ICCAD)*, 185–192. 10.1109/ICCAD.2011.6105324

Cong, J., Zhang, P., & Zou, Y. (2012). Optimizing memory hierarchy allocation with loop transformations for high-level synthesis. *DAC Design Automation Conference 2012*, 1229–1234. 10.1145/2228360.2228586

Coyle, S., Lau, K.-T., Moyna, N., O'Gorman, D., Diamond, D., Di Francesco, F., ... Bini, C. (2010, March). BIO- TEX—Biosensing Textiles for Personalised Healthcare Management. *IEEE Transactions on Information Technology in Biomedicine*, *14*(2), 364–370. doi:10.1109/TITB.2009.2038484 PMID:20064761

Cruz, S. M. A., Toliyat, H. A., & Cardoso, A. J. M. (2005). DSP implementation of the multiple reference frames theory for the diagnosis of stator faults in a DTC induction motor drive. *IEEE Transactions on Energy Conversion*, *20*(2), 329–335. doi:10.1109/TEC.2005.845531

Curone, D., Secco, E. L., Tognetti, A., Loriga, G., Dudnik, G., Risatti, M., ... Magenes, G. (2010, May). Smart Garments for Emergency Operators: The ProeTEX Project. *IEEE Transactions on Information Technology in Biomedicine*, *14*(3), 694–701. doi:10.1109/TITB.2010.2045003 PMID:20371413

da Silva, Braeken, D'Hollander, & Touhafi. (2013). Performance modeling for fpgas: Extending the roofline model with high-level synthesis tools. *Int. J. Reconfig. Comput.*, *2013*, 7:7–7:7.

Daily, M., Medasani, S., Behringer, R., & Trivedi, M. (2017). Self-Driving Cars. *Computer*, *50*(12), 18–23. doi:10.1109/MC.2017.4451204

Darte, A., Member, I. C. S., Schreiber, R., & Villard, G. (2005). *Lattice-based memory allocation* (Vol. 10). IEEE Transactions on Computers.

Daugman, J. (1993). High Confidence visual recognition of persons by a test of statistical independence. *IEEE Transactions on Pattern Analysis and Machine Intelligence*, *15*(11), 1148–1161. doi:10.1109/34.244676

Deering, S. E., & Hinden, B. (2017, July). *Internet Protocol, Version 6 (IPv6) Specification*. RFC 8200. RFC Editor. Retrieved from rfc-editor.org

Deng, J., & Tu, L. (n.d.). *Improvement of Direct Torque Control Low-speed Performance by Using Fuzzy Logic Technique*. International Conference on Mechatronics and Automation, Luoyang, China.

Depenbrock, M. (1988, October). Direct Self Control of Inverter-Fed Induction Machines. *IEEE Trans. On Power Electr.*, *PE-3*(4), 420–429. doi:10.1109/63.17963

Ding, S., Yuan, J., & Ju, J. (2004). An algorithm for agent-based task scheduling in grid environments. *Proceedings of 2004 International Conference on Machine Learning and Cybernetics* (IEEE Cat. No.04EX826). DOI:10.1109/icmlc.2004.1378510

Dorazio, L., Visintainer, F., & Darin, M. (2011). Sensor Networks on the Car: State of the Art and Future Challenges. *Proceedings of the Design Automation and Test in Europe (DATE) Conference.*

Driessen, B., Guneysu, T., Kavun, E. B., Mischke, O., Paar, C., & Poppelmann, T. (2012, December). IPSecco: A lightweight and reconfigurable IPSec core. In *2012 International Conference on Reconfigurable Computing and FPGAs (ReConFig)* (pp. 1-7). 10.1109/ReConFig.2012.6416757

Eberli, F. (2010). Automotive embedded driver assistance: A real-time low-power FPGA stereo engine using semi-global matching. *Proceedings of the International Conference on Computer Design (ICCD).* 10.1109/ICCD.2010.5647552

Ellison, C. (2010). Public key infrastructure. Handbook of Financial Cryptography and Security. doi:10.1201/9781420059823-c16

Elson, J., & Romer, K. (2003). *Wireless Sensor Networks: A New Regime for Time Synchronization.* ACM SigComm Computer Communications Review. doi:10.1145/774763.774787

Escobedo, J., & Lin, M. (2018). Extracting data parallelism in non-stencil kernel computing by optimally coloring folded memory conflict graph. In *Proceedings of the 55th Annual Design Automation Conference* (pp. 156:1–156:6). ACM.

Escobedo, J., & Lin, M. (2018). Graph-theoretically optimal memory banking for stencil-based computing kernels. In *Proceedings of the 2018 ACM/SIGDA International Symposium on Field-Programmable Gate Arrays* (pp. 199–208). ACM. 10.1145/3174243.3174251

Evans, D. (2011). *The Internet of Things - How the Next Evolution of the Internet is Changing Everything.* Cisco Internet Business Solutions Group.

Farashahi, Rashidi, & Saye. (2014). *FPGA based fast and high-throughput 2-slow retiming 128bit AES encryption algorithm.* Elsevier.

Farooq & Aslam. (2017). Comparative analysis of different AES implementation techniques for efficient resource usage and better performance on FPGA. *Journal of King Saud University-Computer and Information Science,* 295-302.

Feizi, S., Ahmadi, A., & Nemati, A. (2014). *A Hardware Implementation of Simon Cryptography Algorithm.* ICCKE. doi:10.1109/ICCKE.2014.6993386

FlexRay Automotive Communication Bus Overview. (2016). www.ni.com/white-paper/3352/en/

Fons & Fons. (2012). FPGA-based Automotive ECU Design Addresses AUTOSAR and ISO 26262 Standards. *Xcell Journal, 78,* 20–31.

Forest, Ferrari, Audisio, Sabatini, Vincentelli, & Natale. (2008). Physical Architectures of Automotive Systems. *Proceedings of the Design Automation and Test in Europe (DATE) Conference,* 391–395.

Gaddam & Lal. (2011). Development of Bio-Crypto Key From Fingerprints Using Cancelable Templates. *International Journal on Computer Science and Engineering, 3*(2), 775-783.

Gadoue, S. M., Giaouris, D., & Finch, J. W. (2009). Arti⁻cial intelligence-based speed control of DTC induction motor drives: A comparative study. *Electric Power Systems Research*, *79*(1), 210–219. doi:10.1016/j.epsr.2008.05.024

Gallo, L., Cilardo, A., Thomas, D., Bayliss, S., & Constantinides, G. A. (2014). Area implications of memory partitioning for high-level synthesis on fpgas. *2014 24th International Conference on Field Programmable Logic and Applications (FPL)*, 1–4. 10.1109/FPL.2014.6927417

Garcia-Morchon, O., Kumar, S., & Sethi, M. (2018, December). *State-of-the-Art and Challenges for the Internet of Things Security.* Internet Engineering Task Force. Retrieved from www.ietf.org

Gaur, J., Chaudhuri, M., Ramachandran, P., & Subramoney, S. (2017). Nearoptimal access partitioning for memory hierarchies with multiple heterogeneous bandwidth sources. *2017 IEEE International Symposium on High Performance Computer Architecture (HPCA)*, 13–24. 10.1109/HPCA.2017.46

Genkin, D., Pipman, I., & Tromer, E. (2014). Get Your Hands Off My Laptop: Physical Side-Channel Key-Extraction Attacks on PCs. In L. Batina & M. Robshaw (Eds.), *Cryptographic Hardware and Embedded Systems - CHES 2014* (pp. 242–260). Berlin: Springer Berlin Heidelberg. doi:10.1007/978-3-662-44709-3_14

Geyer, T., & Mastellone, S. (2012). Model predictive direct torque control of a five-level ANPC converter drive system. *IEEE Transactions on Industry Applications*, *48*(5), 1565–1575. doi:10.1109/TIA.2012.2210174

Ghosh, A. M., Halder, D., & Hossain, S. K. A. (2016). *Remote Health Monitoring System through IoT (5th ed.).* ICIEV.

Gonzalez, J., Blanco, J. L., Galindo, C., Ortiz-de-Galisteo, A., Fernandez-Madrigal, J. A., Moreno, F. A., & Martinez, J. L. (2007). Combination of UWB and GPS for indoor-outdoor vehicle localization. *Proceedings of the 2007 IEEE International Symposium on Intelligent Signal Processing*, 1–6. 10.1109/WISP.2007.4447550

Good, T., & Benaissa, M. (2007). Pipelined AES on FPGA with support for feedback modes (in a multi-channel environment. *IET, VOL,* *1*(1), 1–10. doi:10.1049/iet-ifs:20060059

Gopalsamy, C., Park, S., Rajamanickam, R., & Jayaraman, S. (1999, September). The Wearable Motherboard™: The first generation of adaptive and responsive textile structures (ARTS) for medical applications. *Virtual Reality (Waltham Cross)*, *4*(3), 152–168. doi:10.1007/BF01418152

Group, N. W. (2006). *US Secure Hash Algorithms (SHA and HMAC-SHA).* Request for Comments. doi:10.1017/CBO9781107415324.004

Gschwind, M., Salapura, V., & Maurer, D. (2001). FPGA proto typing of a RISC processor core for embedded applications. *IEEE Transactions on VLSI Systems*, *9*(2), 241–250. doi:10.1109/92.924027

Guinard, D. (2011). *A Web of Things Application Architecture - Integrating the Real-World into the Web (PhD Th.).* ETH Zurich; doi:10.3929/ethz-a-006713673

Compilation of References

Gullasch, D., Bangerter, E., Krenn, S., Liu, F., Lee, R. B., Wang, Z., ... Fips, N. (2001). *197: Announcing the advanced encryption standard (AES).* Technology Laboratory, National Institute of Standards. doi:10.1016/S1353-4858(10)70006-4

Guo, Z., Carlson, A., Pang, L. T., Duong, K. T., Liu, T. J. K., & Nikolić, B. (2009). Large-scale SRAM variability characterization in 45 nm CMOS. *IEEE Journal of Solid-State Circuits, 44*(11), 3174–3192. doi:10.1109/JSSC.2009.2032698

Hameed, Abdulwahabe, & Găpuú. (2016). Health Monitoring System Based on Wearable Sensors and Cloud Platform. *20th ICSTCC.*

Hamid, Zamzuri, & Limbu. (2018). Internet of Vehicle (IoV) Applications in Expediting the Implementation of Smart Highway of Autonomous Vehicle: A Survey. *Performability in Internet of Things,* 137-157.

Han, H., & Tseng, C.-W. (2000). A comparison of locality transformations for irregular codes. In Languages, Compilers, and Run-Time Systems for Scalable Computers (pp. 70–84). Springer Berlin Heidelberg. doi:10.1007/3-540-40889-4_6

Helfmeier, C., Boit, C., Nedospasov, D., & Seifert, J. P. (2013). Cloning physically unclonable functions. *Proceedings of the 2013 IEEE International Symposium on Hardware-Oriented Security and Trust, HOST 2013.* 10.1109/HST.2013.6581556

Hennessy, J. L., & Patterson, D. A. (2012). *Computer Architecture A Quantitative Approach* (5th ed.). Elsevier Inc.

Hercog, D., & Gergič, B. (2014). *A flexible microcontroller-based data acquisition device.* Sensors. doi:10.3390140609755

Hodjat, A., & Verbauwhede, I. (2004). A 21.54 Gbits/s Fully Pipelined AES Processor on FPGA *Proceedings of the 12th Annual IEEE Symposium on Field-Programmable Custom Computing Machines.* 10.1109/FCCM.2004.1

Holcomb, D. E., Burleson, W. P., & Fu, K. (2009). Power-Up SRAM state as an identifying fingerprint and source of true random numbers. *IEEE Transactions on Computers, 58*(9), 1198–1210. doi:10.1109/TC.2008.212

Hosseinkhani & Javadi. (2012). Using Cipher Key to Generate Dynamic S-Box in AES Cipher Syst. *International Journal of Computer Science and Security, 6*(1).

Hsiu-Jay, Ho., & Lin, W.-M. (2004). A performance-optimizing scheduling technique for mesh-connected multicomputers based on real-time job size distribution. *Proceedings. Tenth International Conference on Parallel and Distributed Systems, 2004. ICPADS 2004.* DOI:10.1109/ICPADS.2004.1316150

Huang, Chang, Lin, & Tai. (2007). Compact FPGA Implementation of 32-bits AES Algorithm Using Block RAM. IEEE.

Huq & Islam. (2010). Home area network technology assessment for demand response in smart grid environment. *Universities Power Engineering Conference*, 1-6.

Idris, N. R. N., & Yatim, A. H. M. (2004, August). Direct torque control of induction machines with constant switching frequency and reduced torque ripple. *IEEE Transactions on Industrial Electronics*, *51*(4), 758–767. doi:10.1109/TIE.2004.831718

Inoue, Y., Morimoto, S., & Sanada, M. (2010). Examination and linearization of torque control system for direct torque controlled IPMSM. *IEEE Transactions on Industry Applications*, *46*(1), 159–166. doi:10.1109/TIA.2009.2036540

Interagency International Cybersecurity Standardization Working Group. (2018). *Interagency Report on the Status of International Cybersecurity Standardization for the Internet of Things (IoT)*. National Institute of Standards and Technology. Retrieved from www.nist.gov

International Organisation for Standardisation (ISO). (1994). *Road Vehicles— Interchange of Digital Information— Controller Area Network for High-Speed Communication*. Author.

Ipek, E., Mutlu, O., Martínez, J. F., & Caruana, R. (2008). Self-optimizing memory controllers: A reinforcement learning approach. *Proceedings - International Symposium on Computer Architecture*. 10.1109/ISCA.2008.21

Jhang, Sun, & Cui. (2010). Application and analysis of ZigBee technology for smart grid. *International conference on Computer and Information Application*, 171-174.

Jidin, A., Idris, N. R. N., Yatim, A. H. M., & Sutikno, T. (2011). An optimized switching strategy for quick dynamic torque control in DTC-hysteresis-based induction machines. IEEE Trans. Ind. Electron., 58(8), 3391–3400.

Jidin, A. (2010). Torque ripple minimization in DTC induction motor drive using constant frequency torque controller. *Proc. Int. Conf. Electr. Machines Syst.*, 919–924.

Jindal & Singh. (2015). *Analyzing the Security Performance Tradeoff in Block Ciphers*. ICCCA.

Johnson, A. P., Chakraborty, R. S., & Mukhopadhyay, D. (2015, April). A PUF-Enabled Secure Architecture for FPGA-Based IoT Applications. *IEEE Transactions on Multi-Scale Computing Systems*, *1*(2), 110–122. doi:10.1109/TMSCS.2015.2494014

Juan, E., & Lin, M. (2017). Tessellating memory space for parallel access. ASP-DAC.

Kang, J. W., & Sul, S. K. (2001, June). Analysis and prediction of inverter switching frequency in direct torque control of induction machine based on hysteresis bands and machine parameters. *IEEE Transactions on Industrial Electronics*, *48*(3), 545–553. doi:10.1109/41.925581

Kapoor, C., Graves-Abe, T. L., & Pei, J.-S. (2006). A low-cost off-the-shelf FGPA-based smart wireless sensing unit. Health Monitoring and Smart Nondestructive Evaluation of Structural and Biological Systems V. doi:10.1117/12.658923

Kato, S., Lakshmanan, K., Ishikawa, Y., & Rajkumar, R. (2011). Resource Sharing in GPU-Accelerated Windowing Systems. *2011 17th IEEE Real-Time and Embedded Technology and Applications Symposium*. DOI:10.1109/rtas.2011.26

Kdhanuka, Sachdeva, & Sheikhnitk. (2015). Cryptographic algorithm optimization. *IEEE-IACC*.

Khan, & Owen, & Hughes. (1993). FPGA architectures for ASIC hardware emulators. *Proceedings of the ASIC Conference and Exhibit*, 336- 340. 10.1109/ASIC.1993.410733

Kopetz, H. (1999). Automotive electronics. *Proceedings of the 11th Euromicro Conference on Real-Time Systems*, 132–140. 10.1109/EMRTS.1999.777459

Krawczyk, H., Bellare, M., & Canetti, R. (1997). *HMAC: Keyed-Hashing for Message Authentication*. doi:10.17487/rfc2104

Krim. (2014). Real Time Implementation of High Performance's Direct Torque Control of Induction Motor on FPGA. *International Review of Electrical Engineering*, 9(5), 919–629.

Krim, S., Gdaim, S., Mtibaa, A., & Mimouni, M. F. (2015). Design and implementation of directtorque control based on an intelligent technique of induction motor on FPGA. *Journal of Electrical Engineering & Technology*, 10(4), 1527–1539. doi:10.5370/JEET.2015.10.4.1527

Kuo, W. H., Chen, Y. S., Jen, G. T., & Lu, T. W. (2010). An intelligent positioning approach: RSSI-based indoor and outdoor localization scheme in Zigbee networks. *Proceedings of the 2010 International Conference on Machine Learning and Cybernetics*, 2754–2759. 10.1109/ICMLC.2010.5580783

Kyo-Beum, L., & Blaabjerg, F. (2008). Sensorless DTC-SVM for Induction Motor Driven by a Matrix Converter Using a Parameter Estimation Strategy. *IEEE Transactions on Industrial Electronics*, 55(2), 512–521. doi:10.1109/TIE.2007.911940

Lara-Nino, C. A., Diaz-Perez, A., & Morales-Sandoval, M. (2018, September). Energy and Area Costs of Lightweight Cryptographic Algorithms for Authenticated Encryption in WSN. *Security and Communication Networks*, 2018, 1–14. doi:10.1155/2018/5087065

Lara-Nino, C. A., Diaz-Perez, A., & Morales-Sandoval, M. (2019). Energy/Area-Efficient Scalar Multiplication with Binary Edwards Curves for the IoT. *Sensors (Basel)*, 19(3), 720. doi:10.339019030720 PMID:30744202

Lascu, C., Boldea, I., & Blaabjerg, F. (2000, January–February). A modified direct torque control for induction motor sensorless drive. *IEEE Transactions on Industry Applications*, 36(1), 122–130. doi:10.1109/28.821806

Latré, B., Braem, B., Moerman, I., Blondia, C., & Demeester, P. (2011). A survey on wireless body area networks. *Wireless Networks*, 17(1), 1–18. doi:10.100711276-010-0252-4

Lee & Lee. (2015). *The Internet of Things (iot): Applications, investments, and challenges for enterprises*. Academic Press.

Lee, E. A., & Seshia, S. a. (2011). *Introduction to Embedded Systems - A Cyber-Physical Systems Approach. LeeSeshia.org.* doi:10.1002/9781118557624.ch1

Lee, D. S., Fahey, D. W., Forster, P. M., Newton, P. J., Wit, R. C. N., & Lim, L. L. … Sausen, R. (2009). Aviation and global climate change in the 21st century. *Atmospheric Environment.* doi:10.1016/j.atmosenv.2009.04.024

Lee, I., & Sokolsky, O. (2010). Medical cyber physical systems. *Proceedings of the 47th Design Automation Conference on - DAC '10.* 10.1145/1837274.1837463

Lee, J., Bagheri, B., & Kao, H. A. (2015). A Cyber-Physical Systems architecture for Industry 4.0-based manufacturing systems. *Manufacturing Letters, 3,* 18–23. doi:10.1016/j.mfglet.2014.12.001

Leen, G., & Heffernan, D. (2002). Expanding automotive electronic systems. *Computer, 35*(1), 88–93. doi:10.1109/2.976923

Leen, G., Heffernan, D., & Dunne, A. (1999). Digital networks in the automotive vehicle. *Computing & Control Engineering Journal, 10*(6), 257–266. doi:10.1049/cce:19990604

Leinberger, W., Karypis, G., & Kumar, V. (1999). Job scheduling in the presence of multiple resource requirements. *Proceedings of the 1999 ACM/IEEE Conference on Supercomputing (CDROM) - Supercomputing '99.* 10.1145/331532.331579

Leinmuller, T., Buttyan, L., Hubaux, J.-P., Kargl, F., Kroh, R., Papadimitratos, P., ... Schoch, E. SEVECOM – Secure Vehicle Communication. *Proceedings of the IST Mobile and Wireless Communication Summit.*

Leung, B. (2011). *VLSI for Wireless Communication.* VLSI for Wireless Communication. doi:10.1007/978-1-4614-0986-1

Li, W., Yang, F., Zhu, H., Zeng, X., & Zhou, D. (2018). An efficient data reuse strategy for multi-pattern data access. In *Proceedings of the International Conference on Computer-Aided Design* (pp. 118:1–118:8). ACM. 10.1145/3240765.3240778

Lianbing, L. (2002). A high-performance direct torque control based on DSP in permanent magnet synchronous motor drive. *Proc. 4th World Congress Intell. Control Automat., 2,* 1622–1625. 10.1109/WCICA.2002.1020862

Li, F., Qiao, W., Sun, H., Wan, H., Wang, J., & Xia, Y., … Zhang, P. (2010). Smart transmission grid: Vision and framework. *IEEE Transactions on Smart Grid.* doi:10.1109/TSG.2010.2053726

Lin, L., Songhua, S., Shengping, L., Qiang, L., & Wei, L. (2006). Stator Resistance Identification of Induction Motor in DTC System Based on Wavelet Network. *Intelligent Control and Automation, 2006. WCICA 2006. 2006 IEEE.*

Li, T.-H. S., Chang, S.-J., & Chen, Y.-X. (2003). Implementation of Human-like Driving Skills by Autonomous Fuzzy Behavior Control on an FPGA-Based Car-Like Mobile Robot. *IEEE Transactions on Industrial Electronics, 50*(5), 867–880. doi:10.1109/TIE.2003.817490

Liu, J., Wickerson, J., & Constantinides, G. A. (2017). Tile size selection for optimized memory reuse in high-level synthesis. *2017 27th International Conference on Field Programmable Logic and Applications (FPL)*, 1–8. 10.23919/FPL.2017.8056810

Liu, J., Ming, Z., Bian, J., & Xue, H. (2001). A debug sub-system for embedded-system co-verification. *Proceedings of the Conference on ASIC*, 777–780.

Liu, J., Wickerson, J., Bayliss, S., & Constantinides, G. A. (2018, September). Polyhedralbased dynamic loop pipelining for high-level synthesis. *IEEE Transactions on Computer-Aided Design of Integrated Circuits and Systems*, *37*(9), 1802–1815. doi:10.1109/TCAD.2017.2783363

Liu, Q., Constantinides, G. A., Masselos, K., & Cheung, P. Y. K. (2007). Automatic on-chip memory minimization for data reuse. *15th Annual IEEE Symposium on Field-Programmable Custom Computing Machines (FCCM 2007)*, 251–260. 10.1109/FCCM.2007.18

Liu, Q., Constantinides, G. A., Masselos, K., & Cheung, P. Y. K. (2009, March). Combining data reuse with data-level parallelization for fpga-targeted hardware compilation: A geometric programming framework. *IEEE Transactions on Computer-Aided Design of Integrated Circuits and Systems*, *28*(3), 305–315. doi:10.1109/TCAD.2009.2013541

Liu, Y., Jin, Y., & Makris, Y. (2013, November). Hardware Trojans in wireless cryptographic ICs: Silicon demonstration & detection method evaluation. In *2013 IEEE/ACM International Conference on Computer-Aided Design (ICCAD)* (pp. 399-404). 10.1109/ICCAD.2013.6691149

Li, Z., & Gong, G. (2013). *On the Node Clone Detection in Wireless Sensor Networks*. IEEE. doi:10.1109/TNET.2012.2233750

Luis, R., Antoni, A., Emiliano, A., & Marcel, G. (2003, June). Novel Direct Torque Control (DTC) Sheme With Fuzzy Adaptive Torque- Ripple Reduction. *IEEE Transactions on Industrial Electronics*, *50*(3).

Lymberis. (2005). Progress in R&D on Wearable and Implantable Biomedical Sensors for Better Healthcare and Medicine. *Proceeding of the 3rd Annual International IEEE EMBS Special Topic Conference on Microtechnologies in Medicine and Biology*.

Maes, R., & Verbauwhede, I. (2010). P*hysically Unclonable Functions: A Study on the State of the Art and Future Research Directions*. In A.-R. Sadeghi & D. Naccache (Eds.), *Towards Hardware-Intrinsic Security: Foundations and Practice* (pp. 3–37). Berlin: Springer Berlin Heidelberg. doi:10.1007/978-3-642-14452-3_1

Mahfouz, To, & Khun. (2012). Smart instruments: wireless technology invades the operating room. *IEEE Topical conference on Biomedical Wireless Technologies, Networks and Sensing Systems*, 33-36.

Maletsky, K. (2015). *Attack Methods to Steal Digital Secrets*. Atmel Corporation. Retrieved from www.microchip.com

Management, M. (2005). 15. Memory Mapping and DMA. *Memory*.

Manoj, B. C. (2013). A Trust System for Broadcast Communications in SCADA. *International Journal of Engineering and Computer Science, 2*(12), 3534-3537.

Marzouqi, Al-Qutayri, Salah, Schinianakis, & Stouraitis. (2015). A HighSpeed FPGA Implementation of an RSD-Based ECC Processor. *IEEE Transaction.*

McKay, K. A., Bassham, L., Turan, M. S., & Mouha, N. (2017). *Report on Lightweight Cryptography.* National Institute of Standards and Technology. Retrieved from www.nist.gov

Meeus, W., & Stroobandt, D. (2014). Automating data reuse in high-level synthesis. 2014 Design, Automation Test in Europe Conference Exhibition (DATE), 1–4.

Meng, C., Yin, S., Ouyang, P., Liu, L., & Wei, S. (2015). Efficient memory partitioning for parallel data access in multidimensional arrays. *Proceedings of the 52Nd Annual Design Automation Conference.* 10.1145/2744769.2744831

Merletti, R., & Farina, A. (2009). Analysis of Intramuscular electromyogram signals. *Philosophical Transactions - Royal Society. Mathematical, Physical, and Engineering Sciences, 367*(1887), 357–368. doi:10.1098/rsta.2008.0235 PMID:19008187

Micali, S., & Reyzin, L. (2004). Physically Observable Cryptography. In M. Naor (Ed.), *Theory of Cryptography* (pp. 278–296). Berlin: Springer Berlin Heidelberg. doi:10.1007/978-3-540-24638-1_16

Michael, R. (1988, September). Biomedical Sensors in Interventional Systems: Present Problems and Future Strategies. *Proceedings of the IEEE, 76*(9).

Miettinen, M., Marchal, S., Hafeez, I., Asokan, N., Sadeghi, A.-R., & Tarkoma, S. (2017). IoT SENTINEL: Automated Device-Type Identification for Security Enforcement in IoT. *2017 IEEE 37th International Conference on Distributed Computing Systems (ICDCS).* doi:10.1109/icdcs.2017.283

Milford, M., & McAllister, J. (2016, August). Constructive synthesis of memory-intensive accelerators for fpga from nested loop kernels. *IEEE Transactions on Signal Processing, 64*(16), 4152–4165. doi:10.1109/TSP.2016.2566608

Millner, H., Ebelt, R., Hoffmann, G., & Vossiek, M. (2009). Wireless 3D localization of animals for trait and behaviour analysis in indoor and outdoor areas. *Proceedings of the IEEE MTT-S International Microwave Workshop on Wireless Sensing, Local Positioning, and RFID, 1–4.*

Mirkovic, J., & Reiher, P. (2004, April). A Taxonomy of DDoS Attack and DDoS Defense Mechanisms. *Computer Communication Review, 34*(2), 39–53. doi:10.1145/997150.997156

Mohammad, M. R., & Mahmoud, N. (2009). Hard Real-Time Multiobjective Scheduling in Heterogeneous Systems Using Genetic Algorithms. *International CSI Computer Conference,* 437-445.

Mohammed, Lung, Ocneanu, Thakral, Jones, & Adler. (2014). *Internet of Things: Remote Patient Monitoring Using Internet Services and Cloud Computing.* Academic Press.

Monmasson, E., & Cirstea, M. (2007). FPGA design methodology for industrial control systems—A review. *IEEE Transactions on Industrial Electronics, 54*(4), 1824–1842. doi:10.1109/TIE.2007.898281

Monmasson, E., Idkhajine, L., Cirstea, M. N., Bahri, I., Tisan, A., & Naouar, M. W. (2011). FPGAs in industrial control applications. *IEEE Transactions on Industrial Informatics, 7*(2), 224–243. doi:10.1109/TII.2011.2123908

Morioka & Satoh. (2003). An Optimized S-Box Circuit Architecture for Low Power AES Design. Springer-Verlag.

Morkel & Eloff. (2002). *Encryption Techniques: A Timeline Approach.* Information and Computer Security Architecture (ICSA) Research Group Department of Computer Science University of Pretoria.

Musavi, S. H. A., Chowdhry, B. S., Kumar, T., Pandey, B., & Kumar, W. (2015). IoTs Enable Active Contour Modeling Based Energy Efficient and Thermal Aware Object Tracking on FPGA. *Wireless Personal Communications, 85*(2), 529–543. doi:10.100711277-015-2753-z

Nane, R., Sima, V. M., Pilato, C., Choi, J., Fort, B., & Canis, A. … Bertels, K. (2016). A Survey and Evaluation of FPGA High-Level Synthesis Tools. *IEEE Transactions on Computer-Aided Design of Integrated Circuits and Systems.* doi:10.1109/TCAD.2015.2513673

Nascimento, dos Santos, & Moreno. (2015). A VHDL implementation of the Lightweight Cryptographic Algorithm. *HIGHT.*

National Institute of Standards and Technology. (2015). *FIPS PUB 202: SHA-3 Standard: Permutation-Based Hash and Extendable-Output Functions.* Gaithersburg, MD: National Institute of Standards and Technology. Retrieved from www.nist.gov

Nazran, Pauzi & Ali. (2014). Study of S-box properties in block cipher. *International Conference on Computer, Communications and Control Technology.*

Noguchi, Yamamoto, Kondo, & Takahashi. (1999). Enlarging switching frequency in direct torque-controlled inverter by means of dithering. *IEEE Trans. Ind. Appl., 35*(6), 1358–1366.

Noguchi, T., Yamamoto, M., Kondo, S., & Takahashi, I. (1999, November–December). Enlarging switching frequency in direct torque-controlled inverter by means of dithering. *IEEE Transactions on Industry Applications, 35*(6), 1358–1366. doi:10.1109/28.806050

Otto, C., Milenković, A., Sanders, C., & Jovanov, E. (2006). System architecture of a wireless body area sensor network for ubiquitous health monitoring. *Journal of Mobile Multimedia.*

Overill, R. E. (2005). Review: Advances in Elliptic Curve Cryptography. *Journal of Logic and Computation, 15*(5), 815. doi:10.1093/logcom/exi047

Ovilla-Martinez, B. (2015). *Seguridad en Redes de Sensores Inalambricos Basada en Funciones Fisicamente No-Clonables* (Unpublished doctoral dissertation). CINVESTAV Tamaulipas.

Ovilla-Martinez, B., Diaz-Perez, A., & Garza-Saldaña, J. J. (2013, October). Key establishment protocol for a patient monitoring system based on PUF and PKG. In *2013 10th International Conference and Expo on Emerging Technologies for a Smarter World (CEWIT)* (pp. 1-6). 10.1109/CEWIT.2013.6713752

Peemen, M., Mesman, B., & Corporaal, H. (2015). Inter-tile reuse optimization applied to bandwidth constrained embedded accelerators. 2015 Design, Automation Test in Europe Conference Exhibition (DATE), 169–174. doi:10.7873/DATE.2015.1033

Peng, T., Leckie, C., & Ramamohanarao, K. (2007, April). Survey of Network-based Defense Mechanisms Countering the DoS and DDoS Problems. *ACM Computing Surveys*, *39*(1), 3. doi:10.1145/1216370.1216373

Pilato, C., Mantovani, P., Di Guglielmo, G., & Carloni, L. P. (2014). System-level memory optimization for high-level synthesis of component-based socs. *2014 International Conference on Hardware/Software Codesign and System Synthesis (CODES+ISSS)*, 1–10. 10.1145/2656075.2656098

Ploennigs, J., Ryssel, U., & Kabitzsch, K. (2010). Performance analysis of the EnOcean wireless sensor network protocol. *IEEE Conf. on Emerging Technologies and Factory Automation*, 1-9. 10.1109/ETFA.2010.5641313

Pouchet, L.-N., Bondhugula, U., Bastoul, C., Cohen, A., Ramanujam, J., Sadayappan, P., & Vasilache, N. (2011, January). Loop transformations: Convexity, pruning and optimization. *SIGPLAN Notices*, *46*(1), 549–562. doi:10.1145/1925844.1926449

Pouchet, L.-N., Zhang, P., Sadayappan, P., & Cong, J. (2013). Polyhedral-based data reuse optimization for configurable computing. In *Proceedings of the ACM/SIGDA International Symposium on Field Programmable Gate Arrays* (pp. 29–38). ACM. 10.1145/2435264.2435273

Preindl, M., & Bolognani, S. (2013). Model predictive direct torque control with finite control set for PMSM drive systems, part: Maximum torque perampere operation. *IEEE Transactions on Industrial Informatics*, *9*(4), 1912–1921. doi:10.1109/TII.2012.2227265

Rakotonirainy, A. (2014), Car hacking - Car hacking: The security threat facing our vehicles. *Popular Science*. https://www.sciencedaily.com/releases/2014/09/140917120705.htm

Rao, M., Newe, T., & Grout, I. (2014). Secure hash algorithm-3(SHA-3) implementation on Xilinx FPGAS, suitable for IoT applications. *Proceedings of the International Conference on Sensing Technology, ICST*. 10.21307/ijssis-2019-018

Ren, H., Meng, M. Q.-H., & Chen, X. (2005). Physiological Information Acquisition through Wireless Biomedical Sensor Networks. *Proceedings of the 2005 IEEE International Conference on Information Acquisition*.

Robert Bosch GmbH. (1991). *CAN Specification, Version 2.0*. Author.

Rodriguez-Andina, J. J., Moure, M. J., & Valdes, M. D. (2007). Features, design tools, and application domains of FPGAs. *IEEE Transactions on Industrial Electronics*, *54*(4), 1810–1823. doi:10.1109/TIE.2007.898279

Roy, D. B., Das, P., & Mukhopadhyay, D. (2016). ECC on Your Fingertips: A Single Instruction Approach for Lightweight ECC Design in GF(p). In O. Dunkelman & L. Keliher (Eds.), *Selected Areas in Cryptography - SAC 2015* (pp. 161–177). Cham: Springer International Publishing. doi:10.1007/978-3-319-31301-6_9

Saber, Soufien, & Abdellatif. (2015a). FPGA implementation of the direct torque control with constant switching frequency of induction motor. In Systems, Signals & Devices (SSD), 2015 12th International Multi-Conference on. IEEE.

Saber, Soufien, & Abdellatif. (2015b). Hardware Implementation of a Predictive DTC-SVM with a Sliding Mode Observer of an Induction Motor on the FPGA. *WSEAS Transactions on Systems and Control, 10*, 249-269.

Saber, Soufien, & Abdellatif. (2018). Control with high performances based DTC strategy: FPGA implementation and experimental validation. *EPE Journal*, 1–17.

Saber, K. R. I. M. (2017). Implementation on the FPGA of DTC-SVM Based Proportional Integral and Sliding Mode Controllers of an Induction Motor: A Comparative Study. *Journal of Circuits, Systems, and Computers*, *26*(3).

Saber, K. R. I. M., Soufien, G. D. A. I. M., & Abdellatif, M. T. I. B. A. A. (2017). Modeling and Hardware Implementation on the FPGA of a Variable Structure Control Associated with a DTC-SVM of an Induction Motor. *Electric Power Components and Systems*, *45*(16), 1806–1821. doi:10.1080/15325008.2017.1351010

Sahana, S. K., Khowas, M., & Sinha, K. (2018). *Budget Optimization and Allocation: An Evolutionary Computing Based Model.* Doi:10.2174/97816810870781180101

Saidani, T., Atri, M., Dia, D., & Tourki, R. (2010). Using Xilinx System Generator for Real Time Hardware Co-simulation of Video Processing System. *Electronic Engineering and Computing Technology*, *60*, 227–236. doi:10.1007/978-90-481-8776-8_20

Salim, S., AlDabbagh, M., & Shaikhli, I. F. T. A. (2014). *OLBCA: A New Lightweight Block Cipher Algorithm.* ICACSAT.

Salman, A., Ferozpuri, A., Homsirikamol, E., Yalla, P., Kaps, J., & Gaj, K. (2017, December). A scalable ECC processor implementation for high-speed and lightweight with side-channel countermeasures. In *2017 International Conference on Reconfigurable Computing and FPGAs (ReConFig)* (pp. 1-8). 10.1109/RECONFIG.2017.8279769

Sander, Becker, Hubner, Dreschmann, Luka, Traub, & Weber. (2001). *Modular system concept for a FPGA-based Automotive Gateway.* Academic Press.

Sander, O., Hubner, M., Becker, J., & Traub, M. (2008). Reducing latency times by accelerated routing mechanisms for an FPGA gateway in the automotive domain. *Proceedings of the International Conference on ICECE Technology (FPT)*, 97–104. 10.1109/FPT.2008.4762371

Saraswat, P. K., & Gupta, P. (2006). Design and Implementation of a Process Scheduler Simulator and an Improved Process Scheduling Algorithm for Multimedia Operating Systems. *2006 International Conference on Advanced Computing and Communications*. 10.1109/ADCOM.2006.4289946

Schramm, M., & Grzemba, A. (2013, September). On the implementation of a lightweight generic FPGA ECC crypto-core over GF(p). In *2013 international Conference on Applied Electronics* (pp. 1-4). Academic Press.

Schwiebert, L. (2001). Research Challenges in Wireless Networks of Biomedical Sensor. Academic Press.

Selimis, G., Konijnenburg, M., Ashouei, M., Huisken, J., De Groot, H., Van Der Leest, V., … Tuyls, P. (2011). Evaluation of 90nm 6T-SRAM as Physical Unclonable Function for secure key generation in wireless sensor nodes. *Proceedings - IEEE International Symposium on Circuits and Systems*. 10.1109/ISCAS.2011.5937628

Shannon, C. E. (1948). A Mathematical Theory of Communication. *The Bell System Technical Journal*, 27(4), 623–656. doi:10.1002/j.1538-7305.1948.tb00917.x

Shannon, C. E. (1949). Communication Theory of Secrecy Systems. *Bell Sysit. Tech*, 5(28), 656–715.

Shi, W., Cao, J., Zhang, Q., Li, Y., & Xu, L. (2016, October). Edge Computing: Vision and Challenges. *IEEE Internet of Things Journal*, 3(5), 637–646. doi:10.1109/JIOT.2016.2579198

Shi, W., & Dustdar, S. (2016, May). The Promise of Edge Computing. *Computer*, 49(5), 78–81. doi:10.1109/MC.2016.145

Shreejith, Anshuman, A., & Fahmy. (2016). Accelerated Artificial Neural Networks on FPGA for fault detection in automotive systems. *Design, Automation & Test in Europe Conference & Exhibition (DATE)*.

Shreejith, S., Fahmy, A., & Lukasiewycz, M. (2013). Accelerating Validation of Time Triggered Automotive Systems on FPGAs, *Proceedings of the International Conference on Field Programmable Technology (FPT)*, 4. 10.1109/FPT.2013.6718322

Shyu, K. K., Lin, J. K., Pham, V. T., & Yang, M. J. (2010). Global minimum torque ripple design for direct torque control of induction motor drives. *IEEE Transactions on Industrial Electronics*, 57(9), 3148–3156. doi:10.1109/TIE.2009.2038401

Singh, B., Jain, S., & Dwivedi, S. (2013). Torque ripple reduction technique with improved flux response for a direct torque control induction motor drive. *IET Power Electronics*, 6(2), 326–342. doi:10.1049/iet-pel.2012.0121

Song, I., Gowan, K., Nery, J., Han, H., Sheng, T., Li, H., & Karray, F. (2006). Intelligent Parking System Design Using FPGA. *Proceedings of the International Conference on Field Programmable Logic and Applications*, 1-6.

Sood, S. K., Sarje, A. K., & Singh, K. (2010). An Improvement of Liou et al.'s Authentication Scheme Using Smart Cards. *International Journal of Computers and Applications*, *1*(8), 16–23.

Struik, R. (2018, November). *Alternative Elliptic Curve Representations*. Internet Engineering Task Force. Retrieved from www.ietf.org

Suh, G. E., & Devadas, S. (2007). Physical unclonable functions for device authentication and secret key generation. *Proceedings - Design Automation Conference*. 10.1109/DAC.2007.375043

Su, J., Yang, F., Zeng, X., Zhou, D., & Chen, J. (2017, October). Efficient memory partitioning for parallel data access in fpga via data reuse. *IEEE Transactions on Computer-Aided Design of Integrated Circuits and Systems*, *36*(10), 1674–1687. doi:10.1109/TCAD.2017.2648838

Sun, L., Zhang, D., Li, B., Guo, B., & Li, S. (2010). Activity recognition on an accelerometer embedded mobile phone with varying positions and orientations. In *Ubiquitous Intelligence and Computing* (pp. 548–562). Berlin, Germany: Springer. doi:10.1007/978-3-642-16355-5_42

Tada, Y., Amano, Y., Sato, T., Saito, S., & Inoue, M. (2015, November). A smart shirt made with conductive ink and conductive foam for the measurement of electrocardiogram signals with unipolar precordial leads. *Fibers (Basel, Switzerland)*, *3*(4), 463–477. doi:10.3390/fib3040463

Takahashi, I., & Noguchi, T. (1986). A new quick-response and high efficiency control strategy of an induction motor. IEEE Trans., 22(5). doi:10.1109/TIA.1986.4504799

Tatikonda, R. R., & Kulkarni, V. B. (2016). FPGA based exhaust gas analysis for automotive vehicles. *International Conference on Internet of Things and Applications (IOTA)*. 10.1109/IOTA.2016.7562721

Tehranipoor, M., & Koushanfar, F. (2010, January). A Survey of Hardware Trojan Taxonomy and Detection. *IEEE Design & Test of Computers*, *27*(1), 10–25. doi:10.1109/MDT.2010.7

Thakor, N. V., & Tong, S. (2004). E Lectroencephalogram a Nalysis M Ethods. *Review - Americas Society*. doi:10.1146/annurev.bioeng.5.040202.121601 PMID:15255777

Toh, C., Idris, N., Yatim, A., Muhamad, N., & Elbuluk, M. (2005). Implementation of a New Torque and Flux Controllers for Direct Torque Control (DTC) of Induction Machine Utilizing Digital Signal Processor (DSP) and Field Programmable Gate Arrays (FPGA). *Power Electronics Specialists Conference, 2005. IEEE 36th*. 10.1109/PESC.2005.1581843

Tripathi, A., Khambadkone, A. M., & Panda, S. K. (2005, March). Torque ripple analysis and dynamic performance of a space vector modulation based control method for AC-drives. *IEEE Transactions on Power Electronics*, *20*(2), 485–492. doi:10.1109/TPEL.2004.842956

Trujillo-Olaya, V., Sherwood, T., & Koc, C. K. (2012). Analysis of performance versus security in hardware realizations of small elliptic curves for lightweight applications. *Journal of Cryptographic Engineering, 2*(3), 179–188. doi:10.100713389-012-0039-x

Uddin, N., & Hafeez, M. (2012). FLC-based DTC scheme to improve the dynamic performance of an IM drive. *IEEE Transactions on Industry Applications, 48*(2), 823–831. doi:10.1109/TIA.2011.2181287

Udgata, S. K., Mubeen, A., & Sabat, S. L. (2011). *Wireless Sensor Network Security model using Zero Knowledge Protocol*. IEEE. doi:10.1109/icc.2011.5963368

Varchola, M., Guneysu, T., & Mischke, O. (2011, November). MicroECC: A Lightweight Reconfigurable Elliptic Curve Cryptoprocessor. In *2011 International Conference on Reconfigurable Computing and FPGAs* (pp. 204-210). 10.1109/ReConFig.2011.61

Vestias, M., & Neto, H. (2014). Trends of CPU, GPU, and FPGA for high-performance computing. *2014 24th International Conference on Field Programmable Logic and Applications (FPL).* DOI:10.1109/fpl.2014.6927483

Vipin, K., Shreejith, S., Fahmy, S. A., & Easwaran, A. (2014). Mapping Time-Critical Safety-Critical Cyber Physical Systems to Hybrid FPGAs. *Proceedings of the International Conference on Cyber Physical Systems, Networks, and Applications (CPSNA)*, 31–36. 10.1109/CPSNA.2014.14

Voas, J., Kuhn, R., Laplante, P., & Applebaum, S. (2018). *Internet of Things (IoT) Trust Concerns*. National Institute of Standards and Technology. Retrieved from www.nist.gov

Wang, Y., Li, P., Zhang, P., Zhang, C., & Cong, J. (2013). Memory partitioning for multidimensional arrays in high-level synthesis. In *Proceedings of the 50th Annual Design Automation Conference* (pp. 12:1–12:8). ACM. 10.1145/2463209.2488748

Wang, J. (2010). *High-Speed Wireless Communications*. High-Speed Wireless Communications. doi:10.1017/cbo9780511754609

Wang, Y., Li, H., & Shi, X. (n.d.). Direct Torque Control with Space Vector Modulation for Induction Motors Fed by Cascaded Multilevel Inverters. *32nd IEEE Annual Conference on Industrial Electronics IECON*, 1575-9. 10.1109/IECON.2006.347240

Wang, Y., Li, P., & Cong, J. (2014). Theory and algorithm for generalized memory partitioning in high-level synthesis. *Proceedings of the 2014 ACM/SIGDA International Symposium on Field-programmable Gate Arrays*, 199–208. 10.1145/2554688.2554780

Want, R., Nath, B., & Reynolds, F. (2006, January). RFID Technology and Applications. *IEEE Pervasive Computing, 5*(1), 22–24. doi:10.1109/MPRV.2006.13

Wavenis Technology Homepage. (n.d.). http://www.coronis.com/ en/wavenis_technology.html

Wenger, E., Korak, T., & Kirschbaum, M. (2013). Analyzing Side-Channel Leakage of RFID-Suitable Lightweight ECC Hardware. In M. Hutter & J.-M. Schmidt (Eds.), *Radio Frequency Identification: Security and Privacy Issues - RFIDsec 2013* (pp. 128–144). Berlin: Springer Berlin Heidelberg. doi:10.1007/978-3-642-41332-2_9

Whitman, M. E. (2003, August). Enemy at the Gate: Threats to Information Security. *Communications of the ACM, 46*(8), 91–95. doi:10.1145/859670.859675

Williams, S., Waterman, A., & Patterson, D. (2009, April). Roofline: An insightful visual performance model for multicore architectures. *Communications of the ACM, 52*(4), 65–76. doi:10.1145/1498765.1498785

Willis, B. (2014). Understanding Automotive Electronics. *Microelectronics International.* doi:10.1108/mi.2004.21821aae.002

Wilson, C., Hargreaves, T., & Hauxwell-Baldwin, R. (2015). Smart homes and their users: A systematic analysis and key challenges. *Personal and Ubiquitous Computing, 19*(2), 463–476. doi:10.100700779-014-0813-0

Wolf, M., & Gendrullis, T. (2012). Design, Implementation, and Evaluation of a Vehicular Hardware Security Module. *Proceedings of the International Conference on Information Security and Cryptology (ICISC)*, 302–318. 10.1007/978-3-642-31912-9_20

Wood, C. C., & Banks, W. W. Jr. (1993). Human error: An overlooked but significant information security problem. *Computers & Security, 12*(1), 51–60. doi:10.1016/0167-4048(93)90012-T

Wurz, P., Abplanalp, D., Tulej, M., & Lammer, H. (2012). A neutral gas mass spectrometer for the investigation of lunar volatiles. Planetary and Space Science. doi:10.1016/j.pss.2012.05.016

Xia, C., Zhao, J., Yan, Y., & Shi, T. (2014). A novel direct torque control of matrix converter-fed PMSM drives using duty cycle control for torque ripple reduction. *IEEE Transactions on Industrial Electronics, 61*(6), 2700–2713. doi:10.1109/TIE.2013.2276039

Xilinx Inc. (2013). *UG909: Vivado Design Suite User Guide: Partial Reconfiguration.* www.xilinx.com

Xilinx System Generator v2.1 for Simulink User's Guide Online. (n.d.). www.mathworks.com/applications/dsp_comm/xilinx_ref_guide.pdf

Xilinx. (2009). *Xilinx UG190 Virtex-5 FPGA User Guide. UG190.* Author.

Xu, W., & Lorenz, R. D. (2014). Dynamic loss minimization using improved deadbeat-direct torque and flux control for interior permanent-magnet synchronous machines. *IEEE Transactions on Industry Applications, 50*(2), 1053–1065. doi:10.1109/TIA.2013.2272052

Yalcin, T. (2016). Compact ECDSA engine for IoT applications. *Electronics Letters, 52*(15), 1310–1312. doi:10.1049/el.2016.0760

Yang, H.-J., Fleming, K., Winterstein, F., Chen, A. I., Adler, M., & Emer, J. (2017). Automatic construction of program-optimized fpga memory networks. In *Proceedings of the 2017 ACM/SIGDA International Symposium on FieldProgrammable Gate Arrays* (pp. 125–134). ACM. 10.1145/3020078.3021748

Yang, S., & Verbauwhede, I. M. (2004). *Secure Fuzzy Vault Based Fingerprint Verification System*. IEEE.

Yick, J., Mukherjee, B., & Ghosal, D. (2008). Wireless sensor network survey. *Computer Networks*, *52*(12), 2292–2330. doi:10.1016/j.comnet.2008.04.002

Yoo, B. S., & Das, C. R. (2001). Efficient processor management schemes for mesh-connected multicomputers. *Parallel Computing*, *27*(8), 1057–1078. doi:10.1016/S0167-8191(01)00078-3

Yu, W., Liang, F., He, X., Hatcher, W. G., Lu, C., Lin, J., & Yang, X. (2017). A Survey on the Edge Computing for the Internet of Things. *IEEE Access: Practical Innovations, Open Solutions*. doi:10.1109/ACCESS.2017.2778504

Zeadally, S., Hunt, R., Chen, Y.-S., Irwin, A., & Hassan, A. (2012, August). Vehicular ad hoc networks (VANETS): Status, results, and challenges. *Telecommunication Systems*, *50*(4), 217–241. doi:10.100711235-010-9400-5

Zezulka, F., Marcon, P., Vesely, I., & Sajdl, O. (2016). Industry 4.0 – An Introduction in the phenomenon. *IFAC-PapersOnLine*, *49*(25), 8–12. doi:10.1016/j.ifacol.2016.12.002

Zhang & Parhi. (n.d.). High-Speed VLSI Architectures for the AES Algorithm. *IEEE Transactions on Very Large Scale Integration Systems, 12*(9).

Zhang, Bao, Lin, Rijmen, Yang, & Verbauwhede. (2014). *RECTANGLE: A Bit-slice Ultra-Lightweight Block Cipher Suitable for Multiple Platforms*. Academic Press.

Zhang, H. (2013). Environmental Effect Removal Based Structural Health Monitoring in the Internet of Things. Academic Press.

Zhang, X., Park, J., Parisi-Presicce, F., & Sandhu, R. (2004). *A logical specification for usage control*. doi:10.1145/990036.990038

Zhang, W., Liao, X., Li, P., Jin, H., Lin, L., & Zhou, B. B. (2018). Fine-Grained Scheduling in Cloud Gaming on Heterogeneous CPU-GPU Clusters. *IEEE Network*, *32*(1), 172–178. doi:10.1109/MNET.2017.1700047

Zhang, Y., Zhu, J., Zhao, Z., & Xu, W. (2012). An improved direct torque control for three-level inverter fed induction motor sensorless drive. *IEEE Transactions on Power Electronics*, *27*(3), 1502–1513. doi:10.1109/TPEL.2010.2043543

Zhang, Z., Tang, R., Bai, B., & Xie, D. (2010). Novel direct torque control based on space vector modulation with adaptive stator flux observer for induction motors. *IEEE Transactions on Magnetics*, *46*(8), 3133–3134. doi:10.1109/TMAG.2010.2051142

Zheng, J., Gao, D. W., & Lin, L. (2013). Smart meters in smart grid: An overview. *IEEE Green Technologies Conference*. 10.1109/GreenTech.2013.17

Zheng, X., Zhou, Z., Yang, X., Lan, Z., & Wang, J. (2016). Exploring Plan-Based Scheduling for Large-Scale Computing Systems. *2016 IEEE International Conference on Cluster Computing (CLUSTER)*. 10.1109/CLUSTER.2016.43

Zhou, Y., Al-Hawaj, K. M., & Zhang, Z. (2017). A new approach to automatic memory banking using trace-based address mining. In *Proceedings of the 2017 ACM/SIGDA International Symposium on Field-Programmable Gate Arrays* (pp. 179–188). ACM. 10.1145/3020078.3021734

Zhu, H., Xiao, X., & Li, Y. (2012). Torque ripple reduction of the torque predictive control scheme for permanent-magnet synchronous motors. *IEEE Transactions on Industrial Electronics*, *59*(2), 871–877. doi:10.1109/TIE.2011.2157278

Related References

To continue our tradition of advancing information science and technology research, we have compiled a list of recommended IGI Global readings. These references will provide additional information and guidance to further enrich your knowledge and assist you with your own research and future publications.

Aasi, P., Rusu, L., & Vieru, D. (2017). The Role of Culture in IT Governance Five Focus Areas: A Literature Review. *International Journal of IT/Business Alignment and Governance, 8*(2), 42-61. doi:10.4018/IJITBAG.2017070103

Abdrabo, A. A. (2018). Egypt's Knowledge-Based Development: Opportunities, Challenges, and Future Possibilities. In A. Alraouf (Ed.), *Knowledge-Based Urban Development in the Middle East* (pp. 80–101). Hershey, PA: IGI Global. doi:10.4018/978-1-5225-3734-2.ch005

Abu Doush, I., & Alhami, I. (2018). Evaluating the Accessibility of Computer Laboratories, Libraries, and Websites in Jordanian Universities and Colleges. *International Journal of Information Systems and Social Change, 9*(2), 44–60. doi:10.4018/IJISSC.2018040104

Adeboye, A. (2016). Perceived Use and Acceptance of Cloud Enterprise Resource Planning (ERP) Implementation in the Manufacturing Industries. *International Journal of Strategic Information Technology and Applications, 7*(3), 24–40. doi:10.4018/IJSITA.2016070102

Adegbore, A. M., Quadri, M. O., & Oyewo, O. R. (2018). A Theoretical Approach to the Adoption of Electronic Resource Management Systems (ERMS) in Nigerian University Libraries. In A. Tella & T. Kwanya (Eds.), *Handbook of Research on Managing Intellectual Property in Digital Libraries* (pp. 292–311). Hershey, PA: IGI Global. doi:10.4018/978-1-5225-3093-0.ch015

Adhikari, M., & Roy, D. (2016). Green Computing. In G. Deka, G. Siddesh, K. Srinivasa, & L. Patnaik (Eds.), *Emerging Research Surrounding Power Consumption and Performance Issues in Utility Computing* (pp. 84–108). Hershey, PA: IGI Global. doi:10.4018/978-1-4666-8853-7.ch005

Afolabi, O. A. (2018). Myths and Challenges of Building an Effective Digital Library in Developing Nations: An African Perspective. In A. Tella & T. Kwanya (Eds.), *Handbook of Research on Managing Intellectual Property in Digital Libraries* (pp. 51–79). Hershey, PA: IGI Global. doi:10.4018/978-1-5225-3093-0.ch004

Agarwal, R., Singh, A., & Sen, S. (2016). Role of Molecular Docking in Computer-Aided Drug Design and Development. In S. Dastmalchi, M. Hamzeh-Mivehroud, & B. Sokouti (Eds.), *Applied Case Studies and Solutions in Molecular Docking-Based Drug Design* (pp. 1–28). Hershey, PA: IGI Global. doi:10.4018/978-1-5225-0362-0.ch001

Ali, O., & Soar, J. (2016). Technology Innovation Adoption Theories. In L. Al-Hakim, X. Wu, A. Koronios, & Y. Shou (Eds.), *Handbook of Research on Driving Competitive Advantage through Sustainable, Lean, and Disruptive Innovation* (pp. 1–38). Hershey, PA: IGI Global. doi:10.4018/978-1-5225-0135-0.ch001

Alsharo, M. (2017). Attitudes Towards Cloud Computing Adoption in Emerging Economies. *International Journal of Cloud Applications and Computing*, 7(3), 44–58. doi:10.4018/IJCAC.2017070102

Amer, T. S., & Johnson, T. L. (2016). Information Technology Progress Indicators: Temporal Expectancy, User Preference, and the Perception of Process Duration. *International Journal of Technology and Human Interaction*, 12(4), 1–14. doi:10.4018/IJTHI.2016100101

Amer, T. S., & Johnson, T. L. (2017). Information Technology Progress Indicators: Research Employing Psychological Frameworks. In A. Mesquita (Ed.), *Research Paradigms and Contemporary Perspectives on Human-Technology Interaction* (pp. 168–186). Hershey, PA: IGI Global. doi:10.4018/978-1-5225-1868-6.ch008

Anchugam, C. V., & Thangadurai, K. (2016). Introduction to Network Security. In D. G., M. Singh, & M. Jayanthi (Eds.), Network Security Attacks and Countermeasures (pp. 1-48). Hershey, PA: IGI Global. doi:10.4018/978-1-4666-8761-5.ch001

Anchugam, C. V., & Thangadurai, K. (2016). Classification of Network Attacks and Countermeasures of Different Attacks. In D. G., M. Singh, & M. Jayanthi (Eds.), Network Security Attacks and Countermeasures (pp. 115-156). Hershey, PA: IGI Global. doi:10.4018/978-1-4666-8761-5.ch004

Anohah, E. (2016). Pedagogy and Design of Online Learning Environment in Computer Science Education for High Schools. *International Journal of Online Pedagogy and Course Design*, 6(3), 39–51. doi:10.4018/IJOPCD.2016070104

Anohah, E. (2017). Paradigm and Architecture of Computing Augmented Learning Management System for Computer Science Education. *International Journal of Online Pedagogy and Course Design*, 7(2), 60–70. doi:10.4018/IJOPCD.2017040105

Anohah, E., & Suhonen, J. (2017). Trends of Mobile Learning in Computing Education from 2006 to 2014: A Systematic Review of Research Publications. *International Journal of Mobile and Blended Learning*, 9(1), 16–33. doi:10.4018/IJMBL.2017010102

Assis-Hassid, S., Heart, T., Reychav, I., & Pliskin, J. S. (2016). Modelling Factors Affecting Patient-Doctor-Computer Communication in Primary Care. *International Journal of Reliable and Quality E-Healthcare*, 5(1), 1–17. doi:10.4018/IJRQEH.2016010101

Bailey, E. K. (2017). Applying Learning Theories to Computer Technology Supported Instruction. In M. Grassetti & S. Brookby (Eds.), *Advancing Next-Generation Teacher Education through Digital Tools and Applications* (pp. 61–81). Hershey, PA: IGI Global. doi:10.4018/978-1-5225-0965-3.ch004

Balasubramanian, K. (2016). Attacks on Online Banking and Commerce. In K. Balasubramanian, K. Mala, & M. Rajakani (Eds.), *Cryptographic Solutions for Secure Online Banking and Commerce* (pp. 1–19). Hershey, PA: IGI Global. doi:10.4018/978-1-5225-0273-9.ch001

Baldwin, S., Opoku-Agyemang, K., & Roy, D. (2016). Games People Play: A Trilateral Collaboration Researching Computer Gaming across Cultures. In K. Valentine & L. Jensen (Eds.), *Examining the Evolution of Gaming and Its Impact on Social, Cultural, and Political Perspectives* (pp. 364–376). Hershey, PA: IGI Global. doi:10.4018/978-1-5225-0261-6.ch017

Banerjee, S., Sing, T. Y., Chowdhury, A. R., & Anwar, H. (2018). Let's Go Green: Towards a Taxonomy of Green Computing Enablers for Business Sustainability. In M. Khosrow-Pour (Ed.), *Green Computing Strategies for Competitive Advantage and Business Sustainability* (pp. 89–109). Hershey, PA: IGI Global. doi:10.4018/978-1-5225-5017-4.ch005

Basham, R. (2018). Information Science and Technology in Crisis Response and Management. In M. Khosrow-Pour, D.B.A. (Ed.), Encyclopedia of Information Science and Technology, Fourth Edition (pp. 1407-1418). Hershey, PA: IGI Global. doi:10.4018/978-1-5225-2255-3.ch121

Batyashe, T., & Iyamu, T. (2018). Architectural Framework for the Implementation of Information Technology Governance in Organisations. In M. Khosrow-Pour, D.B.A. (Ed.), Encyclopedia of Information Science and Technology, Fourth Edition (pp. 810-819). Hershey, PA: IGI Global. doi:10.4018/978-1-5225-2255-3.ch070

Bekleyen, N., & Çelik, S. (2017). Attitudes of Adult EFL Learners towards Preparing for a Language Test via CALL. In D. Tafazoli & M. Romero (Eds.), *Multiculturalism and Technology-Enhanced Language Learning* (pp. 214–229). Hershey, PA: IGI Global. doi:10.4018/978-1-5225-1882-2.ch013

Bennett, A., Eglash, R., Lachney, M., & Babbitt, W. (2016). Design Agency: Diversifying Computer Science at the Intersections of Creativity and Culture. In M. Raisinghani (Ed.), *Revolutionizing Education through Web-Based Instruction* (pp. 35–56). Hershey, PA: IGI Global. doi:10.4018/978-1-4666-9932-8.ch003

Bergeron, F., Croteau, A., Uwizeyemungu, S., & Raymond, L. (2017). A Framework for Research on Information Technology Governance in SMEs. In S. De Haes & W. Van Grembergen (Eds.), *Strategic IT Governance and Alignment in Business Settings* (pp. 53–81). Hershey, PA: IGI Global. doi:10.4018/978-1-5225-0861-8.ch003

Bhatt, G. D., Wang, Z., & Rodger, J. A. (2017). Information Systems Capabilities and Their Effects on Competitive Advantages: A Study of Chinese Companies. *Information Resources Management Journal*, 30(3), 41–57. doi:10.4018/IRMJ.2017070103

Bogdanoski, M., Stoilkovski, M., & Risteski, A. (2016). Novel First Responder Digital Forensics Tool as a Support to Law Enforcement. In M. Hadji-Janev & M. Bogdanoski (Eds.), *Handbook of Research on Civil Society and National Security in the Era of Cyber Warfare* (pp. 352–376). Hershey, PA: IGI Global. doi:10.4018/978-1-4666-8793-6.ch016

Boontarig, W., Papasratorn, B., & Chutimaskul, W. (2016). The Unified Model for Acceptance and Use of Health Information on Online Social Networks: Evidence from Thailand. *International Journal of E-Health and Medical Communications*, 7(1), 31–47. doi:10.4018/IJEHMC.2016010102

Brown, S., & Yuan, X. (2016). Techniques for Retaining Computer Science Students at Historical Black Colleges and Universities. In C. Prince & R. Ford (Eds.), *Setting a New Agenda for Student Engagement and Retention in Historically Black Colleges and Universities* (pp. 251–268). Hershey, PA: IGI Global. doi:10.4018/978-1-5225-0308-8.ch014

Burcoff, A., & Shamir, L. (2017). Computer Analysis of Pablo Picasso's Artistic Style. *International Journal of Art, Culture and Design Technologies*, 6(1), 1–18. doi:10.4018/IJACDT.2017010101

Byker, E. J. (2017). I Play I Learn: Introducing Technological Play Theory. In C. Martin & D. Polly (Eds.), *Handbook of Research on Teacher Education and Professional Development* (pp. 297–306). Hershey, PA: IGI Global. doi:10.4018/978-1-5225-1067-3.ch016

Calongne, C. M., Stricker, A. G., Truman, B., & Arenas, F. J. (2017). Cognitive Apprenticeship and Computer Science Education in Cyberspace: Reimagining the Past. In A. Stricker, C. Calongne, B. Truman, & F. Arenas (Eds.), *Integrating an Awareness of Selfhood and Society into Virtual Learning* (pp. 180–197). Hershey, PA: IGI Global. doi:10.4018/978-1-5225-2182-2.ch013

Carlton, E. L., Holsinger, J. W. Jr, & Anunobi, N. (2016). Physician Engagement with Health Information Technology: Implications for Practice and Professionalism. *International Journal of Computers in Clinical Practice, 1*(2), 51–73. doi:10.4018/IJCCP.2016070103

Carneiro, A. D. (2017). Defending Information Networks in Cyberspace: Some Notes on Security Needs. In M. Dawson, D. Kisku, P. Gupta, J. Sing, & W. Li (Eds.), Developing Next-Generation Countermeasures for Homeland Security Threat Prevention (pp. 354-375). Hershey, PA: IGI Global. doi:10.4018/978-1-5225-0703-1.ch016

Cavalcanti, J. C. (2016). The New "ABC" of ICTs (Analytics + Big Data + Cloud Computing): A Complex Trade-Off between IT and CT Costs. In J. Martins & A. Molnar (Eds.), *Handbook of Research on Innovations in Information Retrieval, Analysis, and Management* (pp. 152–186). Hershey, PA: IGI Global. doi:10.4018/978-1-4666-8833-9.ch006

Chase, J. P., & Yan, Z. (2017). Affect in Statistics Cognition. In *Assessing and Measuring Statistics Cognition in Higher Education Online Environments: Emerging Research and Opportunities* (pp. 144–187). Hershey, PA: IGI Global. doi:10.4018/978-1-5225-2420-5.ch005

Chen, C. (2016). Effective Learning Strategies for the 21st Century: Implications for the E-Learning. In M. Anderson & C. Gavan (Eds.), *Developing Effective Educational Experiences through Learning Analytics* (pp. 143–169). Hershey, PA: IGI Global. doi:10.4018/978-1-4666-9983-0.ch006

Chen, E. T. (2016). Examining the Influence of Information Technology on Modern Health Care. In P. Manolitzas, E. Grigoroudis, N. Matsatsinis, & D. Yannacopoulos (Eds.), *Effective Methods for Modern Healthcare Service Quality and Evaluation* (pp. 110–136). Hershey, PA: IGI Global. doi:10.4018/978-1-4666-9961-8.ch006

Cimermanova, I. (2017). Computer-Assisted Learning in Slovakia. In D. Tafazoli & M. Romero (Eds.), *Multiculturalism and Technology-Enhanced Language Learning* (pp. 252–270). Hershey, PA: IGI Global. doi:10.4018/978-1-5225-1882-2.ch015

Cipolla-Ficarra, F. V., & Cipolla-Ficarra, M. (2018). Computer Animation for Ingenious Revival. In F. Cipolla-Ficarra, M. Ficarra, M. Cipolla-Ficarra, A. Quiroga, J. Alma, & J. Carré (Eds.), *Technology-Enhanced Human Interaction in Modern Society* (pp. 159–181). Hershey, PA: IGI Global. doi:10.4018/978-1-5225-3437-2. ch008

Cockrell, S., Damron, T. S., Melton, A. M., & Smith, A. D. (2018). Offshoring IT. In M. Khosrow-Pour, D.B.A. (Ed.), Encyclopedia of Information Science and Technology, Fourth Edition (pp. 5476-5489). Hershey, PA: IGI Global. doi:10.4018/978-1-5225-2255-3.ch476

Coffey, J. W. (2018). Logic and Proof in Computer Science: Categories and Limits of Proof Techniques. In J. Horne (Ed.), *Philosophical Perceptions on Logic and Order* (pp. 218–240). Hershey, PA: IGI Global. doi:10.4018/978-1-5225-2443-4.ch007

Dale, M. (2017). Re-Thinking the Challenges of Enterprise Architecture Implementation. In M. Tavana (Ed.), *Enterprise Information Systems and the Digitalization of Business Functions* (pp. 205–221). Hershey, PA: IGI Global. doi:10.4018/978-1-5225-2382-6.ch009

Das, A., Dasgupta, R., & Bagchi, A. (2016). Overview of Cellular Computing-Basic Principles and Applications. In J. Mandal, S. Mukhopadhyay, & T. Pal (Eds.), *Handbook of Research on Natural Computing for Optimization Problems* (pp. 637–662). Hershey, PA: IGI Global. doi:10.4018/978-1-5225-0058-2.ch026

De Maere, K., De Haes, S., & von Kutzschenbach, M. (2017). CIO Perspectives on Organizational Learning within the Context of IT Governance. *International Journal of IT/Business Alignment and Governance, 8*(1), 32-47. doi:10.4018/IJITBAG.2017010103

Demir, K., Çaka, C., Yaman, N. D., İslamoğlu, H., & Kuzu, A. (2018). Examining the Current Definitions of Computational Thinking. In H. Ozcinar, G. Wong, & H. Ozturk (Eds.), *Teaching Computational Thinking in Primary Education* (pp. 36–64). Hershey, PA: IGI Global. doi:10.4018/978-1-5225-3200-2.ch003

Deng, X., Hung, Y., & Lin, C. D. (2017). Design and Analysis of Computer Experiments. In S. Saha, A. Mandal, A. Narasimhamurthy, S. V, & S. Sangam (Eds.), Handbook of Research on Applied Cybernetics and Systems Science (pp. 264-279). Hershey, PA: IGI Global. doi:10.4018/978-1-5225-2498-4.ch013

Denner, J., Martinez, J., & Thiry, H. (2017). Strategies for Engaging Hispanic/ Latino Youth in the US in Computer Science. In Y. Rankin & J. Thomas (Eds.), *Moving Students of Color from Consumers to Producers of Technology* (pp. 24–48). Hershey, PA: IGI Global. doi:10.4018/978-1-5225-2005-4.ch002

Devi, A. (2017). Cyber Crime and Cyber Security: A Quick Glance. In R. Kumar, P. Pattnaik, & P. Pandey (Eds.), *Detecting and Mitigating Robotic Cyber Security Risks* (pp. 160–171). Hershey, PA: IGI Global. doi:10.4018/978-1-5225-2154-9.ch011

Dores, A. R., Barbosa, F., Guerreiro, S., Almeida, I., & Carvalho, I. P. (2016). Computer-Based Neuropsychological Rehabilitation: Virtual Reality and Serious Games. In M. Cruz-Cunha, I. Miranda, R. Martinho, & R. Rijo (Eds.), *Encyclopedia of E-Health and Telemedicine* (pp. 473–485). Hershey, PA: IGI Global. doi:10.4018/978-1-4666-9978-6.ch037

Doshi, N., & Schaefer, G. (2016). Computer-Aided Analysis of Nailfold Capillaroscopy Images. In D. Fotiadis (Ed.), *Handbook of Research on Trends in the Diagnosis and Treatment of Chronic Conditions* (pp. 146–158). Hershey, PA: IGI Global. doi:10.4018/978-1-4666-8828-5.ch007

Doyle, D. J., & Fahy, P. J. (2018). Interactivity in Distance Education and Computer-Aided Learning, With Medical Education Examples. In M. Khosrow-Pour, D.B.A. (Ed.), Encyclopedia of Information Science and Technology, Fourth Edition (pp. 5829-5840). Hershey, PA: IGI Global. doi:10.4018/978-1-5225-2255-3.ch507

Elias, N. I., & Walker, T. W. (2017). Factors that Contribute to Continued Use of E-Training among Healthcare Professionals. In F. Topor (Ed.), *Handbook of Research on Individualism and Identity in the Globalized Digital Age* (pp. 403–429). Hershey, PA: IGI Global. doi:10.4018/978-1-5225-0522-8.ch018

Eloy, S., Dias, M. S., Lopes, P. F., & Vilar, E. (2016). Digital Technologies in Architecture and Engineering: Exploring an Engaged Interaction within Curricula. In D. Fonseca & E. Redondo (Eds.), *Handbook of Research on Applied E-Learning in Engineering and Architecture Education* (pp. 368–402). Hershey, PA: IGI Global. doi:10.4018/978-1-4666-8803-2.ch017

Estrela, V. V., Magalhães, H. A., & Saotome, O. (2016). Total Variation Applications in Computer Vision. In N. Kamila (Ed.), *Handbook of Research on Emerging Perspectives in Intelligent Pattern Recognition, Analysis, and Image Processing* (pp. 41–64). Hershey, PA: IGI Global. doi:10.4018/978-1-4666-8654-0.ch002

Related References

Filipovic, N., Radovic, M., Nikolic, D. D., Saveljic, I., Milosevic, Z., Exarchos, T. P., ... Parodi, O. (2016). Computer Predictive Model for Plaque Formation and Progression in the Artery. In D. Fotiadis (Ed.), *Handbook of Research on Trends in the Diagnosis and Treatment of Chronic Conditions* (pp. 279–300). Hershey, PA: IGI Global. doi:10.4018/978-1-4666-8828-5.ch013

Fisher, R. L. (2018). Computer-Assisted Indian Matrimonial Services. In M. Khosrow-Pour, D.B.A. (Ed.), Encyclopedia of Information Science and Technology, Fourth Edition (pp. 4136-4145). Hershey, PA: IGI Global. doi:10.4018/978-1-5225-2255-3.ch358

Fleenor, H. G., & Hodhod, R. (2016). Assessment of Learning and Technology: Computer Science Education. In V. Wang (Ed.), *Handbook of Research on Learning Outcomes and Opportunities in the Digital Age* (pp. 51–78). Hershey, PA: IGI Global. doi:10.4018/978-1-4666-9577-1.ch003

García-Valcárcel, A., & Mena, J. (2016). Information Technology as a Way To Support Collaborative Learning: What In-Service Teachers Think, Know and Do. *Journal of Information Technology Research*, *9*(1), 1–17. doi:10.4018/JITR.2016010101

Gardner-McCune, C., & Jimenez, Y. (2017). Historical App Developers: Integrating CS into K-12 through Cross-Disciplinary Projects. In Y. Rankin & J. Thomas (Eds.), *Moving Students of Color from Consumers to Producers of Technology* (pp. 85–112). Hershey, PA: IGI Global. doi:10.4018/978-1-5225-2005-4.ch005

Garvey, G. P. (2016). Exploring Perception, Cognition, and Neural Pathways of Stereo Vision and the Split–Brain Human Computer Interface. In A. Ursyn (Ed.), *Knowledge Visualization and Visual Literacy in Science Education* (pp. 28–76). Hershey, PA: IGI Global. doi:10.4018/978-1-5225-0480-1.ch002

Ghafele, R., & Gibert, B. (2018). Open Growth: The Economic Impact of Open Source Software in the USA. In M. Khosrow-Pour (Ed.), *Optimizing Contemporary Application and Processes in Open Source Software* (pp. 164–197). Hershey, PA: IGI Global. doi:10.4018/978-1-5225-5314-4.ch007

Ghobakhloo, M., & Azar, A. (2018). Information Technology Resources, the Organizational Capability of Lean-Agile Manufacturing, and Business Performance. *Information Resources Management Journal*, *31*(2), 47–74. doi:10.4018/IRMJ.2018040103

Gianni, M., & Gotzamani, K. (2016). Integrated Management Systems and Information Management Systems: Common Threads. In P. Papajorgji, F. Pinet, A. Guimarães, & J. Papathanasiou (Eds.), *Automated Enterprise Systems for Maximizing Business Performance* (pp. 195–214). Hershey, PA: IGI Global. doi:10.4018/978-1-4666-8841-4.ch011

Gikandi, J. W. (2017). Computer-Supported Collaborative Learning and Assessment: A Strategy for Developing Online Learning Communities in Continuing Education. In J. Keengwe & G. Onchwari (Eds.), *Handbook of Research on Learner-Centered Pedagogy in Teacher Education and Professional Development* (pp. 309–333). Hershey, PA: IGI Global. doi:10.4018/978-1-5225-0892-2.ch017

Gokhale, A. A., & Machina, K. F. (2017). Development of a Scale to Measure Attitudes toward Information Technology. In L. Tomei (Ed.), *Exploring the New Era of Technology-Infused Education* (pp. 49–64). Hershey, PA: IGI Global. doi:10.4018/978-1-5225-1709-2.ch004

Grace, A., O'Donoghue, J., Mahony, C., Heffernan, T., Molony, D., & Carroll, T. (2016). Computerized Decision Support Systems for Multimorbidity Care: An Urgent Call for Research and Development. In M. Cruz-Cunha, I. Miranda, R. Martinho, & R. Rijo (Eds.), *Encyclopedia of E-Health and Telemedicine* (pp. 486–494). Hershey, PA: IGI Global. doi:10.4018/978-1-4666-9978-6.ch038

Gupta, A., & Singh, O. (2016). Computer Aided Modeling and Finite Element Analysis of Human Elbow. *International Journal of Biomedical and Clinical Engineering*, 5(1), 31–38. doi:10.4018/IJBCE.2016010104

H., S. K. (2016). Classification of Cybercrimes and Punishments under the Information Technology Act, 2000. In S. Geetha, & A. Phamila (Eds.), *Combating Security Breaches and Criminal Activity in the Digital Sphere* (pp. 57-66). Hershey, PA: IGI Global. doi:10.4018/978-1-5225-0193-0.ch004

Hafeez-Baig, A., Gururajan, R., & Wickramasinghe, N. (2017). Readiness as a Novel Construct of Readiness Acceptance Model (RAM) for the Wireless Handheld Technology. In N. Wickramasinghe (Ed.), *Handbook of Research on Healthcare Administration and Management* (pp. 578–595). Hershey, PA: IGI Global. doi:10.4018/978-1-5225-0920-2.ch035

Hanafizadeh, P., Ghandchi, S., & Asgarimehr, M. (2017). Impact of Information Technology on Lifestyle: A Literature Review and Classification. *International Journal of Virtual Communities and Social Networking*, 9(2), 1–23. doi:10.4018/IJVCSN.2017040101

Harlow, D. B., Dwyer, H., Hansen, A. K., Hill, C., Iveland, A., Leak, A. E., & Franklin, D. M. (2016). Computer Programming in Elementary and Middle School: Connections across Content. In M. Urban & D. Falvo (Eds.), *Improving K-12 STEM Education Outcomes through Technological Integration* (pp. 337–361). Hershey, PA: IGI Global. doi:10.4018/978-1-4666-9616-7.ch015

Haseski, H. İ., Ilic, U., & Tuğtekin, U. (2018). Computational Thinking in Educational Digital Games: An Assessment Tool Proposal. In H. Ozcinar, G. Wong, & H. Ozturk (Eds.), *Teaching Computational Thinking in Primary Education* (pp. 256–287). Hershey, PA: IGI Global. doi:10.4018/978-1-5225-3200-2.ch013

Hee, W. J., Jalleh, G., Lai, H., & Lin, C. (2017). E-Commerce and IT Projects: Evaluation and Management Issues in Australian and Taiwanese Hospitals. *International Journal of Public Health Management and Ethics*, 2(1), 69–90. doi:10.4018/IJPHME.2017010104

Hernandez, A. A. (2017). Green Information Technology Usage: Awareness and Practices of Philippine IT Professionals. *International Journal of Enterprise Information Systems*, 13(4), 90–103. doi:10.4018/IJEIS.2017100106

Hernandez, A. A., & Ona, S. E. (2016). Green IT Adoption: Lessons from the Philippines Business Process Outsourcing Industry. *International Journal of Social Ecology and Sustainable Development*, 7(1), 1–34. doi:10.4018/IJSESD.2016010101

Hernandez, M. A., Marin, E. C., Garcia-Rodriguez, J., Azorin-Lopez, J., & Cazorla, M. (2017). Automatic Learning Improves Human-Robot Interaction in Productive Environments: A Review. *International Journal of Computer Vision and Image Processing*, 7(3), 65–75. doi:10.4018/IJCVIP.2017070106

Horne-Popp, L. M., Tessone, E. B., & Welker, J. (2018). If You Build It, They Will Come: Creating a Library Statistics Dashboard for Decision-Making. In L. Costello & M. Powers (Eds.), *Developing In-House Digital Tools in Library Spaces* (pp. 177–203). Hershey, PA: IGI Global. doi:10.4018/978-1-5225-2676-6.ch009

Hossan, C. G., & Ryan, J. C. (2016). Factors Affecting e-Government Technology Adoption Behaviour in a Voluntary Environment. *International Journal of Electronic Government Research*, 12(1), 24–49. doi:10.4018/IJEGR.2016010102

Hu, H., Hu, P. J., & Al-Gahtani, S. S. (2017). User Acceptance of Computer Technology at Work in Arabian Culture: A Model Comparison Approach. In M. Khosrow-Pour (Ed.), *Handbook of Research on Technology Adoption, Social Policy, and Global Integration* (pp. 205–228). Hershey, PA: IGI Global. doi:10.4018/978-1-5225-2668-1.ch011

Huie, C. P. (2016). Perceptions of Business Intelligence Professionals about Factors Related to Business Intelligence input in Decision Making. *International Journal of Business Analytics*, *3*(3), 1–24. doi:10.4018/IJBAN.2016070101

Hung, S., Huang, W., Yen, D. C., Chang, S., & Lu, C. (2016). Effect of Information Service Competence and Contextual Factors on the Effectiveness of Strategic Information Systems Planning in Hospitals. *Journal of Global Information Management*, *24*(1), 14–36. doi:10.4018/JGIM.2016010102

Ifinedo, P. (2017). Using an Extended Theory of Planned Behavior to Study Nurses' Adoption of Healthcare Information Systems in Nova Scotia. *International Journal of Technology Diffusion*, *8*(1), 1–17. doi:10.4018/IJTD.2017010101

Ilie, V., & Sneha, S. (2018). A Three Country Study for Understanding Physicians' Engagement With Electronic Information Resources Pre and Post System Implementation. *Journal of Global Information Management*, *26*(2), 48–73. doi:10.4018/JGIM.2018040103

Inoue-Smith, Y. (2017). Perceived Ease in Using Technology Predicts Teacher Candidates' Preferences for Online Resources. *International Journal of Online Pedagogy and Course Design*, *7*(3), 17–28. doi:10.4018/IJOPCD.2017070102

Islam, A. A. (2016). Development and Validation of the Technology Adoption and Gratification (TAG) Model in Higher Education: A Cross-Cultural Study Between Malaysia and China. *International Journal of Technology and Human Interaction*, *12*(3), 78–105. doi:10.4018/IJTHI.2016070106

Islam, A. Y. (2017). Technology Satisfaction in an Academic Context: Moderating Effect of Gender. In A. Mesquita (Ed.), *Research Paradigms and Contemporary Perspectives on Human-Technology Interaction* (pp. 187–211). Hershey, PA: IGI Global. doi:10.4018/978-1-5225-1868-6.ch009

Jamil, G. L., & Jamil, C. C. (2017). Information and Knowledge Management Perspective Contributions for Fashion Studies: Observing Logistics and Supply Chain Management Processes. In G. Jamil, A. Soares, & C. Pessoa (Eds.), *Handbook of Research on Information Management for Effective Logistics and Supply Chains* (pp. 199–221). Hershey, PA: IGI Global. doi:10.4018/978-1-5225-0973-8.ch011

Jamil, G. L., Jamil, L. C., Vieira, A. A., & Xavier, A. J. (2016). Challenges in Modelling Healthcare Services: A Study Case of Information Architecture Perspectives. In G. Jamil, J. Poças Rascão, F. Ribeiro, & A. Malheiro da Silva (Eds.), *Handbook of Research on Information Architecture and Management in Modern Organizations* (pp. 1–23). Hershey, PA: IGI Global. doi:10.4018/978-1-4666-8637-3.ch001

Janakova, M. (2018). Big Data and Simulations for the Solution of Controversies in Small Businesses. In M. Khosrow-Pour, D.B.A. (Ed.), Encyclopedia of Information Science and Technology, Fourth Edition (pp. 6907-6915). Hershey, PA: IGI Global. doi:10.4018/978-1-5225-2255-3.ch598

Jha, D. G. (2016). Preparing for Information Technology Driven Changes. In S. Tiwari & L. Nafees (Eds.), *Innovative Management Education Pedagogies for Preparing Next-Generation Leaders* (pp. 258–274). Hershey, PA: IGI Global. doi:10.4018/978-1-4666-9691-4.ch015

Jhawar, A., & Garg, S. K. (2018). Logistics Improvement by Investment in Information Technology Using System Dynamics. In A. Azar & S. Vaidyanathan (Eds.), *Advances in System Dynamics and Control* (pp. 528–567). Hershey, PA: IGI Global. doi:10.4018/978-1-5225-4077-9.ch017

Kalelioğlu, F., Gülbahar, Y., & Doğan, D. (2018). Teaching How to Think Like a Programmer: Emerging Insights. In H. Ozcinar, G. Wong, & H. Ozturk (Eds.), *Teaching Computational Thinking in Primary Education* (pp. 18–35). Hershey, PA: IGI Global. doi:10.4018/978-1-5225-3200-2.ch002

Kamberi, S. (2017). A Girls-Only Online Virtual World Environment and its Implications for Game-Based Learning. In A. Stricker, C. Calongne, B. Truman, & F. Arenas (Eds.), *Integrating an Awareness of Selfhood and Society into Virtual Learning* (pp. 74–95). Hershey, PA: IGI Global. doi:10.4018/978-1-5225-2182-2.ch006

Kamel, S., & Rizk, N. (2017). ICT Strategy Development: From Design to Implementation – Case of Egypt. In C. Howard & K. Hargiss (Eds.), *Strategic Information Systems and Technologies in Modern Organizations* (pp. 239–257). Hershey, PA: IGI Global. doi:10.4018/978-1-5225-1680-4.ch010

Kamel, S. H. (2018). The Potential Role of the Software Industry in Supporting Economic Development. In M. Khosrow-Pour, D.B.A. (Ed.), Encyclopedia of Information Science and Technology, Fourth Edition (pp. 7259-7269). Hershey, PA: IGI Global. doi:10.4018/978-1-5225-2255-3.ch631

Karon, R. (2016). Utilisation of Health Information Systems for Service Delivery in the Namibian Environment. In T. Iyamu & A. Tatnall (Eds.), *Maximizing Healthcare Delivery and Management through Technology Integration* (pp. 169–183). Hershey, PA: IGI Global. doi:10.4018/978-1-4666-9446-0.ch011

Kawata, S. (2018). Computer-Assisted Parallel Program Generation. In M. Khosrow-Pour, D.B.A. (Ed.), Encyclopedia of Information Science and Technology, Fourth Edition (pp. 4583-4593). Hershey, PA: IGI Global. doi:10.4018/978-1-5225-2255-3. ch398

Khanam, S., Siddiqui, J., & Talib, F. (2016). A DEMATEL Approach for Prioritizing the TQM Enablers and IT Resources in the Indian ICT Industry. *International Journal of Applied Management Sciences and Engineering, 3*(1), 11–29. doi:10.4018/ IJAMSE.2016010102

Khari, M., Shrivastava, G., Gupta, S., & Gupta, R. (2017). Role of Cyber Security in Today's Scenario. In R. Kumar, P. Pattnaik, & P. Pandey (Eds.), *Detecting and Mitigating Robotic Cyber Security Risks* (pp. 177–191). Hershey, PA: IGI Global. doi:10.4018/978-1-5225-2154-9.ch013

Khouja, M., Rodriguez, I. B., Ben Halima, Y., & Moalla, S. (2018). IT Governance in Higher Education Institutions: A Systematic Literature Review. *International Journal of Human Capital and Information Technology Professionals, 9*(2), 52–67. doi:10.4018/IJHCITP.2018040104

Kim, S., Chang, M., Choi, N., Park, J., & Kim, H. (2016). The Direct and Indirect Effects of Computer Uses on Student Success in Math. *International Journal of Cyber Behavior, Psychology and Learning, 6*(3), 48–64. doi:10.4018/IJCBPL.2016070104

Kiourt, C., Pavlidis, G., Koutsoudis, A., & Kalles, D. (2017). Realistic Simulation of Cultural Heritage. *International Journal of Computational Methods in Heritage Science, 1*(1), 10–40. doi:10.4018/IJCMHS.2017010102

Korikov, A., & Krivtsov, O. (2016). System of People-Computer: On the Way of Creation of Human-Oriented Interface. In V. Mkrttchian, A. Bershadsky, A. Bozhday, M. Kataev, & S. Kataev (Eds.), *Handbook of Research on Estimation and Control Techniques in E-Learning Systems* (pp. 458–470). Hershey, PA: IGI Global. doi:10.4018/978-1-4666-9489-7.ch032

Köse, U. (2017). An Augmented-Reality-Based Intelligent Mobile Application for Open Computer Education. In G. Kurubacak & H. Altinpulluk (Eds.), *Mobile Technologies and Augmented Reality in Open Education* (pp. 154–174). Hershey, PA: IGI Global. doi:10.4018/978-1-5225-2110-5.ch008

Lahmiri, S. (2018). Information Technology Outsourcing Risk Factors and Provider Selection. In M. Gupta, R. Sharman, J. Walp, & P. Mulgund (Eds.), *Information Technology Risk Management and Compliance in Modern Organizations* (pp. 214–228). Hershey, PA: IGI Global. doi:10.4018/978-1-5225-2604-9.ch008

Landriscina, F. (2017). Computer-Supported Imagination: The Interplay Between Computer and Mental Simulation in Understanding Scientific Concepts. In I. Levin & D. Tsybulsky (Eds.), *Digital Tools and Solutions for Inquiry-Based STEM Learning* (pp. 33–60). Hershey, PA: IGI Global. doi:10.4018/978-1-5225-2525-7.ch002

Lau, S. K., Winley, G. K., Leung, N. K., Tsang, N., & Lau, S. Y. (2016). An Exploratory Study of Expectation in IT Skills in a Developing Nation: Vietnam. *Journal of Global Information Management*, 24(1), 1–13. doi:10.4018/JGIM.2016010101

Lavranos, C., Kostagiolas, P., & Papadatos, J. (2016). Information Retrieval Technologies and the "Realities" of Music Information Seeking. In I. Deliyannis, P. Kostagiolas, & C. Banou (Eds.), *Experimental Multimedia Systems for Interactivity and Strategic Innovation* (pp. 102–121). Hershey, PA: IGI Global. doi:10.4018/978-1-4666-8659-5.ch005

Lee, W. W. (2018). Ethical Computing Continues From Problem to Solution. In M. Khosrow-Pour, D.B.A. (Ed.), Encyclopedia of Information Science and Technology, Fourth Edition (pp. 4884-4897). Hershey, PA: IGI Global. doi:10.4018/978-1-5225-2255-3.ch423

Lehto, M. (2016). Cyber Security Education and Research in the Finland's Universities and Universities of Applied Sciences. *International Journal of Cyber Warfare & Terrorism*, 6(2), 15–31. doi:10.4018/IJCWT.2016040102

Lin, C., Jalleh, G., & Huang, Y. (2016). Evaluating and Managing Electronic Commerce and Outsourcing Projects in Hospitals. In A. Dwivedi (Ed.), *Reshaping Medical Practice and Care with Health Information Systems* (pp. 132–172). Hershey, PA: IGI Global. doi:10.4018/978-1-4666-9870-3.ch005

Lin, S., Chen, S., & Chuang, S. (2017). Perceived Innovation and Quick Response Codes in an Online-to-Offline E-Commerce Service Model. *International Journal of E-Adoption*, 9(2), 1–16. doi:10.4018/IJEA.2017070101

Liu, M., Wang, Y., Xu, W., & Liu, L. (2017). Automated Scoring of Chinese Engineering Students' English Essays. *International Journal of Distance Education Technologies*, 15(1), 52–68. doi:10.4018/IJDET.2017010104

Luciano, E. M., Wiedenhöft, G. C., Macadar, M. A., & Pinheiro dos Santos, F. (2016). Information Technology Governance Adoption: Understanding its Expectations Through the Lens of Organizational Citizenship. *International Journal of IT/Business Alignment and Governance,* 7(2), 22-32. doi:10.4018/IJITBAG.2016070102

Mabe, L. K., & Oladele, O. I. (2017). Application of Information Communication Technologies for Agricultural Development through Extension Services: A Review. In T. Tossy (Ed.), *Information Technology Integration for Socio-Economic Development* (pp. 52–101). Hershey, PA: IGI Global. doi:10.4018/978-1-5225-0539-6.ch003

Manogaran, G., Thota, C., & Lopez, D. (2018). Human-Computer Interaction With Big Data Analytics. In D. Lopez & M. Durai (Eds.), *HCI Challenges and Privacy Preservation in Big Data Security* (pp. 1–22). Hershey, PA: IGI Global. doi:10.4018/978-1-5225-2863-0.ch001

Margolis, J., Goode, J., & Flapan, J. (2017). A Critical Crossroads for Computer Science for All: "Identifying Talent" or "Building Talent," and What Difference Does It Make? In Y. Rankin & J. Thomas (Eds.), *Moving Students of Color from Consumers to Producers of Technology* (pp. 1–23). Hershey, PA: IGI Global. doi:10.4018/978-1-5225-2005-4.ch001

Mbale, J. (2018). Computer Centres Resource Cloud Elasticity-Scalability (CRECES): Copperbelt University Case Study. In S. Aljawarneh & M. Malhotra (Eds.), *Critical Research on Scalability and Security Issues in Virtual Cloud Environments* (pp. 48–70). Hershey, PA: IGI Global. doi:10.4018/978-1-5225-3029-9.ch003

McKee, J. (2018). The Right Information: The Key to Effective Business Planning. In *Business Architectures for Risk Assessment and Strategic Planning: Emerging Research and Opportunities* (pp. 38–52). Hershey, PA: IGI Global. doi:10.4018/978-1-5225-3392-4.ch003

Mensah, I. K., & Mi, J. (2018). Determinants of Intention to Use Local E-Government Services in Ghana: The Perspective of Local Government Workers. *International Journal of Technology Diffusion, 9*(2), 41–60. doi:10.4018/IJTD.2018040103

Mohamed, J. H. (2018). Scientograph-Based Visualization of Computer Forensics Research Literature. In J. Jeyasekar & P. Saravanan (Eds.), *Innovations in Measuring and Evaluating Scientific Information* (pp. 148–162). Hershey, PA: IGI Global. doi:10.4018/978-1-5225-3457-0.ch010

Moore, R. L., & Johnson, N. (2017). Earning a Seat at the Table: How IT Departments Can Partner in Organizational Change and Innovation. *International Journal of Knowledge-Based Organizations, 7*(2), 1–12. doi:10.4018/IJKBO.2017040101

Mtebe, J. S., & Kissaka, M. M. (2016). Enhancing the Quality of Computer Science Education with MOOCs in Sub-Saharan Africa. In J. Keengwe & G. Onchwari (Eds.), *Handbook of Research on Active Learning and the Flipped Classroom Model in the Digital Age* (pp. 366–377). Hershey, PA: IGI Global. doi:10.4018/978-1-4666-9680-8.ch019

Mukul, M. K., & Bhattaharyya, S. (2017). Brain-Machine Interface: Human-Computer Interaction. In E. Noughabi, B. Raahemi, A. Albadvi, & B. Far (Eds.), *Handbook of Research on Data Science for Effective Healthcare Practice and Administration* (pp. 417–443). Hershey, PA: IGI Global. doi:10.4018/978-1-5225-2515-8.ch018

Na, L. (2017). Library and Information Science Education and Graduate Programs in Academic Libraries. In L. Ruan, Q. Zhu, & Y. Ye (Eds.), *Academic Library Development and Administration in China* (pp. 218–229). Hershey, PA: IGI Global. doi:10.4018/978-1-5225-0550-1.ch013

Nabavi, A., Taghavi-Fard, M. T., Hanafizadeh, P., & Taghva, M. R. (2016). Information Technology Continuance Intention: A Systematic Literature Review. *International Journal of E-Business Research, 12*(1), 58–95. doi:10.4018/IJEBR.2016010104

Nath, R., & Murthy, V. N. (2018). What Accounts for the Differences in Internet Diffusion Rates Around the World? In M. Khosrow-Pour, D.B.A. (Ed.), Encyclopedia of Information Science and Technology, Fourth Edition (pp. 8095-8104). Hershey, PA: IGI Global. doi:10.4018/978-1-5225-2255-3.ch705

Nedelko, Z., & Potocan, V. (2018). The Role of Emerging Information Technologies for Supporting Supply Chain Management. In M. Khosrow-Pour, D.B.A. (Ed.), Encyclopedia of Information Science and Technology, Fourth Edition (pp. 5559-5569). Hershey, PA: IGI Global. doi:10.4018/978-1-5225-2255-3.ch483

Ngafeeson, M. N. (2018). User Resistance to Health Information Technology. In M. Khosrow-Pour, D.B.A. (Ed.), Encyclopedia of Information Science and Technology, Fourth Edition (pp. 3816-3825). Hershey, PA: IGI Global. doi:10.4018/978-1-5225-2255-3.ch331

Nozari, H., Najafi, S. E., Jafari-Eskandari, M., & Aliahmadi, A. (2016). Providing a Model for Virtual Project Management with an Emphasis on IT Projects. In C. Graham (Ed.), *Strategic Management and Leadership for Systems Development in Virtual Spaces* (pp. 43–63). Hershey, PA: IGI Global. doi:10.4018/978-1-4666-9688-4.ch003

Nurdin, N., Stockdale, R., & Scheepers, H. (2016). Influence of Organizational Factors in the Sustainability of E-Government: A Case Study of Local E-Government in Indonesia. In I. Sodhi (Ed.), *Trends, Prospects, and Challenges in Asian E-Governance* (pp. 281–323). Hershey, PA: IGI Global. doi:10.4018/978-1-4666-9536-8.ch014

Odagiri, K. (2017). Introduction of Individual Technology to Constitute the Current Internet. In *Strategic Policy-Based Network Management in Contemporary Organizations* (pp. 20–96). Hershey, PA: IGI Global. doi:10.4018/978-1-68318-003-6.ch003

Okike, E. U. (2018). Computer Science and Prison Education. In I. Biao (Ed.), *Strategic Learning Ideologies in Prison Education Programs* (pp. 246–264). Hershey, PA: IGI Global. doi:10.4018/978-1-5225-2909-5.ch012

Olelewe, C. J., & Nwafor, I. P. (2017). Level of Computer Appreciation Skills Acquired for Sustainable Development by Secondary School Students in Nsukka LGA of Enugu State, Nigeria. In C. Ayo & V. Mbarika (Eds.), *Sustainable ICT Adoption and Integration for Socio-Economic Development* (pp. 214–233). Hershey, PA: IGI Global. doi:10.4018/978-1-5225-2565-3.ch010

Oliveira, M., Maçada, A. C., Curado, C., & Nodari, F. (2017). Infrastructure Profiles and Knowledge Sharing. *International Journal of Technology and Human Interaction*, *13*(3), 1–12. doi:10.4018/IJTHI.2017070101

Otarkhani, A., Shokouhyar, S., & Pour, S. S. (2017). Analyzing the Impact of Governance of Enterprise IT on Hospital Performance: Tehran's (Iran) Hospitals – A Case Study. *International Journal of Healthcare Information Systems and Informatics*, *12*(3), 1–20. doi:10.4018/IJHISI.2017070101

Otunla, A. O., & Amuda, C. O. (2018). Nigerian Undergraduate Students' Computer Competencies and Use of Information Technology Tools and Resources for Study Skills and Habits' Enhancement. In M. Khosrow-Pour, D.B.A. (Ed.), Encyclopedia of Information Science and Technology, Fourth Edition (pp. 2303-2313). Hershey, PA: IGI Global. doi:10.4018/978-1-5225-2255-3.ch200

Özçınar, H. (2018). A Brief Discussion on Incentives and Barriers to Computational Thinking Education. In H. Ozcinar, G. Wong, & H. Ozturk (Eds.), *Teaching Computational Thinking in Primary Education* (pp. 1–17). Hershey, PA: IGI Global. doi:10.4018/978-1-5225-3200-2.ch001

Pandey, J. M., Garg, S., Mishra, P., & Mishra, B. P. (2017). Computer Based Psychological Interventions: Subject to the Efficacy of Psychological Services. *International Journal of Computers in Clinical Practice*, *2*(1), 25–33. doi:10.4018/IJCCP.2017010102

Parry, V. K., & Lind, M. L. (2016). Alignment of Business Strategy and Information Technology Considering Information Technology Governance, Project Portfolio Control, and Risk Management. *International Journal of Information Technology Project Management*, *7*(4), 21–37. doi:10.4018/IJITPM.2016100102

Patro, C. (2017). Impulsion of Information Technology on Human Resource Practices. In P. Ordóñez de Pablos (Ed.), *Managerial Strategies and Solutions for Business Success in Asia* (pp. 231–254). Hershey, PA: IGI Global. doi:10.4018/978-1-5225-1886-0.ch013

Patro, C. S., & Raghunath, K. M. (2017). Information Technology Paraphernalia for Supply Chain Management Decisions. In M. Tavana (Ed.), *Enterprise Information Systems and the Digitalization of Business Functions* (pp. 294–320). Hershey, PA: IGI Global. doi:10.4018/978-1-5225-2382-6.ch014

Paul, P. K. (2016). Cloud Computing: An Agent of Promoting Interdisciplinary Sciences, Especially Information Science and I-Schools – Emerging Techno-Educational Scenario. In L. Chao (Ed.), *Handbook of Research on Cloud-Based STEM Education for Improved Learning Outcomes* (pp. 247–258). Hershey, PA: IGI Global. doi:10.4018/978-1-4666-9924-3.ch016

Paul, P. K. (2018). The Context of IST for Solid Information Retrieval and Infrastructure Building: Study of Developing Country. *International Journal of Information Retrieval Research, 8*(1), 86–100. doi:10.4018/IJIRR.2018010106

Paul, P. K., & Chatterjee, D. (2018). iSchools Promoting "Information Science and Technology" (IST) Domain Towards Community, Business, and Society With Contemporary Worldwide Trend and Emerging Potentialities in India. In M. Khosrow-Pour, D.B.A. (Ed.), Encyclopedia of Information Science and Technology, Fourth Edition (pp. 4723-4735). Hershey, PA: IGI Global. doi:10.4018/978-1-5225-2255-3.ch410

Pessoa, C. R., & Marques, M. E. (2017). Information Technology and Communication Management in Supply Chain Management. In G. Jamil, A. Soares, & C. Pessoa (Eds.), *Handbook of Research on Information Management for Effective Logistics and Supply Chains* (pp. 23–33). Hershey, PA: IGI Global. doi:10.4018/978-1-5225-0973-8.ch002

Pineda, R. G. (2016). Where the Interaction Is Not: Reflections on the Philosophy of Human-Computer Interaction. *International Journal of Art, Culture and Design Technologies, 5*(1), 1–12. doi:10.4018/IJACDT.2016010101

Pineda, R. G. (2018). Remediating Interaction: Towards a Philosophy of Human-Computer Relationship. In M. Khosrow-Pour (Ed.), *Enhancing Art, Culture, and Design With Technological Integration* (pp. 75–98). Hershey, PA: IGI Global. doi:10.4018/978-1-5225-5023-5.ch004

Poikela, P., & Vuojärvi, H. (2016). Learning ICT-Mediated Communication through Computer-Based Simulations. In M. Cruz-Cunha, I. Miranda, R. Martinho, & R. Rijo (Eds.), *Encyclopedia of E-Health and Telemedicine* (pp. 674–687). Hershey, PA: IGI Global. doi:10.4018/978-1-4666-9978-6.ch052

Qian, Y. (2017). Computer Simulation in Higher Education: Affordances, Opportunities, and Outcomes. In P. Vu, S. Fredrickson, & C. Moore (Eds.), *Handbook of Research on Innovative Pedagogies and Technologies for Online Learning in Higher Education* (pp. 236–262). Hershey, PA: IGI Global. doi:10.4018/978-1-5225-1851-8.ch011

Radant, O., Colomo-Palacios, R., & Stantchev, V. (2016). Factors for the Management of Scarce Human Resources and Highly Skilled Employees in IT-Departments: A Systematic Review. *Journal of Information Technology Research*, 9(1), 65–82. doi:10.4018/JITR.2016010105

Rahman, N. (2016). Toward Achieving Environmental Sustainability in the Computer Industry. *International Journal of Green Computing*, 7(1), 37–54. doi:10.4018/IJGC.2016010103

Rahman, N. (2017). Lessons from a Successful Data Warehousing Project Management. *International Journal of Information Technology Project Management*, 8(4), 30–45. doi:10.4018/IJITPM.2017100103

Rahman, N. (2018). Environmental Sustainability in the Computer Industry for Competitive Advantage. In M. Khosrow-Pour (Ed.), *Green Computing Strategies for Competitive Advantage and Business Sustainability* (pp. 110–130). Hershey, PA: IGI Global. doi:10.4018/978-1-5225-5017-4.ch006

Rajh, A., & Pavetic, T. (2017). Computer Generated Description as the Required Digital Competence in Archival Profession. *International Journal of Digital Literacy and Digital Competence*, 8(1), 36–49. doi:10.4018/IJDLDC.2017010103

Raman, A., & Goyal, D. P. (2017). Extending IMPLEMENT Framework for Enterprise Information Systems Implementation to Information System Innovation. In M. Tavana (Ed.), *Enterprise Information Systems and the Digitalization of Business Functions* (pp. 137–177). Hershey, PA: IGI Global. doi:10.4018/978-1-5225-2382-6.ch007

Rao, Y. S., Rauta, A. K., Saini, H., & Panda, T. C. (2017). Mathematical Model for Cyber Attack in Computer Network. *International Journal of Business Data Communications and Networking*, 13(1), 58–65. doi:10.4018/IJBDCN.2017010105

Rapaport, W. J. (2018). Syntactic Semantics and the Proper Treatment of Computationalism. In M. Danesi (Ed.), *Empirical Research on Semiotics and Visual Rhetoric* (pp. 128–176). Hershey, PA: IGI Global. doi:10.4018/978-1-5225-5622-0.ch007

Raut, R., Priyadarshinee, P., & Jha, M. (2017). Understanding the Mediation Effect of Cloud Computing Adoption in Indian Organization: Integrating TAM-TOE- Risk Model. *International Journal of Service Science, Management, Engineering, and Technology, 8*(3), 40–59. doi:10.4018/IJSSMET.2017070103

Regan, E. A., & Wang, J. (2016). Realizing the Value of EHR Systems Critical Success Factors. *International Journal of Healthcare Information Systems and Informatics, 11*(3), 1–18. doi:10.4018/IJHISI.2016070101

Rezaie, S., Mirabedini, S. J., & Abtahi, A. (2018). Designing a Model for Implementation of Business Intelligence in the Banking Industry. *International Journal of Enterprise Information Systems, 14*(1), 77–103. doi:10.4018/IJEIS.2018010105

Rezende, D. A. (2016). Digital City Projects: Information and Public Services Offered by Chicago (USA) and Curitiba (Brazil). *International Journal of Knowledge Society Research, 7*(3), 16–30. doi:10.4018/IJKSR.2016070102

Rezende, D. A. (2018). Strategic Digital City Projects: Innovative Information and Public Services Offered by Chicago (USA) and Curitiba (Brazil). In M. Lytras, L. Daniela, & A. Visvizi (Eds.), *Enhancing Knowledge Discovery and Innovation in the Digital Era* (pp. 204–223). Hershey, PA: IGI Global. doi:10.4018/978-1-5225-4191-2.ch012

Riabov, V. V. (2016). Teaching Online Computer-Science Courses in LMS and Cloud Environment. *International Journal of Quality Assurance in Engineering and Technology Education, 5*(4), 12–41. doi:10.4018/IJQAETE.2016100102

Ricordel, V., Wang, J., Da Silva, M. P., & Le Callet, P. (2016). 2D and 3D Visual Attention for Computer Vision: Concepts, Measurement, and Modeling. In R. Pal (Ed.), *Innovative Research in Attention Modeling and Computer Vision Applications* (pp. 1–44). Hershey, PA: IGI Global. doi:10.4018/978-1-4666-8723-3.ch001

Rodriguez, A., Rico-Diaz, A. J., Rabuñal, J. R., & Gestal, M. (2017). Fish Tracking with Computer Vision Techniques: An Application to Vertical Slot Fishways. In M. S., & V. V. (Eds.), Multi-Core Computer Vision and Image Processing for Intelligent Applications (pp. 74-104). Hershey, PA: IGI Global. doi:10.4018/978-1-5225-0889-2.ch003

Romero, J. A. (2018). Sustainable Advantages of Business Value of Information Technology. In M. Khosrow-Pour, D.B.A. (Ed.), Encyclopedia of Information Science and Technology, Fourth Edition (pp. 923-929). Hershey, PA: IGI Global. doi:10.4018/978-1-5225-2255-3.ch079

Romero, J. A. (2018). The Always-On Business Model and Competitive Advantage. In N. Bajgoric (Ed.), *Always-On Enterprise Information Systems for Modern Organizations* (pp. 23–40). Hershey, PA: IGI Global. doi:10.4018/978-1-5225-3704-5.ch002

Rosen, Y. (2018). Computer Agent Technologies in Collaborative Learning and Assessment. In M. Khosrow-Pour, D.B.A. (Ed.), Encyclopedia of Information Science and Technology, Fourth Edition (pp. 2402-2410). Hershey, PA: IGI Global. doi:10.4018/978-1-5225-2255-3.ch209

Rosen, Y., & Mosharraf, M. (2016). Computer Agent Technologies in Collaborative Assessments. In Y. Rosen, S. Ferrara, & M. Mosharraf (Eds.), *Handbook of Research on Technology Tools for Real-World Skill Development* (pp. 319–343). Hershey, PA: IGI Global. doi:10.4018/978-1-4666-9441-5.ch012

Roy, D. (2018). Success Factors of Adoption of Mobile Applications in Rural India: Effect of Service Characteristics on Conceptual Model. In M. Khosrow-Pour (Ed.), *Green Computing Strategies for Competitive Advantage and Business Sustainability* (pp. 211–238). Hershey, PA: IGI Global. doi:10.4018/978-1-5225-5017-4.ch010

Ruffin, T. R. (2016). Health Information Technology and Change. In V. Wang (Ed.), *Handbook of Research on Advancing Health Education through Technology* (pp. 259–285). Hershey, PA: IGI Global. doi:10.4018/978-1-4666-9494-1.ch012

Ruffin, T. R. (2016). Health Information Technology and Quality Management. *International Journal of Information Communication Technologies and Human Development*, 8(4), 56–72. doi:10.4018/IJICTHD.2016100105

Ruffin, T. R., & Hawkins, D. P. (2018). Trends in Health Care Information Technology and Informatics. In M. Khosrow-Pour, D.B.A. (Ed.), Encyclopedia of Information Science and Technology, Fourth Edition (pp. 3805-3815). Hershey, PA: IGI Global. doi:10.4018/978-1-5225-2255-3.ch330

Safari, M. R., & Jiang, Q. (2018). The Theory and Practice of IT Governance Maturity and Strategies Alignment: Evidence From Banking Industry. *Journal of Global Information Management*, 26(2), 127–146. doi:10.4018/JGIM.2018040106

Sahin, H. B., & Anagun, S. S. (2018). Educational Computer Games in Math Teaching: A Learning Culture. In E. Toprak & E. Kumtepe (Eds.), *Supporting Multiculturalism in Open and Distance Learning Spaces* (pp. 249–280). Hershey, PA: IGI Global. doi:10.4018/978-1-5225-3076-3.ch013

Sanna, A., & Valpreda, F. (2017). An Assessment of the Impact of a Collaborative Didactic Approach and Students' Background in Teaching Computer Animation. *International Journal of Information and Communication Technology Education*, *13*(4), 1–16. doi:10.4018/IJICTE.2017100101

Savita, K., Dominic, P., & Ramayah, T. (2016). The Drivers, Practices and Outcomes of Green Supply Chain Management: Insights from ISO14001 Manufacturing Firms in Malaysia. *International Journal of Information Systems and Supply Chain Management*, *9*(2), 35–60. doi:10.4018/IJISSCM.2016040103

Scott, A., Martin, A., & McAlear, F. (2017). Enhancing Participation in Computer Science among Girls of Color: An Examination of a Preparatory AP Computer Science Intervention. In Y. Rankin & J. Thomas (Eds.), *Moving Students of Color from Consumers to Producers of Technology* (pp. 62–84). Hershey, PA: IGI Global. doi:10.4018/978-1-5225-2005-4.ch004

Shahsavandi, E., Mayah, G., & Rahbari, H. (2016). Impact of E-Government on Transparency and Corruption in Iran. In I. Sodhi (Ed.), *Trends, Prospects, and Challenges in Asian E-Governance* (pp. 75–94). Hershey, PA: IGI Global. doi:10.4018/978-1-4666-9536-8.ch004

Siddoo, V., & Wongsai, N. (2017). Factors Influencing the Adoption of ISO/IEC 29110 in Thai Government Projects: A Case Study. *International Journal of Information Technologies and Systems Approach*, *10*(1), 22–44. doi:10.4018/IJITSA.2017010102

Sidorkina, I., & Rybakov, A. (2016). Computer-Aided Design as Carrier of Set Development Changes System in E-Course Engineering. In V. Mkrttchian, A. Bershadsky, A. Bozhday, M. Kataev, & S. Kataev (Eds.), *Handbook of Research on Estimation and Control Techniques in E-Learning Systems* (pp. 500–515). Hershey, PA: IGI Global. doi:10.4018/978-1-4666-9489-7.ch035

Sidorkina, I., & Rybakov, A. (2016). Creating Model of E-Course: As an Object of Computer-Aided Design. In V. Mkrttchian, A. Bershadsky, A. Bozhday, M. Kataev, & S. Kataev (Eds.), *Handbook of Research on Estimation and Control Techniques in E-Learning Systems* (pp. 286–297). Hershey, PA: IGI Global. doi:10.4018/978-1-4666-9489-7.ch019

Simões, A. (2017). Using Game Frameworks to Teach Computer Programming. In R. Alexandre Peixoto de Queirós & M. Pinto (Eds.), *Gamification-Based E-Learning Strategies for Computer Programming Education* (pp. 221–236). Hershey, PA: IGI Global. doi:10.4018/978-1-5225-1034-5.ch010

Sllame, A. M. (2017). Integrating LAB Work With Classes in Computer Network Courses. In H. Alphin Jr, R. Chan, & J. Lavine (Eds.), *The Future of Accessibility in International Higher Education* (pp. 253–275.). Hershey, PA: IGI Global. doi:10.4018/978-1-5225-2560-8.ch015

Smirnov, A., Ponomarev, A., Shilov, N., Kashevnik, A., & Teslya, N. (2018). Ontology-Based Human-Computer Cloud for Decision Support: Architecture and Applications in Tourism. *International Journal of Embedded and Real-Time Communication Systems*, 9(1), 1–19. doi:10.4018/IJERTCS.2018010101

Smith-Ditizio, A. A., & Smith, A. D. (2018). Computer Fraud Challenges and Its Legal Implications. In M. Khosrow-Pour, D.B.A. (Ed.), Encyclopedia of Information Science and Technology, Fourth Edition (pp. 4837-4848). Hershey, PA: IGI Global. doi:10.4018/978-1-5225-2255-3.ch419

Sohani, S. S. (2016). Job Shadowing in Information Technology Projects: A Source of Competitive Advantage. *International Journal of Information Technology Project Management*, 7(1), 47–57. doi:10.4018/IJITPM.2016010104

Sosnin, P. (2018). Figuratively Semantic Support of Human-Computer Interactions. In *Experience-Based Human-Computer Interactions: Emerging Research and Opportunities* (pp. 244–272). Hershey, PA: IGI Global. doi:10.4018/978-1-5225-2987-3.ch008

Spinelli, R., & Benevolo, C. (2016). From Healthcare Services to E-Health Applications: A Delivery System-Based Taxonomy. In A. Dwivedi (Ed.), *Reshaping Medical Practice and Care with Health Information Systems* (pp. 205–245). Hershey, PA: IGI Global. doi:10.4018/978-1-4666-9870-3.ch007

Srinivasan, S. (2016). Overview of Clinical Trial and Pharmacovigilance Process and Areas of Application of Computer System. In P. Chakraborty & A. Nagal (Eds.), *Software Innovations in Clinical Drug Development and Safety* (pp. 1–13). Hershey, PA: IGI Global. doi:10.4018/978-1-4666-8726-4.ch001

Srisawasdi, N. (2016). Motivating Inquiry-Based Learning Through a Combination of Physical and Virtual Computer-Based Laboratory Experiments in High School Science. In M. Urban & D. Falvo (Eds.), *Improving K-12 STEM Education Outcomes through Technological Integration* (pp. 108–134). Hershey, PA: IGI Global. doi:10.4018/978-1-4666-9616-7.ch006

Stavridi, S. V., & Hamada, D. R. (2016). Children and Youth Librarians: Competencies Required in Technology-Based Environment. In J. Yap, M. Perez, M. Ayson, & G. Entico (Eds.), *Special Library Administration, Standardization and Technological Integration* (pp. 25–50). Hershey, PA: IGI Global. doi:10.4018/978-1-4666-9542-9.ch002

Sung, W., Ahn, J., Kai, S. M., Choi, A., & Black, J. B. (2016). Incorporating Touch-Based Tablets into Classroom Activities: Fostering Children's Computational Thinking through iPad Integrated Instruction. In D. Mentor (Ed.), *Handbook of Research on Mobile Learning in Contemporary Classrooms* (pp. 378–406). Hershey, PA: IGI Global. doi:10.4018/978-1-5225-0251-7.ch019

Syväjärvi, A., Leinonen, J., Kivivirta, V., & Kesti, M. (2017). The Latitude of Information Management in Local Government: Views of Local Government Managers. *International Journal of Electronic Government Research*, *13*(1), 69–85. doi:10.4018/IJEGR.2017010105

Tanque, M., & Foxwell, H. J. (2018). Big Data and Cloud Computing: A Review of Supply Chain Capabilities and Challenges. In A. Prasad (Ed.), *Exploring the Convergence of Big Data and the Internet of Things* (pp. 1–28). Hershey, PA: IGI Global. doi:10.4018/978-1-5225-2947-7.ch001

Teixeira, A., Gomes, A., & Orvalho, J. G. (2017). Auditory Feedback in a Computer Game for Blind People. In T. Issa, P. Kommers, T. Issa, P. Isaías, & T. Issa (Eds.), *Smart Technology Applications in Business Environments* (pp. 134–158). Hershey, PA: IGI Global. doi:10.4018/978-1-5225-2492-2.ch007

Thompson, N., McGill, T., & Murray, D. (2018). Affect-Sensitive Computer Systems. In M. Khosrow-Pour, D.B.A. (Ed.), Encyclopedia of Information Science and Technology, Fourth Edition (pp. 4124-4135). Hershey, PA: IGI Global. doi:10.4018/978-1-5225-2255-3.ch357

Trad, A., & Kalpić, D. (2016). The E-Business Transformation Framework for E-Commerce Control and Monitoring Pattern. In I. Lee (Ed.), *Encyclopedia of E-Commerce Development, Implementation, and Management* (pp. 754–777). Hershey, PA: IGI Global. doi:10.4018/978-1-4666-9787-4.ch053

Triberti, S., Brivio, E., & Galimberti, C. (2018). On Social Presence: Theories, Methodologies, and Guidelines for the Innovative Contexts of Computer-Mediated Learning. In M. Marmon (Ed.), *Enhancing Social Presence in Online Learning Environments* (pp. 20–41). Hershey, PA: IGI Global. doi:10.4018/978-1-5225-3229-3.ch002

Tripathy, B. K. T. R., S., & Mohanty, R. K. (2018). Memetic Algorithms and Their Applications in Computer Science. In S. Dash, B. Tripathy, & A. Rahman (Eds.), Handbook of Research on Modeling, Analysis, and Application of Nature-Inspired Metaheuristic Algorithms (pp. 73-93). Hershey, PA: IGI Global. doi:10.4018/978-1-5225-2857-9.ch004

Turulja, L., & Bajgoric, N. (2017). Human Resource Management IT and Global Economy Perspective: Global Human Resource Information Systems. In M. Khosrow-Pour (Ed.), *Handbook of Research on Technology Adoption, Social Policy, and Global Integration* (pp. 377–394). Hershey, PA: IGI Global. doi:10.4018/978-1-5225-2668-1.ch018

Unwin, D. W., Sanzogni, L., & Sandhu, K. (2017). Developing and Measuring the Business Case for Health Information Technology. In K. Moahi, K. Bwalya, & P. Sebina (Eds.), *Health Information Systems and the Advancement of Medical Practice in Developing Countries* (pp. 262–290). Hershey, PA: IGI Global. doi:10.4018/978-1-5225-2262-1.ch015

Vadhanam, B. R. S., M., Sugumaran, V., V., V., & Ramalingam, V. V. (2017). Computer Vision Based Classification on Commercial Videos. In M. S., & V. V. (Eds.), Multi-Core Computer Vision and Image Processing for Intelligent Applications (pp. 105-135). Hershey, PA: IGI Global. doi:10.4018/978-1-5225-0889-2.ch004

Valverde, R., Torres, B., & Motaghi, H. (2018). A Quantum NeuroIS Data Analytics Architecture for the Usability Evaluation of Learning Management Systems. In S. Bhattacharyya (Ed.), *Quantum-Inspired Intelligent Systems for Multimedia Data Analysis* (pp. 277–299). Hershey, PA: IGI Global. doi:10.4018/978-1-5225-5219-2.ch009

Vassilis, E. (2018). Learning and Teaching Methodology: "1:1 Educational Computing. In K. Koutsopoulos, K. Doukas, & Y. Kotsanis (Eds.), *Handbook of Research on Educational Design and Cloud Computing in Modern Classroom Settings* (pp. 122–155). Hershey, PA: IGI Global. doi:10.4018/978-1-5225-3053-4.ch007

Wadhwani, A. K., Wadhwani, S., & Singh, T. (2016). Computer Aided Diagnosis System for Breast Cancer Detection. In Y. Morsi, A. Shukla, & C. Rathore (Eds.), *Optimizing Assistive Technologies for Aging Populations* (pp. 378–395). Hershey, PA: IGI Global. doi:10.4018/978-1-4666-9530-6.ch015

Wang, L., Wu, Y., & Hu, C. (2016). English Teachers' Practice and Perspectives on Using Educational Computer Games in EIL Context. *International Journal of Technology and Human Interaction, 12*(3), 33–46. doi:10.4018/IJTHI.2016070103

Watfa, M. K., Majeed, H., & Salahuddin, T. (2016). Computer Based E-Healthcare Clinical Systems: A Comprehensive Survey. *International Journal of Privacy and Health Information Management*, *4*(1), 50–69. doi:10.4018/IJPHIM.2016010104

Weeger, A., & Haase, U. (2016). Taking up Three Challenges to Business-IT Alignment Research by the Use of Activity Theory. *International Journal of IT/ Business Alignment and Governance*, *7*(2), 1-21. doi:10.4018/IJITBAG.2016070101

Wexler, B. E. (2017). Computer-Presented and Physical Brain-Training Exercises for School Children: Improving Executive Functions and Learning. In B. Dubbels (Ed.), *Transforming Gaming and Computer Simulation Technologies across Industries* (pp. 206–224). Hershey, PA: IGI Global. doi:10.4018/978-1-5225-1817-4.ch012

Williams, D. M., Gani, M. O., Addo, I. D., Majumder, A. J., Tamma, C. P., Wang, M., ... Chu, C. (2016). Challenges in Developing Applications for Aging Populations. In Y. Morsi, A. Shukla, & C. Rathore (Eds.), *Optimizing Assistive Technologies for Aging Populations* (pp. 1–21). Hershey, PA: IGI Global. doi:10.4018/978-1-4666-9530-6.ch001

Wimble, M., Singh, H., & Phillips, B. (2018). Understanding Cross-Level Interactions of Firm-Level Information Technology and Industry Environment: A Multilevel Model of Business Value. *Information Resources Management Journal*, *31*(1), 1–20. doi:10.4018/IRMJ.2018010101

Wimmer, H., Powell, L., Kilgus, L., & Force, C. (2017). Improving Course Assessment via Web-based Homework. *International Journal of Online Pedagogy and Course Design*, *7*(2), 1–19. doi:10.4018/IJOPCD.2017040101

Wong, Y. L., & Siu, K. W. (2018). Assessing Computer-Aided Design Skills. In M. Khosrow-Pour, D.B.A. (Ed.), Encyclopedia of Information Science and Technology, Fourth Edition (pp. 7382-7391). Hershey, PA: IGI Global. doi:10.4018/978-1-5225-2255-3.ch642

Wongsurawat, W., & Shrestha, V. (2018). Information Technology, Globalization, and Local Conditions: Implications for Entrepreneurs in Southeast Asia. In P. Ordóñez de Pablos (Ed.), *Management Strategies and Technology Fluidity in the Asian Business Sector* (pp. 163–176). Hershey, PA: IGI Global. doi:10.4018/978-1-5225-4056-4.ch010

Yang, Y., Zhu, X., Jin, C., & Li, J. J. (2018). Reforming Classroom Education Through a QQ Group: A Pilot Experiment at a Primary School in Shanghai. In H. Spires (Ed.), *Digital Transformation and Innovation in Chinese Education* (pp. 211–231). Hershey, PA: IGI Global. doi:10.4018/978-1-5225-2924-8.ch012

Yilmaz, R., Sezgin, A., Kurnaz, S., & Arslan, Y. Z. (2018). Object-Oriented Programming in Computer Science. In M. Khosrow-Pour, D.B.A. (Ed.), Encyclopedia of Information Science and Technology, Fourth Edition (pp. 7470-7480). Hershey, PA: IGI Global. doi:10.4018/978-1-5225-2255-3.ch650

Yu, L. (2018). From Teaching Software Engineering Locally and Globally to Devising an Internationalized Computer Science Curriculum. In S. Dikli, B. Etheridge, & R. Rawls (Eds.), *Curriculum Internationalization and the Future of Education* (pp. 293–320). Hershey, PA: IGI Global. doi:10.4018/978-1-5225-2791-6.ch016

Yuhua, F. (2018). Computer Information Library Clusters. In M. Khosrow-Pour, D.B.A. (Ed.), Encyclopedia of Information Science and Technology, Fourth Edition (pp. 4399-4403). Hershey, PA: IGI Global. doi:10.4018/978-1-5225-2255-3.ch382

Zare, M. A., Taghavi Fard, M. T., & Hanafizadeh, P. (2016). The Assessment of Outsourcing IT Services using DEA Technique: A Study of Application Outsourcing in Research Centers. *International Journal of Operations Research and Information Systems*, 7(1), 45–57. doi:10.4018/IJORIS.2016010104

Zhao, J., Wang, Q., Guo, J., Gao, L., & Yang, F. (2016). An Overview on Passive Image Forensics Technology for Automatic Computer Forgery. *International Journal of Digital Crime and Forensics*, 8(4), 14–25. doi:10.4018/IJDCF.2016100102

Zimeras, S. (2016). Computer Virus Models and Analysis in M-Health IT Systems: Computer Virus Models. In A. Moumtzoglou (Ed.), *M-Health Innovations for Patient-Centered Care* (pp. 284–297). Hershey, PA: IGI Global. doi:10.4018/978-1-4666-9861-1.ch014

Zlatanovska, K. (2016). Hacking and Hacktivism as an Information Communication System Threat. In M. Hadji-Janev & M. Bogdanoski (Eds.), *Handbook of Research on Civil Society and National Security in the Era of Cyber Warfare* (pp. 68–101). Hershey, PA: IGI Global. doi:10.4018/978-1-4666-8793-6.ch004

About the Contributors

Preeti Sharma has done a lot of research in the area of IoT and Machine Learning. She is working in Bansal College of Engineering as Assistant Professor which is located at India. She has published many papers and chapters in various international journals and conferences. She is having more than 13 years of academic experience in the field of Computer Science & Electronics & Communication Engineering and also working as a reviewer of reputed International journals. She also received many awards from various organizations for contribution in the field of academics. Currently she is working on different project which are based on IoT and machine learning.

Rajit Nair has done a lot of research in the area of IoT, Machine Learning and Blockchain. He is working in Jagran Lakecity University as Assistant Professor which is located at India. He has published many papers and chapters in various international journals and conferences. He is having more than 13 years of academic experience in the field of Computer Science & Engineering and also working as a reviewer of reputed International journals. He also received many awards from various organizations for contribution in the field of academics. Currently he is working on different project which are based on IoT and machine learning.

* * *

Banuselvasaraswathy B. completed B.E in Electronics and Communication Engineering in 2012 and M.E in VLSI design in 2014.Area of Interest includes VLSI Design, Cryptography and Network Security.

Arul Murugan C. received his Bachelor of Engineering degree in Electronics and Communication Engineering in the year 2010 from Anna University, Chennai and his Master of Engineering degree from Anna University, Chennai in the year 2012. He is pursuing Ph.D in the area of Cryptography and Network Security. He joined Karpagam College of Engineering, Coimbatore, India in 2012. He is now

Assistant Professor in Electronics and Telecommunication Engineering. He is a member of ISTE, IAENG, ISRD, and SDIWC.

Anjali Daisy is a Research Scholar, School of Management, SASTRA Deemed University.

P. Dananjayan received Bachelor of Science from University of Madras in 1979, Bachelor of Technology in 1982 and Master of Engineering in 1984 from the Madras Institute of Technology, Chennai and Ph.D. degree from Anna University, Chennai in 1998. He is currently working as a Principal and Professor in the Department of Electronics and Communication Engineering, Pondicherry Engineering College, Pondicherry, India. He is also as a visiting professor to AIT, Bangkok. He has more than 110 publications in National and International Journals. He has presented more than 130 papers in National and International Conferences. He has guided 19 Ph.D candidates and is currently guiding 6 Ph.D students. His research interests include Spread Spectrum Techniques, Wireless Communication, Wireless Adhoc and Sensor Networks.

Arturo Diaz-Perez received the Ph.D. degree in electrical engineering from CINVESTAV, Mexico, in 1998. He is currently a full-time Professor with CINVESTAV Guadalajara.

Juan Escobedo Contreras is a Researcher at UCF. Working on Ph.D. in EE doing research in HLS.

Ashok Kumar K. received Bachelor of Technology from Jawaharlal Nehru Technical University in 2009 and Master of Technology in 2011 from Jawaharlal Nehru Technical University. He worked 3 years as an Assistant Professor in Malla Reddy Institute of Engineering and Technology. Currently, he is working as Research Scholar in the Department of Electronics and Communication Engineering, Pondicherry Engineering College, Pondicherry, India. He has 5 publications in International Journals. His research interests include VLSI system design, Spread Spectrum Techniques, Communication Networks.

Saber Krim received the Electrical Engineering Diploma, the Master, and the Ph.D. degrees in 2011, 2013, and 2017, respectively, all in electrical engineering from the National Engineering School of Monastir, University of Monastir, Tunisia. He is a member of the Research Unit of Industrial Systems study and Renewable Energy, University of Monastir. His current research interests include rapid prototyping and reconfigurable architecture for real-time control applications of electrical systems.

Carlos Andres Lara-Nino received the master's degree in computer science from CINVESTAV Tamaulipas, Mexico, in 2016, where he is currently pursuing the Ph.D. degree.

Mingjie Lin received his B.S. in engineering from the Xi'an Jiaotong University, Xi'an, China, the M.S. degree in Mechanical Engineering and the M.S. degree in Electrical Engineering from Clemson University in 2001, and the PhD in Electrical Engineering from Stanford University in 2008. From 2008 to 2009, he worked at an FPGA startup---Tabula Inc. for one year as a senior engineer. Missing the atmosphere of academic research, he returned to academia at the beginning of 2009 and worked as a post-doctoral scholar at EECS of UC Berkeley for two years. Mingjie's previous research involves VLSI reconfigurable array architecture, bio-inspired/ neuromorphic arrays, and monolithically stacked 3D-IC. His current research focuses on exploring novel ways to construct scalable embedded computing machine with high performance and low power consumption. To this end, his research activities spanned across Computer Architecture/Compiler, Reconfigurable Computing, Integrated Circuit, and System Design.

Miguel Morales-Sandoval received the Ph.D. degree from the National Institute for Astrophysics, Optics, and Electronics, Mexico, in 2008. He is currently a full-time researcher at CINVESTAV Tamaulipas.

Chandrasekaran R. has completed his bachelor of Engineering in Biomedical Engineering in Anna University and Completed his Master of Engineering in Biomedical Engineering in Anna University. He has two years of Teaching Experience and One year of Industrial Experience. His Research areas include Biomedical Instrumentation, Bio-Signal Processing

Saravanan Sivasankaran is working as an Associate Professor in the Department of ISE, CMRIT, Bengaluru, India. He did his Ph.D in Test Pattern Compression for Low power System-on-chip (SoC) Design Testing. He has 18 years of experience in both teaching and research. So far, he has published 2 patents in IoT domain and 3 SCI research papers. He also published 65+ SCOPUS indexed research articles in National and International journals. His research interest focuses on VLSI design and testing, Embedded Systems, IoT, FPGA design, and Security issues in hardware.

Index

A

B

C

D

E

F

G

H

I

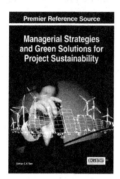

IGI Global Author Services

Providing a high-quality, affordable, and expeditious service, IGI Global's Author Services enable authors to streamline their publishing process, increase chance of acceptance, and adhere to IGI Global's publication standards.

Benefits of Author Services:

- **Professional Service:** All our editors, designers, and translators are experts in their field with years of experience and professional certifications.
- **Quality Guarantee & Certificate:** Each order is returned with a quality guarantee and certificate of professional completion.
- **Timeliness:** All editorial orders have a guaranteed return timeframe of 3-5 business days and translation orders are guaranteed in 7-10 business days.
- **Affordable Pricing:** IGI Global Author Services are competitively priced compared to other industry service providers.
- **APC Reimbursement:** IGI Global authors publishing Open Access (OA) will be able to deduct the cost of editing and other IGI Global author services from their OA APC publishing fee.

Author Services Offered:

English Language Copy Editing
Professional, native English language copy editors improve your manuscript's grammar, spelling, punctuation, terminology, semantics, consistency, flow, formatting, and more.

Scientific & Scholarly Editing
A Ph.D. level review for qualities such as originality and significance, interest to researchers, level of methodology and analysis, coverage of literature, organization, quality of writing, and strengths and weaknesses.

Figure, Table, Chart & Equation Conversions
Work with IGI Global's graphic designers before submission to enhance and design all figures and charts to IGI Global's specific standards for clarity.

Translation
Providing 70 language options, including Simplified and Traditional Chinese, Spanish, Arabic, German, French, and more.

Hear What the Experts Are Saying About IGI Global's Author Services

"Publishing with IGI Global has been *an amazing experience* for me for sharing my research. The *strong academic production* support ensures quality and timely completion." – **Prof. Margaret Niess, Oregon State University, USA**

"The service was *very fast, very thorough, and very helpful* in ensuring our chapter meets the criteria and requirements of the book's editors. I was *quite impressed and happy* with your service." – **Prof. Tom Brinthaupt, Middle Tennessee State University, USA**

Learn More or Get Started Here:

For Questions, Contact IGI Global's Customer Service Team at cust@igi-global.com or 717-533-8845

IGI Global
PUBLISHER of TIMELY KNOWLEDGE
www.igi-global.com

Publisher of Peer-Reviewed, Timely, and
Innovative Academic Research Since 1988

IGI Global's Transformative Open Access (OA) Model:
How to Turn Your University Library's Database Acquisitions Into a Source of OA Funding

Well in advance of Plan S, IGI Global unveiled their OA Fee Waiver (Read & Publish) Initiative. Under this initiative, librarians who invest in IGI Global's InfoSci-Books and/or InfoSci-Journals databases will be able to subsidize their patrons' OA article processing charges (APCs) when their work is submitted and accepted (after the peer review process) into an IGI Global journal.

How Does it Work?

Step 1: **Library Invests in the InfoSci-Databases:** A library perpetually purchases or subscribes to the InfoSci-Books, InfoSci-Journals, or discipline/subject databases.

Step 2: **IGI Global Matches the Library Investment with OA Subsidies Fund:** IGI Global provides a fund to go towards subsidizing the OA APCs for the library's patrons.

Step 3: **Patron of the Library is Accepted into IGI Global Journal (After Peer Review):** When a patron's paper is accepted into an IGI Global journal, they option to have their paper published under a traditional publishing model or as OA.

Step 4: **IGI Global Will Deduct APC Cost from OA Subsidies Fund:** If the author decides to publish under OA, the OA APC fee will be deducted from the OA subsidies fund.

Step 5: **Author's Work Becomes Freely Available:** The patron's work will be freely available under CC BY copyright license, enabling them to share it freely with the academic community.

Note: *This fund will be offered on an annual basis and will renew as the subscription is renewed for each year thereafter. IGI Global will manage the fund and award the APC waivers unless the librarian has a preference as to how the funds should be managed.*

Hear From the Experts on This Initiative:

"I'm very happy to have been able to make one of my recent research contributions *freely available* along with having access to the *valuable resources* found within IGI Global's InfoSci-Journals database."

— **Prof. Stuart Palmer,**
Deakin University, Australia

"Receiving the support from IGI Global's OA Fee Waiver Initiative *encourages me to continue my research work without any hesitation*."

— **Prof. Wenlong Liu,** College of Economics and Management at Nanjing University of Aeronautics & Astronautics, China

For More Information, Scan the QR Code or Contact:
IGI Global's Digital Resources Team at eresources@igi-global.com.

IGI Global
PUBLISHER of TIMELY KNOWLEDGE

Printed in the United States
by Baker & Taylor Publisher Services